DYING JUSTICE

Dying Justice

A Case for Decriminalizing Euthanasia and Assisted Suicide in Canada

JOCELYN DOWNIE

UNIVERSITY OF TORONTO PRESS
Toronto Buffalo London

© University of Toronto Press Incorporated 2004
Toronto Buffalo London
Printed in Canada

ISBN 0-8020-3760-7

Printed on acid-free paper

National Library of Canada Cataloguing in Publication

Downie, Jocelyn Grant, 1962–
Dying justice : a case for decriminalizing euthanasia and assisted
suicide in Canada / Jocelyn Downie.

Includes bibliographical references and index.
ISBN 0-8020-3760-7

1. Euthanasia – Law and legislation – Canada.   2. Assisted suicide –
Law and legislation – Canada.   3. Decriminalization – Canada.   I. Title.

KE3654.E87D69 2004   344.71'04197   C2003-907474-9
KF3827.E87D69 2004

University of Toronto Press acknowledges the financial assistance to its
publishing program of the Canada Council for the Arts and the
Ontario Arts Council.

University of Toronto Press acknowledges the financial support for its
publishing activities of the Government of Canada through the
Book Publishing Industry Development Program (BPIDP).

For Brad

Contents

Acknowledgments

In order to write a book, one needs extraordinary support – intellectual, financial, practical, and emotional. I have been fortunate to receive such support from numerous sources.

For intellectual and emotional support, I would like to thank Abbyann Lynch, Susan Sherwin, and Françoise Baylis. Abbyann Lynch gave me my first real job in bioethics and I am deeply indebted to her for early encouragement and assistance. Susan Sherwin started as a role model and has become a valued colleague and friend. I have been honoured to collaborate with her on various projects and I am grateful for her supportive critical reflections on the book manuscript. Françoise Baylis – my closest collaborator and friend – stimulated me intellectually, challenged me to live up to my ideals, and provided emotional support through it all.

For financial support, I am indebted to the Social Sciences and Humanities Research Council, the Jean Royce Fellowship program at Queen's University, the Nova Scotia Health Research Foundation, and Dalhousie University.

For practical support, I would like to thank Barbara Carter, the administrative secretary at the Dalhousie Health Law Institute. Barbara's skill, good nature, and dedication made it possible for me to find the time and space necessary to complete this book.

For a mixture of intellectual, emotional, and practical support, I would like to thank my colleagues in the Health Law Institute and the Faculty of Law at Dalhousie University. I am most fortunate to work in a stimulating intellectual environment with colleagues who are also dear friends. In relation to this book, Elaine Gibson in particular deserves special thanks for her work as associate director of the

Institute – her cheerful and selfless contributions to the running of the Institute were invaluable.

For emotional support, I would like to thank my family. My parents and sisters have nourished me throughout my education and career. They encouraged me to follow my interests and to get back up whenever I was knocked down. They taught me to care for others and to try to make the world a better place. My sons Sam and Nick kept me focused on what really matters.

For extraordinary support of all kinds, I am most grateful to my partner Brad Abernethy. He read many, many drafts of the manuscript and made critical but constructive comments time and again. He believed in me and my ability to complete the project even when I did not. Quite simply, this book is being published because of him.

DYING JUSTICE

Introduction

THE NEED FOR CLARIFICATION AND REFORM

The legal status of assisted death in Canada requires clarification and reform. Consider first the need for clarification. The absence of a clear legislative or judicial statement on withholding and withdrawing potentially life-sustaining treatment and providing for potentially life-shortening palliative treatment is causing at least six serious harms.[1] First, under the current system, some people are getting unwanted treatment because their health care providers do not know whether they will violate the *Criminal Code* if they do not do everything in their power to sustain life.[2]

Second, patients across the country, even within a single hospital, are getting significantly different treatment or non-treatment (whether this be removing respirators, providing massive amounts of morphine, or providing potassium chloride). Given the confusion around legalities, some health care providers do not respect refusals of potentially life-sustaining treatment whereas others respect refusals of all kinds of treatment. Other health care providers respect refusals of artificial ventilation but not refusals of artificial hydration and nutrition. Some health care providers respect refusals of treatment from competent adults but not from surrogate decision-makers for incompetent patients. Others respect refusals from all decision-makers. Some health care providers respect refusals of treatment from terminally ill patients but not from patients who, with the treatment, would have excellent prognoses. Others respect refusals from all individuals regardless of diagnosis and prognosis. In short, the treatment options may depend solely on which health care institution patients happen to be in, or which health care providers they are assigned.

Third, some people are not getting adequate pain control for a variety of reasons, including that health care providers do not know whether it is legal to provide analgesics in doses or ways that may shorten life.[3]

Fourth, health care providers are under the constant threat of legal liability. Lawyers may sit in their offices and comfortably say, 'Oh no, withholding and withdrawing life-sustaining treatment is legal' or 'the provision of potentially life-shortening palliative treatment is legal,' but they are not the ones who might be charged or sued. Because this threat adds stress to health care providers' lives it may affect their treatment decisions, thereby harming patients, too. It harms patients too, because health care providers may be tempted to practise defensive medicine rather than serving their patient's best interests or wishes.

Fifth, law is being made on the backs of individuals compelling them to expend precious financial, emotional, and physical resources going to court to challenge the system. Consider, for example, the burden borne by Nancy B.[4] Paralysed and suffering from Guillain-Barré syndrome, Nancy B. wanted her respirator removed. She went to court and, with her family, endured a very public debate about her right to refuse life-sustaining treatment. She ultimately won her case and, in so doing, helped establish the right to refuse life-sustaining treatment in Canada,[5] but she paid a significant personal price for the victory. Leadership should be demonstrated by those with more financial, emotional, and physical resources than patients. It should be demonstrated by legislators, organizations of health care professionals, and healthy individuals.

Sixth, law is being made on a narrow case-by-case basis – with all of that method's attendant limitations. The courts are situated to resolve legal rather than moral issues; legislatures are charged with resolving both. While legislatures can consider a wide range of facts, courts are constrained by the facts of the case at bar and the abilities and positions of the parties before them.[6]

Clarification of the legal status of assisted death would contribute significantly to the ending of these six harms.

Consider now the need for reform. First, as will be demonstrated by the review of Canadian cases presented in Chapter 1, instances of assisted suicide and euthanasia are being treated inconsistently. Health care providers in Nova Scotia and Ontario might perform exactly the same acts yet be tried for murder in Nova Scotia while being allowed to plead guilty to the administration of a noxious substance in Ontario. Indeed, even within a single province, there is considerable variation in opinion and attitudes between Crown attorneys. Dr James Cairns, Deputy Chief Coroner, Province of Ontario, told an illuminating anecdote to the Special Senate Committee on Euthanasia and Assisted Suicide: 'Following those three cases [described in Chapter 1], we had a summer school involving all of the senior Crown attorneys. When we presented these three cases to them, we asked 60 of the senior Crown attorneys in the province what they would do, given similar circumstances. They were as divided as everyone else as to what they would do in terms of the appropriate charge.'[7] Inconsistent responses to very similar cases make legal reform crucial.

Second, there is inconsistency between the *Criminal Code* and the actual administration of justice. Although euthanasia is murder with a mandatory minimum life sentence according to the *Criminal Code*, it is treated as a far less serious crime across the country.[8] Either euthanasia deserves a punishment less than at least twenty-five years in jail (in which case the *Criminal Code* should be amended to reflect that) or it deserves a punishment of at least twenty-five years in jail (in which case the pattern of accepting pleas to lesser charges should be stopped). The current approach of keeping euthanasia under the homicide provisions in the *Criminal Code* but prosecuting it under manslaughter or administration of a noxious substance provisions is hypocritical. Note that I am not arguing that there should be no prosecutorial discretion around charging. Rather, I am arguing against a situation in which prosecutorial discretion is taken to an extreme, and no cases are taken under the provision of the *Criminal Code* under which they *prima facie* belong.

Third, under the current system, we are failing the dying, along with their families, friends, and health care providers. People are dying in excruciating pain because they are not being given adequate pain medication.[9] People attempting suicide fail and end up in worse shape than before their attempt.[10] People taking desperate steps to help their patients or loved ones are finding themselves facing the potential of imprisonment for life with no possibility of parole for twenty-five years.[11] People refusing life-sustaining treatment are being forced to stay alive in situations in which they think that life is no longer worth living. People may be committing suicide earlier than they would if assisted suicide were legal because they fear getting to that point where they would need, but would not have access to, assisted suicide. People are turning to Jack Kevorkian, the American physician notorious for providing individuals with assistance in committing suicide as well as for his frequent collisions with the American legal system.[12]

The law concerning all forms of assisted death is in need of both clarification and reform. If this is to take place, I believe the process should be informed by a careful, thorough, and thoughtful analysis of the issues – hence this book.

TERMINOLOGY

Much of the confusion in the contemporary debate on assisted death stems from confusion over the meanings of the terms being used. For example, one person may say that euthanasia should be allowed and another person may say that it should not be. They appear to disagree. However, upon closer examination, we may find that the first person takes the word to mean only 'withholding and withdrawing life-sustaining treatment,' while the second person would also include providing a lethal injection. It turns out that they may not actually disagree on substance; they may agree that withholding and withdrawing potentially life-sustaining treatment should be allowed but the provision of lethal injections should not. By stipulating definitions at the outset, I seek to avoid some of the unnecessary, unproductive, and superficial disagreements that have plagued many discussions of these issues.[13]

- *Assisted death* – the umbrella term for death that requires an intentional act or omission of a second person
- *Withholding of potentially life-sustaining treatment* – the failure to start treatment that has the potential to sustain a person's life
- *Withdrawal of potentially life-sustaining treatment* – stopping treatment that has the potential to sustain a person's life
- *Potentially life-shortening palliative treatment* – the provision of analgesics, with the motive of relieving a person's suffering, in amounts that may, but are not certain to, shorten that person's life
- *Assisted suicide* – the act of intentionally killing oneself with the assistance (i.e., the provision of knowledge and/or means) of another
- *Euthanasia* – an act undertaken by one person with the motive of relieving another person's suffering and the knowledge that the act will end the life of that person

- *Voluntary* – in accordance with the wishes expressed by a competent person or through a valid advance directive
- *Non-voluntary* – without the knowledge of the wishes of a competent or incompetent person
- *Involuntary* – against the wishes expressed by a competent person or through a valid advance directive
- *Competent* – capable of understanding the nature and consequences of the decision to be made
- *Incompetent* – not capable of understanding the nature and consequences of the decision to be made
- *Advance directive* – a document through which a competent person sets out what and/or how health care decisions are to be made in the event that she or he becomes incompetent. There are two types of advance directives:
  - *instruction directives* (commonly known as 'living wills') set out *what* decisions are to be made
  - *proxy directives* (commonly known as 'durable powers of attorney') set out *who* is to make decisions

Before moving on from setting out terminology, I should say a few words about the definition of 'potentially life-shortening palliative treatment' and the voluntary/non-voluntary/involuntary distinction.

The most common definition of 'potentially life-shortening palliative treatment' is 'the provision of drugs designed for pain control in dosages that the provider knows may hasten death for which the intention is to ease pain and is not to cause death.' The problem with this definition is its use of intention. The purpose of the category of 'potentially life-shortening palliative care' is to distinguish between a situation in which a health care provider gives a patient a series of injections of morphine at ever-increasing doses, knowing that this might kill the patient, and a situation in which a health care provider gives a patient an injection of potassium chloride, knowing that this will kill the patient.

The language of intention, however, does not draw this distinction. Intention can be understood in at least two ways. First, following the conventional meaning in criminal law, intention can be understood as knowledge of consequences. In both of the two scenarios outlined above, it can be forcefully argued that the health care provider intended the death (i.e., knew that death was a possible consequence of the action). Second, following the more colloquial meaning, intention can be understood as motive or purpose. In both of these scenarios, it can be forcefully argued that the motive of the health care provider is to alleviate suffering – in the case of ever-increasing doses of morphine, through analgesia, and in the case of potassium chloride, through certain death. The significant distinction that remains between the two situations is the level of certainty around the causing of death. The former *may* shorten life and the latter *will*. I therefore redefine the category as 'the provision of analgesics, with the motive of relieving a person's suffering, in dosages or in ways that may (but are not certain to) shorten the person's life.' Much more will be said about intention in Chapter 8.

It should be noted here that some have suggested that there is no such thing as potentially life-shortening palliative treatment. That is, they argue that palliative treatment, properly administered, will carry no risk of causing death. In support of this claim, they acknowledge that morphine and other opiates used for pain control are respiratory depressants, but argue that, properly administered, their respiratory effect will be counteracted by respiratory tolerance. It is certainly true that proper administration can reduce the risk of causing death; it is not, however, true that proper administration can eliminate that risk. As noted by the neurologist James Bernat, 'occasionally a patient's pulmonary failure is so severe that the small respiratory suppressant effect may become clinically significant. In these cases, it is conceivable that the high-dose opiates necessary to control pain or dyspnea might accelerate death.'[14] I therefore consider this a valid category of assisted death.

With regard to the voluntary/non-voluntary/involuntary distinction, it must be noted that all too frequently the debate about assisted death is conducted using only the categories of voluntary and involuntary assisted death. However, the distinction between involuntary and non-voluntary is too important to lose. Involuntary euthanasia breaches a competent individual's autonomy, while non-voluntary euthanasia might not. Non-voluntary euthanasia might not be in the individual's best interests, but, although important, that is another matter entirely. It is important to keep involuntariness and non-voluntariness separate, so that the different attributes of the cases (a certain breach of autonomy vs a possible breach of autonomy and a possible failure to act in someone's best interests) can be taken into account in the analysis.

AN OVERVIEW OF THE BOOK

This book has three parts. In Part I, I review the current legal status of assisted death for competent individuals in Canada in relation to the common law (i.e., judge-made law) and relevant federal and provincial legislation. I will follow the traditional categorization in terms of the nature of the acts because the legislation and common law, inasmuch as they discuss assisted death, use these traditional categories. Part I will therefore examine the law on the following four issues: (1) withholding and withdrawing potentially life-sustaining treatment; (2) potentially life-shortening palliative treatment; (3) assisted suicide; and (4) euthanasia.

In Part II, I begin addressing the question of what the law should be with respect to assisted death by first drawing a set of values out of the common law, the *Canadian Charter of Rights and Freedoms*, and other relevant legislation. Out of these same sources, I then draw out the approach taken to resolve conflicts among values. Finally, I explore the legal regime that these values and the approach to resolution of values conflicts imply for the issue of voluntary withholding and withdrawing potentially life-sustaining treatment. I argue that if a free and informed refusal of treatment is made by a competent individual, it must be respected. I argue further that the following elements should *not* be included in the test for respecting refusal: a bleak prognosis (e.g., terminal illness); a particular type of treatment being withheld or withdrawn (e.g., mechanical ventilation vs artificial hydration and nutrition); the presence of unrelievable physical pain; the absence of any reasonable alternative (as perceived by third parties); and age.

It should be stressed here that I am, in this book, arguing for a permissive regime with respect only to *voluntary* assisted death. I limit the scope of my alternative approach in this way because my analysis of voluntary assisted death is significantly different than that of non-voluntary assisted death. I believe that the case for a permissive regime with respect to voluntary assisted death hangs largely on the principle of respect for autonomy. I believe that the case for a permissive regime with respect to non-voluntary assisted death does not involve autonomy, but rather hangs largely on the principle of beneficence and the corollary best interests approach to substitute decision-making. Furthermore, the case law and legislation relevant to the analysis of voluntary assisted death are also significantly different from the case law and legislation relevant to the analysis of non-voluntary assisted death. For example, when one moves to non-voluntary assisted death, the constitutional protection of autonomy falls away and the *parens patriae* jurisdiction of the courts comes into play. In addition, the provincial legislation concerning children and dependent adults takes on increasing importance.

I am in this book also arguing for a permissive regime with respect only to currently competent individuals. I limit the scope of my alternative approach in this way because the case for a permissive regime with respect to previously competent individuals is related to the case for currently competent individuals, but is nonetheless distinct. For example, the philosophical arguments for respecting current autonomy as opposed to past autonomy are somewhat different. There is distinct common law and legislation regarding refusals of treatment by or on behalf of previously competent individuals, and the core values of the legal system could play out differently with respect to current as opposed to past autonomy.

To properly develop the arguments for a permissive regime with respect to voluntary assisted death for competent individuals alone will consume the entire length of a book. Thus, the development of the arguments for a permissive regime with respect to non-voluntary assisted death and voluntary assisted death for previously competent individuals (e.g., through advance directives) must remain an enterprise for another time. Nothing in this book, however, should be taken to suggest that a permissive regime for such forms of assisted death could not be defended.[15]

It is important to note, nevertheless, that in limiting the scope of my alternative approach to voluntary assisted death, I am not limiting the scope of the discussion in the book to voluntary assisted death. I will, of course, discuss non-voluntary and involuntary assisted death in considerable depth in a variety of places (e.g., in Chapter 11 on the slippery slope argument against the decriminalization of assisted suicide and euthanasia). Concerns about slippage from a permissive voluntary regime to a permissive non-voluntary or involuntary regime are very real and require serious consideration.

It should also be noted here that, throughout the book, I take 'should be' to mean 'should be *in order to be consistent with the core values and values hierarchy of the Canadian legal system.*' The question of what the law should be will be answered on the legal system's own terms. That is, I will not discuss what the law should be in a moral sense, but rather what the law should be given the overarching legal regime within which that law will reside. It is well beyond the scope of this book to set out and defend a set of moral values as the set of values that ought to guide public policy. I cannot, for example, objectively defend the adoption of the values in liberal individualism as opposed to communitarianism as opposed to socialist feminism. However, given the context of this book (i.e., law and policy rather than moral theory), it seems reasonable to look to ground the answer to what the law should be in the values found in the common law, legislation, and the Constitution. More will be said about this approach and about concerns about positivism that might be raised about it in the overview of Part II.

In Part III, I explore what the legal regime with respect to assisted suicide and voluntary euthanasia should be. First, I reject the five distinctions most commonly drawn by those who attempt to distinguish between withholding and withdrawing potentially life-sustaining treatment, on the one hand, and assisted suicide and euthanasia, on the other. These distinctions are: passive versus active; natural versus unnatural death; certainty versus possibility of death; alleviation of suffering versus the ending of life; and violation of bodily integrity versus absence of such violation.[16]

Second, I argue that many of the arguments made against decriminalizing assisted suicide and voluntary euthanasia apply just as much to withholding and withdrawing potentially life-sustaining treatment. If the arguments do not preclude a permissive regime with respect to withholding or withdrawing potentially life-sustaining treatment, then they ought not be taken to preclude a permissive regime with respect to assisted suicide and voluntary euthanasia either. Concerns about freedom, competence, and equality in the context of decisions about assisted death are serious and valid, but they apply just as much to withholding and withdrawing potentially life-sustaining treatment as they do to assisted suicide and voluntary euthanasia.

Third, I deal with arguments that apply just as much to withholding and withdrawal of potentially life-sustaining treatment as they do to assisted suicide and euthanasia *and* have serious flaws regardless of application. I explore arguments based on, for example, the value of suffering and the sanctity of life.

Fourth, I then reject the slippery slope arguments commonly made against decriminalizing assisted suicide and voluntary euthanasia. For example, I provide a detailed analysis of the data from, and literature about, the Netherlands – the country most frequently cited as evidence of the dangers of the slippery slope. I consider the slippery slope arguments separately from other arguments made against decriminalizing assisted suicide and voluntary euthanasia; although they could fit into one or more of the other categories of arguments mentioned above, the slippery slope arguments deserve separate consideration because so many people find them so very compelling.[17] Because I wish to do the slippery slope argument justice and treat it with respect, I not only present it as completely and forcefully as I can, but also attempt to respond to it as completely and forcefully as I can.

Finally, I argue that a legislative regime permitting withholding and withdrawing potentially life-sustaining treatment but prohibiting assisted suicide and voluntary euthanasia violates the *Canadian Charter of Rights and Freedoms.*[18]

My goal is to convince readers that voluntary assisted suicide and euthanasia should no longer be completely prohibited. They should be treated, in law, in the same fashion as voluntary withholding and withdrawal of potentially life-sustaining treatment: (1) access to them should not be restricted on the basis of a bleak prognosis, the nature of the treatment proposed, the presence of unrelievable physical pain, the absence of any reasonable alternative, or age; and (2) access to them should be permitted when a competent individual makes a free and informed request for an assisted death.

Under the alternative regime I propose, there would be variations with regard to legal status and level and process of scrutiny between individual cases, but the variations would be due not to the nature of the act but, rather, to the nature of the decision. So, the type of voluntary assisted death involved – for example, whether someone is refusing life-sustaining treatment as opposed to seeking assistance with suicide – would be irrelevant to the legal status and the scrutiny of the decision. By contrast, whether there is some reason to be concerned about incompetence, coercion, or lack of information would be highly relevant. The lower the competence, freedom, and level of information, the greater the scrutiny of the decision and the lower the likelihood that assisting with the death would be legal (whatever the form of assistance). Conversely, the higher the competence, freedom, and level of information, the less the scrutiny and the greater the likelihood that assisting with the death would be legal (whether the assistance be removing a feeding tube or providing a lethal injection of potassium chloride).

In the end, compared with the current legal regime, my proposed regime is therefore *less* permissive with respect to withholding and withdrawal of potentially life-sustaining treatment and *more* permissive with respect to euthanasia and assisted suicide.

PART ONE

What the Law Is

CHAPTER ONE

The Withholding and Withdrawal of Potentially Life-Sustaining Treatment from Competent Persons

When assessing the legal status of withholding and withdrawing treatment from competent persons, one must consider two relevant categories of persons: competent adults and mature minors. Before turning to these two categories, however, consider the *Criminal Code*[1] backdrop against which the entire discussion of the legal status of the withholding and withdrawal of potentially life-shortening treatment takes place.

THE *CRIMINAL CODE* BACKDROP

At first glance, the *Criminal Code* appears to preclude respecting an individual's refusal of potentially life-sustaining treatment. The section titled 'Duties Tending to Preservation of Life' contains the following provisions:

215(1) Every one is under a legal duty ...

    (c) to provide necessaries of life to a person under his charge if that person

        (i) is unable, by reason of detention, age, illness, mental disorder or other cause, to withdraw himself from that charge, and

        (ii) is unable to provide himself with necessaries of life.

    (2) Every one commits an offence who, being under a legal duty within the meaning of subsection (1), fails without lawful excuse, the proof of which lies on him, to perform that duty, if ...

(b) with respect to a duty imposed by paragraph (1)(c), the failure to perform the duty endangers the life of the person to whom the duty is owed or causes or is likely to cause the health of that person to be injured permanently.

216 Every one who undertakes to administer surgical or medical treatment to another person or to do any other lawful act that may endanger the life of another person is, except in cases of necessity, under a legal duty to have and to use reasonable knowledge, skill and care in so doing.

217 Every one who undertakes to do an act is under a legal duty to do it if an omission to do the act is or may be dangerous to life.

Other *prima facie* relevant *Criminal Code* provisions include the following:

219(1) Every one is criminally negligent who
    (a) in doing anything, or
    (b) in omitting to do anything that it is his duty to do,

shows wanton or reckless disregard for the lives or safety of other persons.

(2) For the purposes of this section, 'duty' means a duty imposed by law.

220 Every person who by criminal negligence causes death to another person is guilty of an indictable offence and liable

(a) where a firearm is used in the commission of the offence, to imprisonment for life and to a minimum punishment for a term of four years; and
(b) in any other case, to imprisonment for life.

222(5) A person commits culpable homicide when he causes the death of a human being ...

(b) by criminal negligence

Courts have held that potentially life-sustaining treatment constitutes 'necessaries of life'[2] and that patients are understood to be 'in the charge of' health care providers.[3] Therefore, following section 215, one might consider the withholding or withdrawal of potentially life-sustaining treatment without lawful excuse a failure to provide necessaries of life.

Following section 219, one might consider the withdrawal of potentially life-sustaining treatment as showing wanton or reckless disregard for life and thus as criminal negligence (and, if the withdrawal caused death, criminal negligence causing death under section 220 and/or culpable homicide under section 222). The withholding of potentially life-sustaining treatment that the health care provider has a legal duty to provide (e.g., under section 215 of the *Code*) could be seen as showing wanton or reckless disregard for life and thus as criminal negligence, criminal negligence causing death, and/or culpable homicide. That much is clear.

What constitutes a 'lawful excuse' and what constitutes 'wanton and reckless disregard for life' in the context of assisted death and, from that, what constitutes illegal withholding and withdrawal of potentially life-sustaining treatment remains unclear simply on the face of the *Criminal Code*. We must therefore look beyond the text of the *Criminal Code*. When the case law, common law, and provincial legislation speak to these questions, then health care providers can practise without fear that withholding or withdrawal of potentially life-sustaining treatment will attract criminal liability. However, when the case law, common law, and provincial legislation conflict or say nothing on these questions, criminal liability for withholding or withdrawal of potentially life-sustaining treatment remains possible and chills the practice of medicine.

COMPETENT ADULTS

The Case Law Re: The *Criminal Code*

Two cases have addressed the issue of the meaning of the *Criminal Code* for the withholding and withdrawal of potentially life-sustaining treatment from competent adults.[4]

In *Nancy B.* v. *Hôtel-Dieu de Québec,*[5] a young woman sought an injunction to compel the hospital and her physician to respect her request to discontinue the use of a respirator. Nancy B. suffered from irreversible paralysis from the neck down caused by Guillain-Barré

Syndrome. With respirator support, she might live for quite some time. Without it, she would die very quickly. Justice Dufour took the following basic approach to statutory interpretation: '[i]n this country, we have a coherent legal system. In interpreting texts of law, it is necessary to first determine the meaning that logic gives them.'[6] He assumed that one should not interpret the law in a way that leads to absurdities, and he asserted that interpreting the *Criminal Code* to prohibit respect for refusals of potentially life-sustaining treatment in at least some circumstances would lead to absurdity.[7] He concluded that the *Criminal Code* should not be interpreted as entirely prohibitive. Second, he argued that both the common law doctrine of informed consent and the *Civil Code* require respect for at least some refusals of treatment. Assuming a necessary relationship of coherence between the *Criminal Code* and these other sources of legal rights and responsibilities, Justice Dufour concluded that the *Criminal Code* should not be interpreted as entirely prohibitive. Thus, he concluded that 'the conduct of a physician who stops the respiratory support treatment of his patient at the freely given and informed request of the patient'[8] should not be characterized as unreasonable and that such conduct should not be taken to denote wanton and reckless disregard for life. Therefore, he concluded, such conduct should not attract liability under the *Criminal Code*.

In *British Columbia (Attorney General)* v. *Astaforoff,* Justice Bouck of the British Columbia Supreme Court held that the corrections authorities did not have a legal duty (under what is now section 215 of the *Criminal Code*) to forcibly feed Mary Astaforoff (a Doukhobor prisoner on a hunger strike) even though she was likely to die without force-feeding: 'According to the province, it made available to the prisoner the necessaries of life but she chooses not to accept them. In reply, the respondents contend that the law should be interpreted to read that the province must forcibly provide her with these necessaries. I do not think the *Criminal Code* should be defined to mean that provincial jail officials and others having someone under their care and control must force the necessaries of life upon that person.'[9]

Thus, on the basis of the limited case law directed towards the interpretation of the *Criminal Code*, as it applies to the context of the withholding or withdrawal of potentially life-sustaining treatment from competent adults, one can conclude that courts will not interpret the *Criminal Code* as precluding respect for refusals of treatment from competent adults.

Provincial Legislation

Three provinces have passed and proclaimed comprehensive legislation dealing with the range of issues related to consent to health care treatment.[10] The Ontario *Health Care Consent Act* provides:

> Sec. 10. No treatment without consent. – A health practitioner who proposes a treatment for a person shall not administer the treatment, and shall take reasonable steps to ensure that it is not administered, unless,
>
> (a) he or she is of the opinion that the person is capable with respect to the treatment, and the person has given consent.

The legislation also anticipates the withdrawal of consent:

> Sec. 14. Withdrawal of consent. – A consent that has been given by or on behalf of the person for whom the treatment was proposed may be withdrawn at any time,
>
> (a) by the person, if the person is capable with respect to the treatment at the time of the withdrawal;
>
> Sec. 2. Definitions ...
>
> 'plan of treatment' means a plan that ...
>
> (c) provides for the administration to the person of various treatments or courses of treatment and may, in addition, provide for the withholding or withdrawal of treatment in light of the person's current health condition.

Competent adults in Ontario thus have a clear statutorily protected right to refuse potentially life-sustaining treatment. The legislation in British Columbia and Prince Edward Island establishes the same right. Both the PEI and BC legislation state that every patient/adult (respectively) who is capable of giving or refusing consent to treatment has the right 'to give consent or to refuse consent on any grounds, including moral or religious grounds, even if the refusal will result in death.'[11]

Other provinces have passed and proclaimed less than comprehensive legislation that deals with consent to health care treatment but they have done so almost in passing. For example, the Nova Scotia *Hospitals Act* provides: 'Sec. 54. Consent to hospital treatment required. – (1) No person admitted to a hospital shall receive treatment unless he consents to such treatment.' This provision lies buried in an Act that deals with everything from approval for construction of a hospital[12] to notice of non-entitlement to insured services[13] to processes for involuntary committal of persons to psychiatric facilities.[14] Like similar provisions in other provincial Acts, it provides only a minimal statutory requirement for respect for refusals of treatment.

Except in Ontario, British Columbia, and Prince Edward Island, provincial legislation has provided relatively little guidance with respect to the withholding and withdrawal of potentially life-sustaining treatment from competent adults.

The Common Law

In 1993, Justice Sopinka, writing for the majority in *Rodriguez* v. *British Columbia (Attorney General)* – a case discussed in greater detail in Chapter 3 – made three statements to the effect that Canadians have a common law right to refuse even potentially life-sustaining treatment:

> That there is a right to choose how one's body will be dealt with, even in the context of beneficial medical treatment, has long been recognized by the common law. To impose medical treatment on one who refuses constitutes battery, and our common law has recognized the right to demand that medical treatment which would extend life be withheld or withdrawn.[15]

> Canadian courts have recognized a common law right of patients to refuse consent to medical treatment, or to demand that treatment, once commenced, be withdrawn or discontinued (*Ciarlariello* v. *Schacter*, [1993] 2 S.C.R. 119). This right has been specifically recognized to exist even if the withdrawal from or refusal of treatment may result in death (*Nancy B.* v. *Hôtel-Dieu de Québec* (1992), 86 D.L.R. (4th) 385 (Que. S.C.); *Malette* v. *Shulman* (1990), 72 O.R. (2d) 417 (C.A.).[16]

> Whether or not one agrees that the active vs passive distinction is maintainable, however, the fact remains that under our common law, the physician has no choice but to accept the patient's instructions to discontinue treatment. To continue to treat the patient when the patient has withdrawn consent to that treatment constitutes battery (*Ciarlariello* and *Nancy B., supra*).[17]

These statements resolve the confusion generated by the apparently conflicting earlier jurisprudence.[18] One could debate what the earlier cases actually stood for but *Rodriguez* made such debate irrelevant for the purposes of this chapter. *Rodriguez* established that there is a common law right for adults to refuse potentially life-sustaining treatment.[19]

Conclusion

There is clearly a common law right for competent adults to refuse potentially life-sustaining treatment, and no provincial legislation conflicts with this common law right. Although one might read the *Criminal Code* as restricting the withholding and withdrawal of some potentially life-sustaining treatment, standard principles of statutory interpretation imply that one should not (and the Supreme Court of Canada would not) read it that way with regard to refusals by competent adults.

MATURE MINORS

Provincial Legislation

Six provinces have legislation relevant to mature minors'[20] refusals of potentially life-sustaining treatment.[21] Under the Ontario *Health Care Consent Act*, anyone able to understand the information relevant to making a health care decision and able to appreciate the reasonably foreseeable consequences of the decision must have his or her decision respected.[22] Thus, in Ontario, mature minors have the statutory right to refuse potentially life-sustaining treatment regardless of whether the courts or health care providers consider it in the minors' best interests.

At first glance, the provisions in the New Brunswick *Medical Consent of Minors Act*[23] and the British Columbia *Infants Act*[24] appear similar to those of the Ontario legislation; the consent of a minor appears as effective as that of an adult if the minor can understand the nature and consequences of the treatment decision. Further inspection, however, reveals that these Acts provide minors with only a limited statutory right. The New Brunswick legislation limits the right with respect to minors under the age of 16.[25] The British Columbia legislation limits the right in a similar way for all minors.[26] Thus, in New Brunswick and British Columbia, consent of a mature minor is necessary and sufficient *where the health care provider considers the refusal of treatment in the best interests of the minor.*

Recent amendments to the Manitoba *Child and Family Services Act* import a mature minor rule regarding children who have been apprehended under the Act. Under the amended Act, the agency shall not authorize medical treatment for children 16 years or older without the consent of the child.[27] The agency may apply to the court to authorize such treatment but the court will not do so unless it is satisfied that the child is not able: '(a) to understand the information that is relevant to making a decision to consent or not consent to the medical examination or the medical or dental treatment; or (b) to appreciate the reasonably foreseeable consequences of making a decision to consent or not consent to the medical examination or the medical or dental treatment.'[28] Thus, an unlimited mature minor rule applies in Manitoba to minors 16 years or older who have been apprehended by Child and Family Services.

Under the Quebec *Civil Code*, the age of consent for medical treatment is 14.[29] Therefore, minors 14 years of age and older can consent to medical treatment on their own behalf. However, the *Code* also requires that the court authorize treatment in cases in which a minor 14 years of age or older refuses medical treatment and the court is explicitly not required to respect the minor's refusal.[30]

The Alberta *Child Welfare Act* takes the opposite approach to the legislation discussed earlier in this section B – rather than legislating even a limited mature minor rule, it replaces the common law mature minor rule so far as it relates to individuals under the age of 18 who are in need of essential medical treatment.[31] While a mature minor is entitled to an opportunity to express his or her opinion on the matter and the minor's opinion should be considered by the surrogate decision-maker, his or her consent is neither necessary nor sufficient.[32]

In the other provinces and the territories, provincial legislation provides no guidance on this issue.

The Common Law

The common law right to refuse potentially life-sustaining treatment clearly extends to competent adults. But does it extend beyond competent adults? In *Rodriguez*, Justice Sopinka spoke of 'patients' having the right to refuse treatment. Did he intend to include mature minors in the category of 'patients' given that he said 'patients' rather than 'adults'? I would argue that he did not intend to include mature minors in the category of 'patients.' Pointing to the common law foundation for his statements, he referred only to cases involving adults and did not refer to cases in which mature minors had been found to have at least a limited right to refuse treatment.[33] From this omission, one can infer that he did not intend to extend the common law right to refuse treatment to mature minors. Indeed, extending the right to refuse treatment to mature minors would have taken the common law right in a somewhat controversial direction rather than simply endorsing a position taken by a number of courts[34] and considered uncontroversial by most.[35] It is extremely unlikely that Justice Sopinka would have done so without explicitly referring to the relevant cases, particularly in a situation where such an extension would not be relevant to the analysis of the case before him – the case in which Justice Sopinka made these remarks about withholding and withdrawal of potentially life-sustaining treatment is a case involving an adult with amyotrophic lateral sclerosis challenging the constitutionality of the assisted suicide provision of the *Criminal Code*.

Without Supreme Court of Canada guidance on this issue, we must turn to the lower courts. In *Johnston v. Wellesley Hospital*,[36] the Ontario High Court held that, at common law, parental consent was not necessary for an individual under the age of majority who could nevertheless understand the nature and consequences of the proposed treatment. The minor's consent was sufficient.[37] In *J.S.C. v. Wren*,[38] the Alberta Court of Appeal found that a 16-year-old girl could give a valid consent to a therapeutic abortion against her parents' wishes.[39] These cases introduced what is known as 'the mature minor rule' into Canadian law – under the common law, when a minor is capable of understanding the nature and consequences of a treatment decision, the minor's consent is necessary and sufficient. However, cases involving *refusals of treatment* rather than *consent to treatment* and some other *very recent* cases suggest that the mature minor rule might be more limited than it at first appears.

The 'mature minor trilogy' consists of three cases in which courts in three different provincial jurisdictions first dealt with mature minors and refusals of treatment under the common law.[40] All of these cases involved young Jehovah's Witnesses who were refusing chemotherapy because of the blood transfusions it necessitated. Lisa K. and Joshua Walker had acute myeloid leukemia, and Adrian Yeatts had acute B cell lymphocytic leukemia. All had extremely poor prognoses, were refusing burdensome treatment, and were refusing treatment on religious grounds. In all of these cases, the courts held that treatment could not be provided.

At first blush, the decisions look like they embrace the mature minor rule as articulated above, but a closer look reveals the possibility of an additional feature of the rule. The first two cases, *L.D.K.* and *Re A.Y.*, came to the courts by way of applications by Child and Family Services agencies under provincial child protection legislation. Although both decisions were grounded in the legislation, the courts nevertheless made comments about the maturity of the minors and the law beyond the legislation. In *L.D.K.*, Justice Main of the Ontario Provincial Court (Family Division) made much of Lisa's maturity[41] and found: 'Given the intelligence, state of mind and position taken by L., all of which were known to this hospital, she ought to have been consulted before being transfused. She was not. I must find that she has been discriminated against on the basis of her religion and her age pursuant to s.15(1) [the equality provision of the *Charter*]. In these circumstances, upon being given a blood transfusion, her right to the security of her person pursuant to s.7 [the life, liberty, and security of the person provision of the *Charter*] was infringed.'[42] In *A.Y.*, the court held that 'I am also satisfied that it is proper under the *Act, and in law generally*, for me to take into consideration his wishes, and I do so.'[43] The Court ordered that 'the boy is declared to be a mature minor whose wish to receive medical treatment without blood or blood products is to be respected.'[44]

The third case considered the common law in somewhat more depth. In *Walker*, Chief Justice Hoyt of the New Brunswick Court of Appeal, writing for the majority, said: 'In Canada, the common law recognizes the doctrine of a mature minor, namely, one who is capable of understanding the nature and consequences of the proposed treatment. Accordingly, a minor, if mature, does have the legal capacity to consent to his or her own medical treatment ... At common law, when a minor is mature, no parental consent is required.'[45]

These decisions have frequently been taken[46] as establishing an unlimited common law mature minor rule for Canada but this conclusion is not wholly warranted. In fact, the court's endorsement of the refusal of treatment in each of these cases was also grounded in a belief that the treatment refused was not necessarily in the best interests of the child. In *L.D.K.*, the legal basis for Justice Main's decision was not a finding that Lisa was a mature minor and therefore had a right to refuse treatment but rather that, in pursuing a treatment plan other than that proposed by the health care team, Lisa's parents were acting in her best interests.[47] Therefore, Lisa was not a child in need of protection under the *Child Welfare Act*,[48] and therefore, her parents' refusal was sufficient to preclude the hospital from treating her. Like Justice Main in *L.D.K.*, Justice Wells in *A.Y.* took into account Adrian's maturity but grounded his decision in a consideration under the New Brunswick legislation of what he thought was in Adrian's best interests.[49] In *Walker*, Chief Justice Hoyt based his decision on the fact that Joshua was sufficiently mature *and* on the fact that the proposed alternative treatment plan was in his best interests.[50] Thus, the courts take seriously the issue of the maturity of the minor, but they seem to retain for themselves the authority to override the mature minor's decision if the court considers it not in the best interests of the minor. What we have, apparently, is a limited mature minor rule – unlike a competent adult, a mature minor only has the right to refuse treatment that the court considers in his or her best interests to refuse.

This limit seems to have been placed more explicitly on the mature minor rule in some very recent cases.[51] In *Ney* v. *Canada (Attorney General)*, the British Columbia Supreme Court considered the common law position on consent to medical treatment on or on behalf of children and concluded:

> In summary, at common law a child is capable of consenting to medical treatment if he or she has sufficient intelligence and maturity to fully appreciate the nature and consequences of a medical procedure to be performed for his or her benefit. It appears that the medical practitioner is to make this determination. If the child is incapable of meeting this test then the parents' consent will be required for treatment. It is not clear whether parental control yields to the child's independence or whether they are concurrent powers of consent. But it is clear that the parents may not veto treatment to which a capable child consents, and that neither child nor parents can require a medical practitioner to treat. Apart from s.16, this rule is modified only to the extent that the decision of a child or parents may be overridden under the provisions of the Family and Child Service Act *or by the court acting under its parens patriae jurisdiction.*[52]

The decision in *Ney* has been enthusiastically endorsed by McEachern C.J.B.C. in *R.* v. *D.D.W.*[53] and Jewers J. of the Manitoba Court of Queen's Bench in *Kennett Estate* v. *Manitoba (Attorney General)*.[54]

In another recent mature minor case, *Van Mol (Guardian ad litem of)* v. *Ashmore*,[55] confusion remains. Justice Lambert, for himself but in the majority in the result, did not endorse the best interests and concurrent parental consent limits. Rather, he restated the common law rule and, for his restatement relied heavily on the cases already discussed in this chapter. He explicitly rejected the limit of concurrent parental consent but ignored the best interests limit found in the very cases he relied on. Was the dropping of the best interests limit intentional or not? I would argue that it was unintentional, as Justice Lambert's reasons give no indication that he saw that there was a best interests limit in the earlier cases. In contrast, Justice Huddart, in concurring reasons, restated her position – expressed previously in *Ney* – that there is residual *parens patriae* jurisdiction.[56]

Thus, at the end of the common law review, a number of significant questions remain. Would courts in jurisdictions that have not yet considered this issue embrace the mature minor rule if presented with a case involving a mature minor? In the face of a good as opposed to a bleak prognosis, would the courts be so willing to allow mature minors to refuse potentially life-sustaining treatment? What would the courts do in the face of a trivial rather than burdensome treatment or in the face of a decision not grounded in religious conviction? For example, a case involving a 15-year-old paraplegic refusing antibiotics for an easily treatable infection because he no longer wishes to live as a paraplegic would be a test of the courts' commitment to respecting the autonomy of mature minors. Would the courts find only a limited right of refusal (i.e., a right only to make decisions others regard as good decisions)? Or would the courts simply find the minor to be insufficiently mature (using what they regard to be a poor decision as evidence of immaturity)? Or would the courts respect the refusal? Significant uncertainty surrounds the common law status of the withholding and withdrawal of potentially life-sustaining treatment from mature minors.

Conclusion

The status and scope of the right of competent minors to refuse potentially life-sustaining treatment remain somewhat unclear in most of Canada. Minors who understand the nature and consequences of the decision to refuse treatment will likely have their refusals enforced by the courts if the courts consider the refusals to be in the minors' best interests. Apart from those limited circumstances, however, uncertainty remains as to what will be done with respect to mature minors' refusals.[57]

UNILATERAL WITHHOLDING OR WITHDRAWAL

When a competent person wants treatment but the health care team believes that treatment would not serve the person's best interests, the law is not nearly as clear as when the roles are reversed. Until recently, this issue had not been considered by any court in Canada but in the past few years, two relevant cases have surfaced.

In November 1997, the Court of Appeal in Manitoba decided a case involving a child in a persistent vegetative state.[58] The physicians wished to enter a Do Not Resuscitate (DNR) order on his chart; the parents disagreed, and legal action ensued. The trial judge agreed that a DNR order was in the child's best interests and authorized the placement of the order. On appeal, the Court of Appeal overturned the trial judge's decision to authorize, not on the grounds that the DNR order was not in the child's best interests, but rather on the grounds that the physicians had the authority to enter it on the child's chart without going to court. Justice Twaddle found, for the court, that consent from the parents of an infant was not necessary for the physician to enter a DNR order on the child's chart. On a broader note, Justice Twaddle wrote: '[N]either consent nor a court order in lieu is required for a medical doctor to issue a non-resuscitation direction where, in his or her judgment, the patient is in a persistent vegetative state. Whether or not such a direction should be issued is a judgment call for the doctor to make having regard to the patient's history and condition, and the doctor's evaluation of the hopelessness of the case. The wishes of the patient's family or guardians should be taken into account, but neither their consent nor the approval of a court is required.'[59]

In the second case,[60] Mr Sawatzky, was an elderly man with Parkinson's disease and numerous other health problems. His physicians placed a DNR order on his chart without notifying his wife. When she discovered the order, Mrs Sawatzky sought an interlocutory injunction to have the order removed from her husband's chart. In November 1998 Justice Beard of the Manitoba Court of the Queen's Bench issued an interlocutory injunction ordering the lifting of the DNR order and ordering the parties to seek additional independent medical opinions and recommending that the parties attempt to resolve the matter out of court.

Given that Justice Beard was hearing a motion for an interlocutory injunction, she did not decide the issue of the legal status of unilateral DNR orders. However, she did make it quite clear that she believes that the law is unsettled in this arena. She noted: 'Based on the case law to date, the courts have stated that a decision not to provide treatment is exclusively within the purview of the doctor and is not a decision to be made by the courts. Thus, it appears that the courts would not interfere with a medical decision not to provide treatment.'[61] And: 'I think that many Canadians have been surprised to learn that a doctor can make a 'do not resuscitate' order without the consent of a patient or his or her family, yet that appears to be the current state of the law in Canada, Britain, and the United States.'[62]

She also noted the deficiencies in the case law to date: '[C]ounsel have referred to only three cases in which the facts and issues are at least somewhat closely related to this matter, although even then there are some clear differences. There is only one case from a Canadian court, being the *CFS v. RL and SLH* decision and that case did not consider either the effect of rights under the *Charter of Rights and Freedoms* (the *Charter*) or the Manitoba *Human Rights Code*, CCSM, c. H175.'[63]

Justice Beard effectively left open the question of what would be found to be the legal status of unilateral DNR orders at trial. In the end, without a trial, the parties agreed to have Mr Sawatzky transferred to another facility. Mr Sawatzky subsequently died and so the case went no further.

As these are the only two cases in Canada on the issue of unilateral withholding and withdrawal of potentially life-sustaining treatment, they can be read as binding precedents only for persons in Manitoba. However, they vividly illustrate the lack of clarity about the law in this area.

CONCLUSION

Thus, we can conclude that the legal right of competent adults to refuse potentially life-sustaining treatment has been clearly established at least at common law. The legal status of refusals for competent minors remains somewhat unclear as does the legal status of demands for potentially life-sustaining treatment made by competent persons (whether adult or minor). This lack of clarity matters, because in the absence of clarity the *Criminal Code* looms large and has a potentially negative effect on medical practice.

CHAPTER TWO

The Provision of Potentially Life-Shortening Palliative Treatment

LEGISLATION

The following sections appear in the *Criminal Code* of Canada.

219(1) Every one is criminally negligent who

  (a) *in doing anything*, or
  (b) in omitting to do anything that it is his duty to do, shows wanton or reckless disregard for the lives or safety of other persons [emphasis added].

220 Every person who by criminal negligence causes death to another person is guilty of an indictable offence and liable

  (a) where a firearm is used in the commission of the offence, to imprisonment for life and to a minimum punishment for a term of four years; and
  (b) in any other case, to imprisonment for life.

222(5) A person commits culpable homicide when he causes the death of a human being ...

  (b) by criminal negligence

229 Culpable homicide is murder

  (a) where the person who causes the death of a human being

(i) means to cause his death, or
(ii) means to cause him bodily harm that he knows is likely to
     cause his death, and is reckless whether death ensues or
     not.

These sections of the *Criminal Code* appear to support the proposition that the law prohibits at least some provision of potentially
life-shortening palliative treatment. Clearly, providing potentially
life-shortening palliative treatment that shows wanton or reckless
disregard for life constitutes criminal negligence (or criminal negligence causing death) and meaning to cause death by providing life-
shortening palliative treatment constitutes culpable homicide. But
what constitutes 'wanton or reckless disregard for life' in this context?
What constitutes 'meaning to cause death'? For answers to these questions, we must look beyond the *Criminal Code*.

FOUR CASES TO CONSIDER

There have been three important cases involving the provision of
potentially life-shortening palliative treatment known to the legal
authorities. None of these resulted in criminal charges.

First, in 1990, Dr Thomas Perry gave an injection of morphine to his
father who was dying of cancer. Dr Perry admitted that the morphine
might have shortened his father's life. The B.C. College of Physicians
and Surgeons investigated the incident and concluded that Dr Perry
did nothing wrong – indeed, they concluded that he provided his
father with good quality palliative care. No criminal charges were
laid.[1]

Second, in 1991, Dr Peter Graaf ordered repeated doses of morphine
and valium for two patients. Both patients died. A British Columbia
coroner reviewed the deaths of Dr Graaf's two patients and concluded
that they both died of morphine overdoses grossly exceeding the
amount necessary to control their pain. The B.C. College of Physicians
and Surgeons investigated the incident and concluded that Dr Graaf
had acted inappropriately in ordering such high dosages and rates of
administration of morphine and valium. However, the college did not
find Dr Graaf guilty of professional misconduct. Again, no charges
were laid.[2]

Third, in 1992, an Ontario coroner launched an inquiry into fifteen
deaths at the Christopher Robin home for severely handicapped chil-

dren. The coroner's jury concluded that when children became ill with treatable diseases, active care was switched to palliative care and a morphine drip was initiated whether or not it was medically indicated. The switch was made without appropriate tests or discussions with the children's families. The coroner's jury concluded that morphine was a possible factor in the cause of death in eleven of the fourteen deaths being investigated and a definite factor in two of the deaths. For only one death was morphine not listed as a factor in the cause of death.[3] No charges were laid, largely because of difficulties in proving causation (there had been an autopsy in only one case and the results were difficult to assess even in that case).[4]

Despite the potential for criminal charges, no charges have ever been laid for the provision of potentially life-shortening palliative treatment. Nevertheless, no conclusions can be drawn about the content of 'wanton and reckless disregard for life' from these cases, because there are a number of reasons other than absence of wanton and reckless disregard for life for not proceeding with a prosecution (e.g., the difficulty with proving causation). We cannot simply assume that the absence of prosecutions means that the conduct in these cases did not demonstrate 'wanton and reckless disregard for life' or that the people involved did not 'mean to cause death.'

More insight and guidance can perhaps be drawn from a fourth case. In *Rodriguez*, Justice Sopinka, for a majority of five of the Supreme Court of Canada, implies that potentially life-shortening palliative treatment is not illegal: 'The administration of drugs designed for pain control in dosages which the physician knows will hasten death constitutes active contribution to death by any standard. However, the distinction drawn here is one based upon intention – in any case of palliative care the intention is to ease pain, which has the effect of hastening death ... In my view, distinctions based upon intent are important, and in fact, form the bases of our criminal law. While factually the distinction may, at times, be difficult to draw, legally it is clear.'[5]

Although later in this book I will argue that Justice Sopinka is mistaken about intent and intention, his statement seems to send the message to prosecutors and health care providers alike that courts are unlikely to conclude that the provision of potentially life-shortening palliative treatment demonstrates wanton and reckless disregard for life. Therefore, there is likely to be no finding of criminal negligence. Similarly, courts are unlikely to consider a person who provides potentially life-shortening palliative treatment to 'mean to cause death.'

Therefore, there is likely to be no finding of culpable homicide. However, the boundaries of Justice Sopinka's conception of 'appropriate palliative care' are unclear. Is consent necessary? Is substituted consent for incompetent patients sufficient? How close to certainty of causing death can a health care provider go without demonstrating 'wanton and reckless disregard for life' or 'meaning to cause death'? Furthermore, we do not know for certain whether the majority of the Supreme Court of Canada, confronted with this practice directly rather than obliquely, would endorse Justice Sopinka's conclusion.

CONCLUSION

The *Criminal Code* takes us to the conclusion that the provision of potentially life-shortening palliative treatment is illegal if it demonstrates wanton and reckless disregard for life or if the person providing it means to cause death. The case law may take us to the conclusion that *some* provision of potentially life-shortening palliative treatment does not demonstrate wanton and reckless disregard for life (for some, it implies, is legal) and that people who provide it do not always mean to cause death.

There are, however, no clear guidelines for the assessment of whether a particular instance of providing potentially life-shortening palliative treatment constitutes 'wanton and reckless disregard' for life or whether a person who provides the treatment 'means to cause death.' As a result, the practice of providing potentially life-shortening palliative treatment continues to be conducted under a shadow of possible criminal liability.

CHAPTER THREE

Assisted Suicide

LEGISLATION

Assisted suicide is quite clearly prohibited by the Canadian *Criminal Code*. The *Criminal Code* provides:

241 Every one who
(a) counsels a person to commit suicide, or
(b) aids or abets a person to commit suicide,
whether suicide ensues or not, is guilty of an indictable offence and liable to imprisonment for a term not exceeding fourteen years.

THREE CASES TO CONSIDER

Three significant cases in Canada involve assisted suicide.[1] In the first, section 241(b) withstood a *Charter* challenge. In the second, an individual was convicted for the first time under section 241(b). In the third, a physician was charged for the first time under section 241(b) and became the first physician in Canada convicted of assisting suicide.

In 1993, the Supreme Court of Canada upheld section 241(b) of the *Criminal Code* by a five to four margin in the face of a challenge brought by Sue Rodriguez (a woman suffering from amyotrophic lateral sclerosis who wished to commit an assisted suicide).[2] The majority found that there was no breach of section 7 of the *Canadian Charter of Rights and Freedoms* ('Everyone has the right to life, liberty and security of the person and the right not to be deprived thereof except in accordance with the principles of fundamental justice'). They assumed without deciding that there was a breach of section 15 ('Every individual is

equal before and under the law and has the right to the equal protection and equal benefit of the law without discrimination and, in particular, without discrimination based on race, national or ethnic origin,
colour, religion, sex, age or mental or physical disability'). But they
found that the breach would be saved by section 1 ('The *Canadian Charter of Rights and Freedoms* guarantees the rights and freedoms set out in
it subject only to such reasonable limits prescribed by law as can be
demonstrably justified in a free and democratic society'). Therefore,
they concluded, section 241(b) was constitutional. Chief Justice Lamer
for himself found a breach of section 15. Justice McLachlin (as she then
was) for herself and Justice L'Heureux-Dubé found a breach of section
7, and Justice Cory for himself found a breach of both sections 7 and 15.
The dissenting judges found that none of the breaches could be saved
under s.1 and therefore they all concluded that section 241(b) was
unconstitutional.

Despite the Supreme Court of Canada decision, Sue Rodriguez ultimately died as a result of an assisted suicide.[3] Svend Robinson, a Member of Parliament from British Columbia, was present at her death and
has said that a physician assisted in the suicide. However, no one was
or will ever be prosecuted in connection with this assisted suicide. Following a review of the evidence in the case and in light of the British
Columbia guidelines for the exercise of prosecutorial discretion reproduced in the Appendix, special prosecutor Robert Johnston concluded:
'The evidence demonstrates that some person or persons must have
assisted Sue Rodriguez to commit suicide on February 12, 1994. The
identity of that person or those persons cannot be established. The fact
that Svend Robinson was present at the suicide, without evidence
which would show that his opportunity to have committed an offence
was exclusive, is not sufficient to lay a charge against him. Speculation
or suspicion does not meet the test of substantial likelihood of conviction. Based on the existing evidence, my decision is that no charges
shall be laid arising out of the suicide of Susan Jane Rodriguez.'[4]

In October 1995, a woman was convicted under section 241(b) for
assisting in the suicide of a friend. The Crown alleged, and the jury
agreed, that Mary Fogarty provided Brenda Barnes, a diabetic, with
syringes and insulin and wrote Barnes's suicide note for her. The
Crown further alleged that Fogarty assisted with the suicide because
she thought (mistakenly) that she stood to benefit from Barnes's
$100,000 life insurance policy. Fogarty claimed that she gave Barnes the
syringes so that she could inject amphetamines. Fogarty speculated

that Barnes took the insulin out of Fogarty's purse. Fogarty admitted writing the suicide note at Barnes's dictation but claimed not to have known it was a suicide note. Fogarty, convicted and sentenced to three years probation and 300 hours of community service,[5] became the first person in over thirty years[6] to be charged and convicted under the assisted suicide provisions of the *Criminal Code.*[7]

On 20 June 1996, Dr Maurice Genereux was charged under section 241(b) of the *Criminal Code* for assisting with the suicide of a patient.[8] In May 1997, additional charges were laid, and he ultimately faced charges of aiding or abetting suicide, counselling to commit suicide, criminal negligence causing death, and criminal negligence causing bodily harm. Dr Genereux was accused of prescribing drugs to two patients he was treating who were HIV positive (one ultimately committed suicide and one attempted suicide). This was the first time that a physician had been charged with assisted suicide in Canada. On 23 December 1997, Dr Genereux pled guilty and became the first physician convicted under section 241(b).[9]

It is worth noting that the two cases in which there have been prosecutions under section 241(b) of the *Criminal Code* are not typical cases of assisted death. Their peculiarities might well explain why these and only these cases have been followed through to convictions. In the Fogarty case, the jury concluded that Fogarty assisted her friend to commit suicide out of self-interest rather than out of a desire to help a competent friend to end a life of unrelenting suffering. In *Genereux*, the prosecutors in Toronto already knew of Dr Genereux, as he had been charged with sexual offences involving his patients. Furthermore, a newspaper carried a story about the successfully assisted suicide written by the partner of the man who killed himself. The publicity and Dr Genereux's past history may have affected the prosecutors' decision to proceed against Dr Genereux. Because of their peculiarities, these two cases may not give much insight into what might happen with a more typical assisted suicide.

Before leaving this review of the case law, we must note the paucity of cases that have been brought under section 241(b) of the *Criminal Code* (just three in over thirty years). We know that assisted suicide is happening in Canada,[10] yet it is not being prosecuted. Is the almost absolute absence of prosecutions under section 241(b) due to prosecutors not knowing about instances of assisted suicide, not having access to sufficient evidence to proceed with prosecutions (because of the private nature of assisted suicides), or choosing for other reasons not to proceed (e.g., disagreeing with the *Criminal Code* or believing that juries will refuse to convict)?

CONCLUSION

Assisted suicide is illegal in Canada. Until either the federal Parliament amends the *Criminal Code* or a differently constituted Supreme Court of Canada[11] hears another case involving assisted suicide and overturns *Rodriguez*,[12] it will remain illegal in Canada.

CHAPTER FOUR

Euthanasia

LEGISLATION

Euthanasia, like assisted suicide, is quite clearly illegal in Canada. The homicide provisions of the *Criminal Code* prohibit it.

229 Culpable homicide is murder

    (a) where the person who causes the death of a human being

        (i) means to cause his death, or
        (ii) means to cause him bodily harm that he knows is likely to cause his death, and is reckless whether death ensues or not;

231(1) Murder is first degree murder or second degree murder.
    (2) Murder is first degree murder when it is planned and deliberate ...

    (7) All murder that is not first degree murder is second degree murder.

Consent does not provide a defence to a murder charge even in a case of euthanasia since section 14 of the *Criminal Code* provides: '14. No person is entitled to consent to have death inflicted on him, and such consent does not affect the criminal responsibility of any person by whom death may be inflicted on the person by whom consent is given.' Similarly, the mercy motive of euthanasia does not provide a defence to a culpable homicide charge. Justice Dickson (as he then was) stated the general rule with respect to motive and the criminal law in *R.* v. *Lewis*, 'In ordinary parlance, the words "intent" and "motive" are frequently used interchangeably, but in the criminal law they are distinct. In most criminal trials, the mental element, the *mens rea* with which the Court is concerned, relates to "intent," i.e., the exercise of a free will to use particular means to produce a particular result, rather than with "motive," i.e., that which precedes and induces the exercise of the will. The mental element of a crime ordinarily involves no reference to motive.'[1] While Justice Dickson's general rule is that 'motive is no part of the crime and is legally irrelevant to criminal responsibility,'[2] there are a number of specific exceptions to this general rule: for some offences, negative inferences about *mens rea* or identity can be drawn from an alleged motive; motive obviously goes to self-defence; and motive may be relevant to sentencing where there is no mandatory minimum sentence.[3] However, none of these specific exceptions provides a defence to a charge of first or second degree murder.[4]

Finally, the common law defence of necessity (brought into the *Criminal Code* through section 8[5]) probably will not provide a defence in a case of euthanasia – indeed the Supreme Court of Canada rejected it in *R.* v. *Latimer*.[6] The *Criminal Code* therefore sends a very strong message that euthanasia will not be tolerated in Canada.

TEN CASES TO CONSIDER

In theory, euthanasia constitutes first or second degree murder. In practice, however, it is almost always dealt with as administering a noxious thing or manslaughter. The *Criminal Code* is being tempered by the exercise of prosecutorial discretion. Euthanasia is *de jure* murder but *de facto* a considerably less serious crime. Consider the following set of cases (including both voluntary and non-voluntary euthanasia cases so as to give the most comprehensive overview of the law before launching into the narrower argument for the decriminalization of voluntary euthanasia).

In Alberta[7] in 1982, Dr Nachum Gal (a paediatric resident) was charged with first degree murder in the death of a severely brain-damaged infant. He fled to Israel and the government of Alberta unsuccessfully sought his extradition. The nurse who actually gave the lethal dose of morphine that he ordered and the supervising nurse with whom the nurse checked the dose were both suspended from the practice of nursing for one year.[8]

In Ontario in 1991, a man dying of cancer was in a hospital on a morphine infusion to control his pain. His son turned up the infusion. A nurse came into the room, discovered the infusion rate, and turned it back down. The man died two days later and the son was charged with attempted murder. He pled guilty to mischief likely to endanger life and was put on probation.[9]

In Ontario in 1991, Nurse Scott Mataya was charged with first degree murder in the death of a terminally ill 78-year-old patient.[10] The patient's family had consented to the withdrawal of his ventilator. Following the withdrawal, the patient began to convulse, twitch, cough, and vomit mucus. Mataya, fearing that the patient's wife would re-enter the room and see her husband suffering, gave him a lethal dose of potassium chloride. Mataya pled guilty to administering a noxious thing with the intent to endanger the life of the patient and was convicted under section 245 of the *Criminal Code*.[11] The maximum sentence possible was fourteen years in jail. Mataya was given a suspended sentence and placed on three years probation (two conditions of which were: 'that he surrender his nursing licence and that he never apply for reinstatement,' and that he not 'seek employment in any health-care occupation or in a geriatric facility').[12]

In Quebec in 1992, a physician gave an injection of potassium chloride to a patient dying of AIDS at the patient's request. The disciplinary committee of the Corporation Professionelle des Médecins du Québec (CPMQ) disciplined the physician.[13] However, the CPMQ recommended against criminal charges and none were ever laid. The committee concluded that the physician had acted in the best interests of the patient and that a jury would not convict even if charges were laid.[14]

In Ontario in 1993, Dr Alberto de la Rocha was charged with second degree murder and administering a noxious thing with the intent to endanger life in the death of a terminally ill 70-year-old woman.[15] The patient had requested the removal of her ventilator. Dr de la Rocha removed the ventilator at the patient's request and, as a palliative measure, gave her morphine. He then asked a nurse to give the patient potassium chloride; the nurse refused, and he gave it to her himself. A plea bargain was arranged such that the Crown would seek a prison term but would drop the second degree murder charge if Dr de la Rocha pled guilty to administering a noxious thing with intent to cause bodily harm. The judge convicted Dr de la Rocha and, despite the Crown's submissions on sentence, placed him on probation for three years with no special conditions (such as the condition of surrender of licence as imposed on Mataya or temporary removal from practice as requested by the Crown in this case).[16]

The prosecutor in this case explained the reasoning behind his exercise of prosecutorial discretion. He identified the following factors as playing a part in his decision:

- the concern about how a jury would react to being asked to cast Dr de la Rocha in the same light as 'real killers – child killers, sex slayers, thrill killers'
- a difficulty finding any physicians willing to 'break ranks' and testify as expert witnesses
- the fact that the Sue Rodriguez case was unfolding at the same time and the Gallup Polls were indicating that eight out of ten favoured her
- the fact that Dr de la Rocha was a well-respected physician in a small northern Ontario community (a community that had a hard time attracting qualified medical personnel) and that the community was split about how to deal with the case
- the concern about what message would be sent to the community if they went to trial and, as in the Morgentaler trials, the jury acquitted Dr de la Rocha
- the fact that, if it went to trial, we would see '12 common folk from Timmins kind of chart the course for euthanasia at this point in time'[17]

With these factors in mind, and with some reluctance, he agreed to the plea bargain that was ultimately accepted in this case.

In Saskatchewan in 1993, Robert Latimer was charged with first degree murder in the death of his daughter. He placed his severely handicapped daughter in the cab of his truck and, with the purpose of alleviating what he believed to be her otherwise unrelievable suffering, asphyxiated her with carbon monoxide. Mr Latimer was convicted of second degree murder and sentenced to the mandatory minimum life sentence with no possibility of parole for ten years.[18] After he successfully appealed his conviction to the Supreme Court of Canada, the Court ordered a new trial.[19] The Court did not, as one might have thought, order the new trial on the grounds that the mandatory minimum life sentence was excessive. Rather, it ordered the new trial on the grounds that the prosecution tampered with the jury by asking the

Royal Canadian Mounted Police to question prospective jurors about their ethical and religious views on euthanasia and abortion. Mr Latimer was tried again on a charge of second degree murder, convicted, and, despite the statutory mandatory minimum life sentence with no possibility of parole for ten years, was sentenced to two years less a day, with one year to be spent in prison and one year under house arrest. This extraordinary sentence was possible because the trial judge granted Latimer a constitutional exemption from the mandatory minimum sentence on the grounds that such a punishment, in the circumstances of this case, would constitute cruel and unusual punishment and thus breach Latimer's section 12 rights under the *Charter*.[20] Mr Latimer appealed against the conviction and the Crown appealed against the sentence. The Court of Appeal dismissed Latimer's appeal, allowed the Crown's appeal, and imposed the mandatory minimum sentence.[21] The Supreme Court of Canada recently denied Latimer's appeal, and Robert Latimer returned to jail to serve at least 10 years.[22] The court unanimously held that the mandatory minimum sentence did not constitute cruel and unusual punishment and therefore did not violate Latimer's constitutional rights.

In Nova Scotia in 1994, Cheryl Myers and her husband Michael Power were charged with second degree murder in the death of Ms Myers's terminally ill father. Following a promise made to him while he was competent, they killed him when he could not function for himself, had to wear adult diapers, and was in great pain. They smothered him with a pillow. Ms Myers and Mr Power pled guilty to manslaughter and were given suspended sentences and placed on probation for three years, and ordered to complete 150 hours of community service.[23] In explaining the exercise of prosecutorial discretion, the judge said: 'The Crown acknowledging that its case on second degree murder was a viable case, but also acknowledging that the sentence which would, of necessity, be imposed should a conviction be entered on second degree murder, that is, a term of incarceration for a minimum period of 10 years would have been unduly harsh given the circumstances of the offence and the circumstances of the offender, has seen fit in his wisdom to accept the plea to the lesser and included offence.'[24]

In Ontario in 1994, Jean Brush was charged with first degree murder in the death of her husband, who was blind and suffering from Alzheimer's disease.[25] In July 1994, Mr and Mrs Brush attempted suicide unsuccessfully. In August, Mrs Brush stabbed her husband and herself.

Her husband died but she survived. Mrs Brush pled guilty to man-slaughter and was given a suspended sentence and placed on proba-tion for eighteen months.

In Alberta in 1994, Robert Cashin was charged with attempted mur-der in the death of his 69-year-old terminally ill mother, Murielle Cashin.[26] Apparently he put a large number of pills in his mother's hand and she put them in her mouth.[27] A home care nurse reported the incident to the police and Murielle Cashin was taken to hospital, where she died three days later. Robert Cashin pled guilty to administering a noxious thing and was given a suspended sentence and placed on pro-bation for two years.[28]

In Nova Scotia in 1997, Dr Nancy Morrison was charged with first degree murder following the death of Paul Mills, a 65-year-old man with cancer of the esophagus, in November 1996. After numerous interventions (including many surgeries), the health care team deter-mined that nothing more could be done for him. With the consent of Mr Mills's family, the team stopped all potentially life-sustaining treat-ment and extubated him. Unfortunately, none of the drugs adminis-tered appeared to alleviate his suffering as he seemed to be in considerable pain and was gasping for breath. In response to this situa-tion of unrelievable suffering, Dr Morrison gave Paul Mills a lethal injection of potassium chloride.

Dr Morrison was released on bail and she returned to a limited prac-tice. Despite the fact that Judge Randall concluded that Dr Morrison gave Mr Mills a lethal dose of potassium chloride, at the end of the pre-liminary hearing, he concluded that 'a Jury properly instructed could not convict the accused of the offence charged, any included offence, or any other offence' and discharged Dr Morrison.[29] The Crown sought an order of *certiorari* to quash Judge Randall's decision. However, because this was a review of a decision at a preliminary inquiry (rather than an appeal), the standard of review was excess of jurisdiction rather than error of law. Thus, while Justice Hamilton found that Judge Randall had made an error of law, she also found that the error was within his jurisdiction and, therefore, she did not have the power to grant the application.[30] The Crown decided not to appeal Justice Hamilton's decision. This closed the case with respect to criminal pro-ceedings. The Nova Scotia College of Physicians and Surgeons then investigated the matter and chose to proceed by way of a letter of rep-rimand. On 30 March 1999, Dr Morrison signed the letter, thereby admitting that she gave a lethal injection of potassium chloride to her patient. The letter remains in her file, but will not prevent her from practising in any way.[31] Thus, the entire case was closed.

These cases present a stark picture of the justice system's treatment of euthanasia: ten deaths and eight murder charges; one murder conviction and six convictions on lesser charges; one prison term. This stands in stark contrast to the strong prohibition of euthanasia found in the *Criminal Code*. Clearly, the *Criminal Code* is being tempered by the exercise of prosecutorial discretion. Euthanasia is illegal but while *de jure* murder, it is *de facto* a considerably less serious crime.

PART TWO

What the Law Should Be for the Voluntary Withholding and Withdrawal of Potentially Life-Sustaining Treatment

OVERVIEW

In this part, I begin to explore what the law *should* be. As mentioned earlier, for the purposes of this book 'should be' means 'should be in order to be consistent with the core values and values hierarchy of the Canadian legal system.' I therefore seek to answer the question of what the law should be on the legal system's own terms. That is, I do not make moral statements about what the law should be but rather, statements of what, given the overarching legal regime within which the law will reside, the law should be.

In this part, I first draw a set of values out of the common law, the *Charter*, and other relevant legislation. From these same sources, I then draw out the approach taken to resolving conflict between these values. Finally, I explore what legal regime the values and the approach taken to resolution of conflicting values imply for the issue of the voluntary withholding and withdrawal of potentially life-sustaining treatment.

This project may, at first glance, seem somewhat odd; there is widespread agreement in North American law and in the North American ethics literature that free and informed refusals of treatment by competent adults should be respected even where respecting the refusal will result in death. However, the project remains necessary for several reasons.

First, it undercuts a charge that might otherwise be made against the conclusion I draw in Part III. Without the contribution from this part, my argument would be:

Premise One: Assisted suicide and euthanasia should be treated in the same fashion as the withholding and withdrawal of potentially life-sustaining treatment.

Premise Two: The withholding and withdrawal of potentially life-sustaining treatment are legally permitted.

Conclusion: Therefore, assisted suicide and euthanasia should be legally permitted.

This argument implicitly presumes that the law is as it should be with respect to the withholding and withdrawal of potentially life-sustaining treatment. This presumption is positivistic and introduces a potentially fatal weakness into the argument.

The charge of positivism, however, loses much of its force against the conclusion I draw in Part III, because my argument actually runs as follows:

Premise One: Assisted suicide and euthanasia should be treated in the same fashion as the withholding and withdrawal of potentially life-sustaining treatment.

Premise Two: The withholding and withdrawal of potentially life-sustaining treatment *should be* legally permitted.

Conclusion: Therefore, assisted suicide and euthanasia *should be* legally permitted.

Note that the argument no longer contains the positivistic presumption.

Second, this part's project remains necessary because it anticipates another possible response to the argument made in Part III. That is, it anticipates the following response from an opponent of the decriminalization of assisted suicide and euthanasia:

Premise One: Assisted suicide and euthanasia should be treated in the same fashion as the withholding and withdrawal of potentially life-sustaining treatment.

Premise Two: The withholding and withdrawal of potentially life-sustaining treatment *should not be* permitted.

Conclusion: Therefore, assisted suicide and euthanasia *should not be* permitted.

If I succeed here in Part II, this response will not be open to opponents of the decriminalization of assisted suicide and euthanasia.

Third, this part's project allows me to clarify a significant grey area in the law, namely, the legal status of refusals of treatment made by mature minors.

Finally, this part's project indirectly lays the foundation for the claims that I will make later about assisted suicide and euthanasia. I will ultimately argue that the legal regime for assisted suicide and euthanasia should be the same as the legal regime for the withholding and withdrawal of potentially life-sustaining treatment, and I will use this part to describe that regime. Specifically, in the course of determining what the law should be with respect to the withholding and withdrawal of treatment, I arrive at a certain test. Later, in Part III, I will propose the use of this same test for assisted suicide and euthanasia.

CHAPTER FIVE

The Values

INTRODUCTION

The values discussed in this chapter are autonomy, dignity, and life. These three values are the most frequently raised in discussions of assisted death and they are the most relevant to a determination of what the law should be with respect to assisted death. Two other values (protection of the vulnerable and equality) might *prima facie* appear relevant but are not discussed as values in this section. Protection of the vulnerable is not considered as a separate value because I believe that it should be considered as a means of protecting the values of autonomy, dignity, and life rather than a value in and of itself – Justice McLachlin, as she then was, in dissent in *Rodriguez v. British Columbia (Attorney General)*[1] makes this same move from protection of the vulnerable to the preservation of life. Those who are more likely to have their autonomy or dignity violated or their lives ended inappropriately are 'the vulnerable' in the context of assisted death. Autonomy, dignity, and life are the values. Protection of the vulnerable is a way to ensure that these values are protected and promoted.

Equality is not considered because, insofar as it is relevant to the issue of assisted death, it is relevant only to euthanasia, assisted suicide, and non-voluntary withholding and withdrawal of potentially life-sustaining treatment. It is not relevant to the voluntary withholding and withdrawal of potentially life-sustaining treatment. That is, it operates as a potential argument for decriminalizing assisted suicide and euthanasia.[2] In much the same way, it also operates as a potential argument for a permissive but regulated regime with respect to non-voluntary withholding and withdrawal of treatment. However, it does not operate as any part of an argument about the appropriate legal response to voluntary refusals of treatment.

AUTONOMY

The Common Law

The legal veneration of autonomy began a number of years ago. In 1980, the Supreme Court of Canada adopted Justice Cardozo's now widely repeated phrase 'every human being of adult years and sound mind has a right to determine what shall be done with his own body.'[3] The Supreme Court of Canada adopted this philosophy in *Hopp* v. *Lepp*[4] and *Reibl* v. *Hughes*[5] and embraced it on numerous occasions since then. For example, in *Ciarlariello* v. *Schacter*, Justice Cory wrote for the Court: 'It should not be forgotten that every patient has a right to bodily integrity. This encompasses the right to determine what medical procedures will be accepted and the extent to which they will be accepted. Everyone has the right to decide what is to be done to one's own body. This includes the right to be free from medical treatment to which the individual does not consent. This concept of individual autonomy is fundamental to the common law.'[6]

This strong commitment to autonomy is also found in the common law quite apart from the context of consent to medical treatment. For example, it can be found in discussions of torts and self-incrimination.

Writing for the majority in *R.* v. *Ewanchuk*, Justice Major linked the right to physical integrity to the value of autonomy and then noted the historical foundation for the right to physical integrity:

> [H]aving control over who touches one's body, and how, lies at the core of human dignity and autonomy ...
>
> The common law has recognized for centuries that the individual's right to physical integrity is a fundamental principle, 'every man's person being sacred, and no other having a right to meddle with it in any the slightest manner': see Blackstone's Commentaries on the Laws of England (4th ed. 1770), Book III, at p. 120.[7]

With respect to self-incrimination, Justice Wilson (writing in dissent in *Thomson Newspapers Ltd.* v. *Canada (Director of Investigation and Research)* but later embraced by Chief Justice Lamer in dissent in *R.* v. *Jones*[8] and then by Justice Iacobucci for the majority in *R.* v. *White*[9]) wrote: 'Having reviewed the historical origins of the rights against compellability and self-incrimination and the policy justifications advanced in favour of their retention in more modern times, I conclude that their preservation is prompted by a concern that the privacy and personal autonomy and dignity of the individual be respected by the state.'[10]

Clearly, there is a strong commitment to autonomy in the common law.

The *Charter*

In *R. v. Morgentaler*, Chief Justice Dickson noted the common law tradition of valuing autonomy and concluded that '"[s]ecurity of the person," in other words, is not a value alien to our legal landscape. With the advent of the *Charter*, security of the person [taken to include autonomy] has been elevated to the status of a constitutional norm.'[11] Through *Morgentaler* and subsequent security of the person cases, this has certainly been proven true. Furthermore, the common law tradition of valuing autonomy has also been carried on through the interpretation of other sections of the *Charter*.

Purpose of the Charter

The jurisprudence makes it clear that the *Charter* must be interpreted in a broad and purposive manner.[12] When the Court discusses the purposes of the *Charter*, autonomy is clearly a central value. Speaking of the general values underlying the *Charter* in *Big M.*, Chief Justice Dickson wrote for the majority:

> Freedom can primarily be characterized by the absence of coercion or constraint. If a person is compelled by the state or the will of another to a course of action or inaction which he would not otherwise have chosen, he is not acting of his own volition and he cannot be said to be truly free. One of the major purposes of the *Charter* is to protect, within reason, from compulsion or restraint. Coercion includes not only such blatant forms of compulsion as direct commands to act or refrain from acting on pain of sanction, coercion includes indirect forms of control which determine or limit alternative courses of conduct available to others. Freedom in a broad sense embraces both the absences of coercion and constraint, and the right to manifest beliefs and practices. Freedom means that, subject to

such limitations as are necessary to protect public safety, order, health, or morals or the fundamental rights and freedoms of others, no one is to be forced to act in a way contrary to his beliefs or his conscience.[13]

Similarly, in *Morgentaler*, Justice Wilson (concurring) wrote for herself: 'Thus, the rights guaranteed in the *Charter* erect around each individual, metaphorically speaking, an invisible fence over which the state will not be allowed to trespass. The role of the courts is to map out, piece by piece, the parameters of the fence.'[14] Both of these statements are classic statements of a liberal individualist philosophy. They convey a strong commitment to the value of autonomy.

Section 7

From an analysis of the purposes of the *Charter*, one can move to a consideration of the content of the specific rights and freedoms guaranteed under the *Charter*. Section 7 is of particular relevance to the project of determining the core values that should ground a legal response to assisted death. Section 7 of the *Charter* provides 'the right to life, liberty, and security of the person and the right not to be deprived thereof except in accordance with the principles of fundamental justice.'

The right to liberty and the right to security of the person are clearly and directly related to autonomy. The Supreme Court of Canada has reflected on the content of these rights in a number of decisions and has concluded that these rights include control over one's physical and mental integrity. In *Morgentaler*, Chief Justice Dickson writing for himself and Justice Lamer (as he then was) wrote: '[S]tate interference with bodily integrity and serious state-imposed psychological stress, at least in the criminal law context, constitute a breach of security of the person.'[15]

Justice Wilson (writing for herself) took a classic liberal individualist approach to this abortion case. Describing the right to liberty, she wrote: 'I would conclude, therefore, that the right to liberty contained in s. 7 guarantees to every individual a degree of personal autonomy over important decisions intimately affecting their private lives.'[16]

Describing the impact of the abortion law on a woman's right to security of the person, she wrote: 'This is not, in my view, just a matter of interfering with her right to liberty in the sense (already discussed) of her right of personal autonomy in decision-making, it is a direct interference with her physical 'person' as well. She is truly being treated as a means – a means to an end which she does not desire but over which she has no control.'[17]

In *Rodriguez*, Justice Sopinka, writing for the majority, embraced both Chief Justice Dickson's narrower and Justice Wilson's more expansive positions as reflected in the passages quoted above. Justice Sopinka summed up the Canadian jurisprudence on security of the person in the following way: 'There is no question, then, that personal autonomy, at least with respect to the right to make choices concerning one's own body, control over one's physical and psychological integrity, and basic human dignity are encompassed within security of the person, at least to the extent of freedom from criminal prohibitions which interfere with these.'[18]

It is clear that section 7 reflects the value of, and demands respect for, autonomy especially with respect to decision-making about one's body.[19]

Section 8

Section 8 provides that 'Everyone has the right to be secure against unreasonable search and seizure.' When exploring the nature and scope of this right, the Supreme Court of Canada has focused on the right to privacy. The Court has then looked behind the right to privacy to the core value of autonomy. Justice La Forest with Chief Justice Dickson (concurring) wrote in *R. v. Dyment*: 'The foregoing approach [to section 8] is altogether fitting for a constitutional document enshrined at a time when, Westin tells us, society has come to realize that privacy is at the heart of liberty in a modern state; see Alan F. Westin, Privacy and Freedom (1970), pp. 349–350. Grounded in man's physical and moral autonomy, privacy is essential for the well-being of the individual. For this reason alone, it is worthy of constitutional protection, but it also has profound significance for the public order. The restraints imposed on government to pry into the lives of the citizen go to the essence of a democratic state.'[20]

Similarly, in *R. v. Plant*, Justice Sopinka for the majority wrote that investigative practices 'have been found to run afoul of the s. 8 right against unreasonable search and seizure in that the dignity, integrity and autonomy of the individual are directly compromised.'[21] The phrase 'dignity, integrity and autonomy' has been picked up in subsequent cases as capturing the value that lies behind the constitutional right to privacy protected by section 8.[22]

The right to privacy lies behind the section 8 right to be secure against unreasonable search and seizure, and respect for autonomy lies behind the right to privacy.

Section 2

The Supreme Court of Canada has clearly identified autonomy as one of the core values behind the freedoms guaranteed in section 2.[23] With respect to freedom of conscience and religion, Chief Justice Dickson writing for the majority in *Big M.* said:

> It should also be noted, however, that an emphasis on individual conscience and individual judgment also lies at the heart of our democratic political tradition. The ability of each citizen to make free and informed decisions is the absolute prerequisite for the legitimacy, acceptability, and efficacy of our system of self-government. It is because of this centrality of the rights associated with freedom of individual consciences both to basic beliefs about human worth and dignity and to a free and democratic political system that American jurisprudence has emphasized the primacy or 'firstness' of the First Amendment. It is this same centrality that in my view underlies their designation in the *Canadian Charter of Rights and Freedoms* as 'fundamental.' They are the *sine qua non* of the political tradition underlying the *Charter.*
>
> Viewed in this context, the purpose of freedom of conscience and religion becomes clear. The values that underlie our political and philosophic traditions demand that every individual be free to hold and to manifest whatever beliefs and opinions his or her conscience dictates, provided *inter alia* only that such manifestations do not injure his or her neighbours or their parallel rights to hold and manifest beliefs and opinions of their own. Religious belief and practice are historically prototypical and, in many ways, paradigmatic of conscientiously-held beliefs and manifestations and are therefore protected by the *Charter.*[24]

With respect to freedom of expression, Justice La Forest for the Court in *C.B.C.* v. *New Brunswick* quoted approvingly from his own dissenting reasons in *R.J.R. MacDonald Inc.* v. *Canada (Attorney General)*:

> Although freedom of expression is undoubtedly a fundamental value, there are other fundamental values that are also deserving of protection and consideration by the courts. When these values come into conflict, as

they tend to do, it is necessary for the courts to make choices based not upon an abstract, platonic analysis, but upon a concrete weighing of the relative significance of each of the relevant values in our community in the specific context. This the Court has done by weighing freedom of expression claims in light of their relative connection to a set of even more fundamental values. In *Keegstra*, supra at pp. 762–63, Dickson CJ identified these fundamental or 'core' values as including the search for political, artistic and scientific truth, the protection of individual *autonomy* and self-development, and the promotion of public participation in the democratic process.[25]

With respect to freedom of association, in *Lavigne* v. *Ontario Public Service Employees Union (OPSEU)*, Justice La Forest, for himself and Justices Sopinka and Gonthier, wrote: 'At the core of the guarantee of freedom of association is the individual's freedom to choose the path of self-actualization. This is an aspect of the *autonomy* of the individual.'[26]

Conclusion

Thus, it can be concluded that the Supreme Court of Canada sees autonomy as one of the core values underlying both the purpose of the *Charter* and a number of its specific rights and freedoms.

Other Relevant Legislation

Consent to treatment legislation found in various provinces across Canada also clearly reflects the value of autonomy.[27] In Ontario, for example, through the *Health Care Consent Act, 1996*, health care providers are instructed not to administer treatment without the consent of a competent patient or, if the patient is incompetent, without the consent of the patient's surrogate decision-maker. Surrogate decision-makers are in turn instructed to make substituted judgments wherever possible (i.e., to make decisions according to what they think the patient would have wanted).[28] Enhancing autonomy is an explicitly stated purpose of this legislation.[29]

The value of autonomy can be seen in legislation other than that concerned with consent to treatment. As noted by Justice L'Heureux-Dubé for herself in *R.* v. *Cuerrier* with respect to the assault provisions in the *Criminal Code*:

[T]he assault scheme [in the *Criminal Code*] is also about protecting and promoting people's physical *autonomy*, by recognizing each individual's power to consent, or to withhold consent, to any touching ...

Parliament has recognized with s. 265(3), that in order to maximize the protection of physical integrity and personal *autonomy*, only consent obtained without negating the voluntary agency of the person being touched is legally valid.[30]

Similarly, Justice Major wrote for the majority in *R. v. Ewanchuk*: 'The rationale underlying the criminalization of assault explains this. Society is committed to protecting the personal integrity, both physical and psychological, of every individual. Having control over who touches one's body, and how, lies at the core of human dignity and *autonomy*. The inclusion of assault and sexual assault in the Code expresses society's determination to protect the security of the person from any non-consensual contact or threats of force.'[31]

Yet again, autonomy surfaces as a core value in the Canadian legal system.

DIGNITY

Dignity is closely related to autonomy in the Canadian legal system. Although frequently bundled together with autonomy,[32] it also appears independently.[33] Like autonomy, it is found in the common law, *Charter* jurisprudence, and a variety of pieces of legislation. Like autonomy, it is considered a core value of the legal system: 'that respect for human *dignity* is one of the underlying principles upon which our society is based is unquestioned.'[34]

The Common Law

Several areas of the common law reflect the value accorded to dignity. As noted by Justice Cory writing for the majority in *R. v. Stillman*, '[t]raditionally, the common law and Canadian society have recognized the fundamental importance of the innate dignity of the individual.'[35] Reference to the common law with respect to search and seizure, defamation, and self-incrimination illustrates this recognition.[36]

The state power of search and seizure is limited at common law by concerns about human dignity. The courts have long weighed the benefits of permitting searches (e.g., crime control) against the harms searches cause to human dignity. As Justice La Forest with Chief Justice Dickson (concurring) noted in *Dyment*: 'The use of a person's body without his consent to obtain information about him, invades an area of personal privacy essential to the maintenance of his human dignity.'[37]

The common law approach to defamation has also focused on dignity. Justice Cory for the majority in *Hill* v. *Church of Scientology of Toronto* linked defamation to dignity through a concern with the preservation of a good reputation:

> At the same time, it [a good reputation] serves the equally or perhaps more fundamentally important purpose of fostering our self-image and sense of self-worth. This sentiment was eloquently expressed by Justice Stewart in Rosenblatt v. Baer, 383 US 75 (1966), who stated at p. 92: 'The right of a man to the protection of his own reputation from unjustified invasion and wrongful hurt reflects no more than our basic concept of the essential dignity and worth of every human being – a concept at the root of any decent system of ordered liberty.'[38]

Finally, the common law approach to self-incrimination has also focused on dignity. The Court has linked a variety of common law rules (e.g., the confessions rule) to the principle against self-incrimination and then linked that principle to the value of dignity. Justice Iacobucci for the majority in *White* wrote: 'The definition of the principle against self-incrimination as an assertion of human freedom is intimately connected to the principle's underlying rationale. As explained by the Chief Justice in *Jones, supra*, at pp. 250–51, the principle has at least two key purposes, namely to protect against unreliable confessions, and to protect against abuses of power by the state. There is both an individual and a societal interest in achieving both of these protections. Both protections are linked to the value placed by Canadian society upon individual privacy, personal autonomy and dignity.'[39]

The *Charter*

The Supreme Court of Canada has, on numerous occasions, indicated that dignity lies at the heart of the *Charter*. Indeed, Justice Cory, writing for the majority in *Hill*, describes the dignity of the individual as 'a concept which underlies all the *Charter* rights.'[40]

The Supreme Court of Canada has also indicated that dignity is the basis of a number of the specific rights and freedoms guaranteed by the *Charter*. The discussion of the value of autonomy as reflected in *Charter* jurisprudence supports the claim that dignity lies behind sections 2, 7, and 8 of the *Charter*. In this section, I will establish that dignity lies behind sections 11, 12, and 15.[41]

Section 11

Justice Sopinka, for the Court, in *Amway* made it clear that dignity underlies the section 11(c) right not to be compelled to be a witness in proceedings against oneself: 'Applying a purposive interpretation to s. 11(c), I am of the opinion that it was intended to protect the individual against the affront to dignity and privacy inherent in a practice which enables the prosecution to force the person charged to supply the evidence out of his or her own mouth.'[42]

Section 12

Similarly, the Court has said the section 12 right not to be subjected to cruel and unusual punishment is concerned with dignity. In *R. v. Smith*, the majority of the Court accepted the proposition that assessments of a sentence against the section 12 standard can depend upon whether the sentence is 'degrading to human dignity.'[43] In *Kindler v. Canada (Minister of Justice)*, Justice Cory held the death penalty up to section 12 scrutiny. He wrote at length about the role of dignity in the Canadian legal system and concluded in relation to section 12 that: '[it] is the principle of human dignity which lies at the heart of s. 12. It is the dignity and importance of the individual which is the essence and the · cornerstone of democratic government.'[44]

Section 15

The Supreme Court of Canada recently took the opportunity presented in *Law v. Canada (Minister of Employment and Immigration)*[45] to summarize and clarify the approach to be taken to claims made under the section 15 equality provision of the *Charter*.[46] Justice Iacobucci, writing for the Court, wrote: 'It may be said that the purpose of s. 15(1) is to prevent the violation of essential human dignity and freedom through the imposition of disadvantage, stereotyping, or political or social prejudice, and to promote a society in which all persons enjoy equal recognition at law as human beings or as members of Canadian society, equally capable and equally deserving of concern, respect and consideration ... In the articulation of the purpose of s. 15(1) just provided on the basis of past cases, a focus is quite properly placed upon the goal of assuring human dignity by the remedying of discriminatory treatment.[47] He then offered the following definition of dignity: 'Human dignity means that an individual or group feels self-respect and self-worth. It is concerned with physical and psychological integrity and empowerment.'[48]

Thus, dignity lies at the heart of the *Charter* and grounds many of the specific rights and freedoms protected by the *Charter*.

Other Relevant Legislation

A wide range of legislation, most notably human rights statutes and the *Criminal Code*, also clearly reflects the value of dignity.[49]

Human rights legislation across the country serves the value of dignity. For example, the stated objectives of the Yukon *Human Rights Act* include:

(a) to further in the Yukon the public policy that every individual is free and equal in dignity and rights ...

(c) to promote recognition of the inherent dignity and worth and of the equal and inalienable rights of all members of the human family.[50]

Similarly, the purposes of the Nova Scotia *Human Rights Act* include: '(a) recognize the inherent dignity and the equal and inalienable rights of all members of the human family.'[51]

A number of provisions of the *Criminal Code* also serve the preservation of dignity. Consider, for example, the objectives of the provisions about criminal libel[52] and the promotion of hatred[53] respectively as described by the Supreme Court of Canada. Justice Cory, for the majority in R. v. *Lucas* noted: 'The protection of an individual's reputation from wilful and false attack recognizes both the innate dignity of the individual and the integral link between reputation and the fruitful participation of an individual in Canadian society. Preventing damage to reputation as a result of criminal libel is a legitimate goal of criminal law.'[54]

In R. v. *Keegstra*, Justice McLachlin commented on the objective of the provision about promotion of hatred: 'As the Attorney General of Canada puts it, the objective of the legislation is, "among other things, to protect racial, religious and other groups from the wilful promotion of hatred and the breakdown of racial and social harmony," and "to prevent the destruction of our multicultural society." These aims are subsumed in the twin values of social harmony and individual dignity.'[55] Justice McLachlin wrote in dissent, but the majority agreed with her on the objective of the legislation.

Dignity is clearly a core value in the Canadian legal system.

LIFE

Respect for life is a core value of the Canadian legal system. However, unlike autonomy and dignity, this value is not reflected in all areas of the legal system. The common law does not express the value of life. At common law, all possibility of litigation for personal injury is extinguished by death.[56]

Section 7 of the *Charter* guarantees 'the right not to be deprived of life, liberty, and security of the person except in accordance with the principles of fundamental justice.' This provision of the *Charter* reflects the value of life in at least two ways: first, as 'the sanctity of life, which is one of the three *Charter* values protected by s. 7,'[57] and second, through the principles of fundamental justice. In *Rodriguez*, Justice Sopinka (for the majority) explored the value of life in his discussion of the principles of fundamental justice: 'What the preceding review [historical and comparative international] demonstrates is that Canada and other Western democracies recognize and apply the principle of the sanctity of life as a general principle.'[58] Thus section 7 demonstrates that the Canadian legal system accords value to life.[59]

The *Criminal Code* has numerous provisions that aim to protect life. As Justice Sopinka noted in *Rodriguez*: 'This purpose [protecting the vulnerable] is grounded in the state interest in protecting life and reflects the policy of the state that human life should not be depreciated by allowing life to be taken. This policy finds expression not only in the provisions of our *Criminal Code* which prohibit murder and other violent acts against others notwithstanding the consent of the victim, but also in the policy against capital punishment and, until its repeal, attempted suicide.'[60]

Part VIII of the *Criminal Code* establishes a series of 'offences against the person' that aim to protect life. These include: violations of duties tending to preservation of life; criminal negligence causing death; murder; manslaughter; and assisted suicide. Furthermore, section 14 provides that 'No person is entitled to consent to have death inflicted on him, and such consent does not affect the criminal responsibility of any person by whom death may be inflicted on the person by whom consent is given.'

Legislation other than the *Criminal Code* also reflects the value of life. For example, a variety of federal and provincial statutes create actions where, at common law under *actio personalis moritur cum persona*, no action lies. For example, survival of actions statutes extend the person's ability to sue beyond death (through his or her estate).[61] Fatal injuries acts generate standing for third parties to sue following the death of another.[62]

Finally, the value accorded to life was revealed through the abolishment of capital punishment. As Justice Sopinka notes in *Rodriguez*:

> To the extent that there is a consensus, it is that human *life* must be respected and we must be careful not to undermine the institutions that protect it.
>
> This consensus finds legal expression in our legal system which prohibits capital punishment. This prohibition is supported, in part, on the basis that allowing the state to kill will cheapen the value of human life and thus the state will serve in a sense as a role model for individuals in society.[63]

Thus, life is clearly a core value in the Canadian legal system.

CHAPTER SIX

Resolution of Conflicts among Values

INTRODUCTION

Conflict may arise whenever there is more than one person and/or more than one fundamental value involved; we must ask how the legal system resolves such conflicts.[1] Two kinds of conflict should concern us here: internal and external conflict. Internal conflict arises when two or more values are in conflict with respect to one individual. For example, to respect a person's autonomous wish to have treatment withdrawn can mean that the life of that person will not be preserved. External conflict arises when the same value applies to more than one person and cannot be realized for all, or when one value applies to one person, another value applies to another person, and both values cannot be realized. For example, two persons' autonomous wishes can be incompatible, making it impossible to respect both persons' autonomy. Also, respecting one person's autonomous wishes can mean that the life of another person will not be preserved.

The Canadian legal system almost always resolves internal conflict by holding that autonomy takes precedence over life. The Canadian legal system resolves external conflict by applying the principle that the harm of not realizing the value for the one person must be weighed against the harm of not realizing the value for the other and the greater harm is to be avoided. To support these claims, I will now review of the limits on life and autonomy.[2]

LIMITS ON LIFE

As shown earlier, the value of life clearly lies at the heart of the Canadian legal system. It is not, however, an absolute value, and it is less important than the values of autonomy and dignity. The legal system's core commitment to protecting life is severely limited.

First, the common law does not express the value of life. As noted previously, tort actions do not survive the death of the tort victim. Second, even where statutes seem to express the value of life in the common law, they do so only in a very limited way. While legislation generates standing to sue for the estate and for third parties, it frequently and severely limits the damages. Most notably, loss of life itself is not a compensable damage. In other words, legislation recognizes the instrumental value of life (e.g., for fatal injuries actions, death of a loved one causes grief, and for survival actions, death results in lost wages and the prospect of a shortened life causes sadness) but not the intrinsic value (e.g., for survival actions, there are no non-pecuniary losses where there was instantaneous death).[3]

Third, the *Criminal Code* does not manifest an unequivocal commitment to life. Suicide is no longer an offence. Killing in self-defence or war is not an offence. Failure to perform the simplest of rescues or to provide the smallest of assistances is not an offence even if the person left unaided dies as a direct consequence of the failure.[4]

Fourth, the alleged consensus about capital punishment that Justice Sopinka referred to in *Rodriguez* may not exist. The legal system does not completely prohibit capital punishment. In 1976 when Parliament abolished the death penalty for all offences under the *Criminal Code*, it explicitly left the death penalty as a penalty for war crimes under the *War Crimes Act*.[5] Furthermore, the public and its elected representatives do not clearly support the prohibition on capital punishment. Public opinion polls put support for capital punishment at 52 per cent.[6] And, as noted by Justice McLachlin in *Kindler*: 'The last execution in Canada was in 1962. Yet, while the death penalty has been formally abolished in this country, its possible return continues to be debated. In 1987, in response to persistent calls to bring back the death penalty, members of Parliament conducted a free vote on a resolution to reinstate capital punishment. The result was a defeat of the motion, but the vote – 148–127 – fell far short of reflecting a broad consensus even among Parliamentarians.'[7]

Fifth, the Supreme Court of Canada has recognized that the sanctity of life principle is not absolute. Writing for the majority in *Rodriguez*, Justice Sopinka endorsed the Law Reform Commission's characterization of the sanctity of life principle as a limited principle:

The Law Reform Commission expressed this philosophy appropriately in its Working Paper 28, Euthanasia, Aiding Suicide and Cessation of Treatment (1982), at p. 36: 'Preservation of human life is acknowledged to be a fundamental value of our society. Historically, our criminal law has changed very little on this point. Generally speaking, it sanctions the principle of the sanctity of human life. Over the years, however, law has come to temper the apparent absolutism of the principle, to delineate its intrinsic limitations and to define its true dimensions.'[8]

Later in the judgment, Justice Sopinka concluded: 'Canada and other Western democracies recognize and apply the principle of the sanctity of life as a general principle which is subject to limited and narrow exceptions in situations in which notions of personal autonomy and dignity must prevail.'[9]

Thus, the value of life may, at least in some circumstances, be outweighed by the value of autonomy and dignity.

LIMITS ON AUTONOMY

Autonomy is also a core value in the Canadian legal system but it too is not an absolute value. There are some limits on the legal system's commitment to respecting autonomy. I will consider these limits within the framework of internal and external conflict discussed previously.

Internal Conflict

The legal system does not generally support restrictions on the autonomy of an individual in order to prevent harm to that individual. Suicide and attempted suicide are legal. Under the common law I can consent to being physically beaten in a boxing match or a hockey game.[10] The common law lets me hang-glide, climb Mount Everest, and engage in other very dangerous activities. The general underlying philosophy is that 'for [...] freedom to be meaningful, people must have the right to make choices that accord with their own values, regardless of how unwise or foolish those choices may appear to others.'[11]

This general philosophy has some exceptions. Most notably, under section 14 of the *Criminal Code*, 'no person is entitled to consent to have death inflicted on him, and such consent does not affect the criminal responsibility of any person by whom death may be inflicted on the person by whom consent is given.' Under contract law, an autonomous decision to sell oneself into slavery or to contract out of human rights will not be enforced.[12] Under mental health legislation in all but one province, competent individuals can be confined against their wishes when they suffer from a mental disorder and pose a danger to themselves.[13] In a few provinces, such individuals can also be treated against their wishes.[14] I concede that these exceptions show that a competent individual's autonomy is sometimes limited solely in order to prevent harm to that individual. However, three counter-arguments may be made in response to the applicability of these exceptions to the issue of refusing potentially life-sustaining treatment.

First, the *Criminal Code*, slavery, and involuntary confinement to psychiatric institutions examples involve restrictions on liberty, but do not involve violations of bodily integrity in order to prevent harm to the individual. And yet, just such a violation is at stake with involuntary potentially life-sustaining treatment. Therefore, these examples do not provide strong support for restricting respect for refusals of potentially life-sustaining treatment.

Second, many would argue that refusing potentially life-sustaining treatment is not the same thing as consenting to have death inflicted upon oneself. Furthermore, if they were the same thing, the legitimacy of section 14 of the *Criminal Code* would be at issue in this book. For the anti-positivist reasons discussed earlier, the section's presence in the *Criminal Code* cannot be used as an argument against removing it from the *Criminal Code*.

Third, in regard to the mental health provisions, it is critical to note that all but one Canadian jurisdiction permit the involuntary confinement of competent individuals,[15] a very small minority permit the involuntary treatment of competent involuntary patients,[16] and none permit treatment against the wishes of competent voluntary patients. Thus, by a very strong margin, the involuntary treatment of competent individuals is not tolerated. Therefore, taken as a whole, the mental health provisions actually *support* the claim that refusals of potentially life-sustaining treatment made by competent individuals should be respected.

Of course, these responses will not persuade everyone. However, even if we assume that they are not persuasive, we can still legitimately conclude that the examples of instances in which autonomy is limited in order to prevent harm to the competent individual do not support the claim that refusals of potentially life-sustaining treatment made by competent individuals should not be respected. In the vast majority of instances (and, in particular, in those instances which involve violations of bodily integrity and are therefore most analogous to refusals of potentially life-sustaining treatment), autonomy is not so limited. Therefore, on the values and the approach taken to resolution of conflicts among values by the current legal system, one should respect refusals of potentially life-sustaining treatment made by competent individuals when the only persons potentially hurt by the refusal are the individuals themselves.

External Conflict

As the saying goes, 'My right to swing my fist ends at the tip of your nose.' In other words, autonomy must be respected unless respecting it will result in greater harm to others. If respecting autonomy will result in harm to others, then that harm must be weighed against the harm of not respecting autonomy. The common law, the *Charter*, and other relevant legislation all manifest this general approach.

For example, at common law, I cannot simply choose to attack another person. The tort of battery restricts my autonomy in order to prevent harm to others. Similarly, concerns about the welfare of others limit my rights and freedoms guaranteed under the *Charter*. Chief Justice Dickson, writing for the majority in *Big M*, described the limits on autonomy under the *Charter* as 'such limitations as are necessary to protect public safety, order, health, or morals or the fundamental rights and freedoms of others.'[17] Finally, under a variety of pieces of legislation, the state's concern for others' well-being limits my autonomy. For example, under the *Criminal Code*, I am prevented from taking another person's property without permission and, under mental health legislation, competent individuals can be confined against their wishes in order to prevent harm to third parties.[18]

Thus, the value of preventing harm to others at least in some circumstances outweighs the value of autonomy. Clearly, we require a balancing of harms when a situation generates an external conflict between the core values in the Canadian legal system. No general formula exists for such balancing. However, we can define a contested context for balancing, explore the legal system's responses to analogous contexts, and then draw conclusions about how the balance should be conducted in the contested context.[19]

For the purposes of this part, the contested context is the withholding or withdrawal of potentially life-sustaining treatment. On the one hand, involuntary treatment breaches the individual's autonomy, specifically self-control over his or her bodily integrity. On the other hand, respecting refusals might also bring about harms.

What has the legal system done in analogous contexts? Specifically, what has the legal system said about balancing violations of bodily integrity against harms to third parties? In brief, the legal system has held that violations of bodily integrity can be outweighed by harms to third parties but only on rare and carefully circumscribed occasions. Consider the following examples of situations in which the legal system does not permit the violation of bodily integrity:

- The state cannot treat pregnant women for drug addiction against their wishes even though the addiction may be placing the fetus at risk.[20]
- In all provinces permitting *inter vivos* transplants, the free and informed consent of competent donors is required. Therefore, even where a child needs a kidney to survive, the state cannot compel a parent who is a match for the child to donate the kidney. Even where one person needs a blood transfusion to survive, the state cannot order another individual who is a match to donate blood.[21]

On the other hand, consider the following examples of situations in which the legal system does permit the violation of bodily integrity:

- Courts have the authority to order the involuntary taking of blood from a competent person suspected of having committed a sexual assault if the conditions set out in the *Criminal Code* have been met.[22]
- Medical officers of health have the authority to order confinement and examination (including blood sampling) against the wishes of competent individuals under the provincial public health legislation.[23]
- Mental health provisions allow the involuntary confinement of competent individuals where they pose a threat of danger to others.[24]

The legal system clearly permits confinement and limits on freedoms to prevent harms to others but only very rarely does it permit involuntary intrusions into bodily integrity. Intrusions are permitted only when authority is clearly established through legislation and when the harm to third parties is severe.[25] When competent individuals refuse treatment, the harms to third parties do not even approach the severity of the harms associated with the examples discussed above. The harms to third parties associated with respecting such refusals are clearly less than the harms for which the state will not allow involuntary intrusions into bodily integrity. Therefore, reasoning by analogy, in the contested context of withholding and withdrawal of potentially life-sustaining treatment, the harm to others will not outweigh the harm of not respecting autonomy. Treatment in the face of an autonomous refusal is therefore not justified.

CONCLUSION

We can now take the relevant core values and the approach taken to the resolution of conflicts among values and apply them to the issue of the voluntary withholding and withdrawal of potentially life-sustaining treatment from competent individuals. In brief, an autonomous refusal of potentially life-sustaining treatment should be respected. The implications of this statement will be spelled out in the next chapter.

CHAPTER SEVEN

A Legal Regime for the Withholding and Withdrawal of Potentially Life-Sustaining Treatment from Competent Individuals

INTRODUCTION

I will begin presenting the first part of my alternative approach to the regulation of voluntary assisted death for competent individuals in Canada by exploring what, on the basis of the values and the approach taken to the resolution of conflicts among values previously discussed, the legal regime with respect to voluntary withholding and withdrawal of potentially life-sustaining treatment from competent individuals should be. Given that, as argued in the previous chapter, an autonomous refusal of potentially life-sustaining treatment should be respected, what should the legal regime be?

First, I will argue that, given the core values and the approach taken to resolving conflicts among values, refusals should be respected when the refusal is made by a competent individual, the refusal is voluntary, and the refusal is informed. I will argue that this approach should be clearly set out in statute and that the operationalizing of the approach should receive much more attention than it has to date. Then I will argue that, again given the core values, the approach taken to resolving conflicts among values, and other considerations that will be spelled out where appropriate, respect for refusals should *not* be limited to the following elements which are sometimes proposed by others working in this field[1]: terminal illness; the particular type of treatment being withheld or withdrawn (e.g., mechanical ventilation vs artificial hydration and nutrition); the presence of unrelievable physical pain; the absence of any reasonable alternative; and age.

A THREE-PART TEST

My earlier review of the legal system established the importance of the values of autonomy, dignity, and life and, in circumstances of internal conflict, the privileging of autonomy over life and in circumstances of external conflict the balancing of harms. From this, I derived the guiding principle that an autonomous refusal of potentially life-sustaining treatment should be respected. From this principle, we can derive a test for when to respect a refusal of potentially life-sustaining treatment. In this section, I will set out the current legal approach, assess it by holding it up to the core values and guiding principle, and suggest a modified approach in light of the assessment.

The Current Legal Approach

Interestingly, the current legal approach consists primarily of common law rather than legislation. As described in Part I, few provinces have consent legislation and the federal *Criminal Code* is at best confusing and, at worst, inconsistent with the common law. Within the common law, Canadian courts have issued a number of decisions on refusals of treatment.[2] Unfortunately, nowhere have they provided a clear, concise, and comprehensive statement of when a refusal of treatment decision must be respected. We must therefore closely read the relevant refusal of treatment cases and extrapolate from the doctrine of informed consent as developed in the context of health care.[3]

Legal Liability of Doctors and Hospitals in Canada, the leading text in this area, sets out the following test for a valid consent:

Consent must be:

(a) given voluntarily (without coercion, undue influence, or fraudulent misrepresentation);
(b) given by a patient who has capacity;
(c) referable both to the treatment and to the person who is to administer that treatment;
and
(d) given by a patient who is informed.[4]

This description has been echoed in legislation[5] and explicitly relied upon in case law.[6] However, this description of the test is not entirely accurate. I would argue for the following alternative description of the current test in the common law. A consent must be:

1 *Informed.* To be informed, there must have been accurate and adequate disclosure of information. Adequacy of disclosure is assessed according to a modified objective standard (i.e., what the reasonable person in the patient's position would want to know).[7] Accurate information is information that describes the treatment itself and the person who is to administer the treatment. Fraudulent misrepresentation of the potential harms or benefits is clearly inaccurate disclosure.[8]

2 *Voluntary.* Examples of influences that can compromise the voluntariness of a decision include force (actual or threatened) and power-imbalance coupled with exploitation.[9]

3 *Made by an individual with the capacity to understand the nature and consequences of the decision.*[10] Examples of influences that can compromise competency include youth[11] and disease (particularly mental illness).

This description differs from the leading text's description in two important ways. First, the requirement that consent be 'referable both to the treatment and to the person who is to administer that treatment' is not treated as a separate element but rather as a part of (a). This is because, to be properly informed, an individual must know exactly what treatment she is consenting to and who will be providing the treatment. Reference to the treatment and the treatment provider serves no more than an informative role.

Second, inaccurate descriptions of the intervention itself or fraudulent misrepresentations of the potential harms or benefits of the intervention are placed under information rather than voluntariness. Inaccurate disclosures go to whether the decision is informed and do not compromise the person's freedom.

At least one major issue remains unsettled with respect to the current test. As discussed in Part I, it is not yet clear whether the courts believe that refusals of treatment by mature minors should be treated differently than refusals of competent adults. Some courts have articulated an unlimited mature minor rule (i.e., if a minor understands the nature and consequences of a particular decision, then the minor's decision should be respected), while others have articulated a limited mature minor rule (i.e., if a minor understands the nature and consequences of a particular decision and the minor's decision is in the minor's best interests from the perspective of the court, then the minor's decision should be respected). The Supreme Court of Canada has not yet addressed this issue.

Assessing the Current Legal Approach

When the current approach is held up to the core values and guiding principle established earlier, it appears to fare quite well: the basic elements of the test (decisions must be informed, voluntary, and made by a competent individual) are clearly and closely aligned with respect for autonomy.[12] However, I would argue that several serious weaknesses remain in the current approach. It is not clear whether the individual must understand the information disclosed. In *Reibl* v. *Hughes*, the Supreme Court of Canada hinted at understanding as a requirement. However, it did so in passing, in the context of language comprehension, and without any clear statement of the nature and scope of the understanding required.[13] Because of this lack of clarity, individuals receive inconsistent treatment (as different health care providers interpret the test differently) and health care providers face inconsistent standards of civil liability.

A second weakness is the lack of clarity in the legal status of refusals of potentially life-sustaining treatment by mature minors. This uncertainty leaves individuals vulnerable to inconsistent treatment and health care providers vulnerable to liability under an uncertain standard.

Third, the test for when a treatment decision must be respected has never been clearly and comprehensively spelled out by the relevant authorities in many Canadian jurisdictions (whether that be the provincial legislatures, provincial courts, or the Supreme Court of Canada). As a result, some confusion remains in practice. Since the test has not been spelled out, it is not applied in a thorough and rigorous way. Because of the law's extraordinary focus on the disclosure of risks, the law tends to focus on the disclosure of information element and pay little attention to the other elements. By setting out a test that must be followed, the courts or the legislatures would contribute to ensuring that all elements of the test are addressed and that autonomous refusals of treatment are respected.

Finally, little guidance is available with respect to operationalizing the test. Consider, for example, the element of competency. As mentioned previously, few provincial statutes and no national statutes clearly direct practice in this arena. No clinical practice guidelines have been adopted by, for example, the Canadian Medical Association. Within the Canadian health professions there is a noted lack of expertise with regard to competency assessments.[14] Furthermore, throughout North American medical practice and education, there are no standardized instruments for competency assessments or competency assessment training.[15] While suggestions for instruments and guidelines have been made in medico-scientific literature, none have been formally adopted in Canada. In the absence of guidance with respect to operationalizing the test, practitioners are left with little guidance or comfort as they decide how to proceed. More importantly, patients are left without the protection that comes from clear procedures set out in a regime specifically designed to protect their rights and interests.

A Modified Approach

I would first argue that for a decision to be informed, there must be an understanding of the information and not just disclosure of information. Therefore, understanding and not just disclosure should be required. An individual may be very intelligent and rational and yet may speak only Inuktitut. Full disclosure may be made to her of all of the risks of a proposed treatment. However, if the disclosure is conducted in English without a translator, she will not understand the information. If she is asked, 'Do you agree?' and she responds by nodding her head up and down, she has not made an autonomous choice.

In light of the preceding discussion, I propose the following modified test. A refusal of potentially life-sustaining treatment should be respected if:

1 the individual is capable of understanding the nature and consequences of the decision to be made;
2 the decision is voluntary; and
3 the decision is informed, where a) there has been accurate and adequate disclosure of information and b) the individual understands the information that has been disclosed.

If any of these features is not present, then the refusal should not *prima facie* be respected. If the missing feature can be corrected, then it should be (e.g., by giving accurate and adequate disclosure) and a subsequent refusal should then be respected. If the missing feature cannot be corrected (e.g., because of permanent incapacity), then the regime governing non-voluntary withholding or withdrawal or voluntary withholding or withdrawal from previously competent individuals must be engaged.

In relation to the criticism regarding mature minors, I would recommend that the legal status of refusals of potentially life-sustaining treatment by mature minors be clarified (later in this chapter, I will argue for the direction of this clarification – that an unlimited mature minor rule should be adopted).

In relation to the criticism that the current test is partial and unclear, I would recommend that the test be spelled out in statute rather than the common law. For a number of reasons, the common law is not well suited to the establishment of a comprehensive and coherent regime for dealing with assisted death.

First, law reform through the common law places the burden for law reform on those individuals who have the resources (financial, emotional, and physical) to go to court and challenge the system. Consider, for example, the burden borne by Nancy B.[16] Paralyzed and suffering from Guillain-Barré syndrome, Nancy B. wanted her respirator removed. She had to go to court and, with her family, endure a very public debate about her right to refuse life-sustaining treatment. She ultimately won the case and, in so doing, helped to establish the right to refuse life-sustaining treatment in Canada. However, she paid a significant price. The burden of leadership for law reform in this arena belongs with the legislatures.

Second, legislatures are not as constrained as the courts. Legislatures can and must take into account a wide range of fact patterns while, on the whole, the courts must consider only the facts before them. Furthermore, the courts are not free to consult widely and are therefore limited by the knowledge, abilities, and positions of the parties and the counsel before them.

Third, legislatures could, with one piece of legislation, clarify all aspects of assisted death. The courts, on the other hand, are permitted to rule on only the issues raised by the case before them. For example, the issue of *parens patriae* jurisdiction and mature minors was raised by the parties in the case of *Sheena B*[17] but since the case involved an infant, the Supreme Court of Canada did not address the issue. Compared with legislation, multiple court cases certainly involve much more time and probably involve far more human resources.

Fourth, the area of assisted death raises a number of moral questions. These are, as the courts have recognized on a number of occasions, best left to the legislatures. As noted by Justice Beard in *Sawatzky v. Riverview Health Centre*: 'Those questions raise serious legal, moral, ethical, medical and practice issues on which there is unlikely to ever be complete agreement ... While the courts may be an appropriate place to start the discussion of these issues in that the courts can clarify the existing state of the law in light of the Charter of Rights and Freedoms, it may be for the government to resolve any moral or ethical questions that remain at the end of the day. The government can ensure a much wider debate including all interested sectors of society, while a court proceeding is, by necessity, relatively narrow and limited even if some interventions are allowed.'[18]

For all of these reasons, I believe that the test for respecting refusals of potentially life-sustaining treatment should be spelled out through statute rather than the common law.

In relation to the final criticism of the current approach (the lack of operationalization), I would recommend a three-part approach. First, more research must be conducted into operationalizing all elements of the legal test. For example, competency is clearly required by the law but how is competency to be assessed? Some, but not enough, research has been conducted. Much more research must be done as the complexity of competency assessments, particularly for populations such as teenagers, individuals at various stages of Alzheimer's disease, and individuals receiving considerable competency-compromising medications, outstrips our understanding of effective tests for competency.

Second, once more research has been done, consensus must be sought. For example, several instruments have been developed and tested with respect to their overall effectiveness in predicting or assessing competency. Salient among these are the Hopkins Competency Assessment Test,[19] the Competency Interview Schedule,[20] the Standardized Mini-Mental Status Examination,[21] and the MacArthur Competency Assessment Tool for Treatment.[22] However, there is no universal or formal agreement on which tests should be used in what circumstances to determine decision-making competency.

Third, once the instruments for operationalizing the test have been established and agreed upon by the medical community, they must be integrated into the core curricula of the health care professions.

A REJECTION OF FIVE COMMON RESTRICTIVE ELEMENTS

Terminal Illness

Some authors have suggested that refusals of treatment should be respected only when there is 'a terminal illness'[23] but this restriction has several problems. First, terminal illness has indeterminate boundaries. It is not at all clear what projected length of survival should take one out of the category of the terminally ill – one year, six months, one week, one day? It is also notoriously difficult to project length of survival, particularly when moving from one day to six months or a year. Finally, and most importantly, if respect for refusals is grounded in respect for autonomy and dignity, then the terminal nature of an illness is irrelevant. Rather, what matters is whether the individual believes his or her life to be no longer worth living, regardless of the projected span. Therefore, respect for refusals of treatment should not be limited to terminal illness.

Type of Treatment

It has been suggested that there is a significant difference between types of treatment and that while extraordinary treatment can be withheld, ordinary treatment cannot. Similarly, while artificial respiration can be withheld, artificial hydration and nutrition cannot.[24] However, problems exist with both of these potential limits on respecting refusals of treatment. Consider each in turn.

'Ordinary' and 'extraordinary' are highly contingent terms that can vary across time, geography, and medical condition. As an example, consider kidney dialysis. Dialysis was extraordinary treatment forty years ago and is, largely, ordinary treatment now.[25] But while it might be ordinary treatment in downtown Toronto it might be extraordinary treatment in a remote outpost in the Yukon Territory. While it is an ordinary treatment in a patient with nothing but renal failure it might be extraordinary treatment in a patient with AIDS. 'Ordinary' and 'extraordinary' are also indeterminate terms. No agreed-upon criteria for ordinariness exists. Finally, as used by many in the context of the assisted death debate, the terms have normative content. In other words, many people use the term 'ordinary treatment' to mean treatment they think ought to be provided, while they use 'extraordinary treatment' to mean treatment that they think it is reasonable to withhold or withdraw. For these people, lacking independent non-normative definitions of the terms, it is circular to use the distinction to justify the differential treatment.[26]

The proposed limit on artificial hydration and nutrition runs into different but equally damaging sorts of problems. It is certainly true that some health care workers experience the withholding or withdrawal of artificial hydration and nutrition as different from the withholding or withdrawal of artificial respiration. However, while this difference might justify a position that precludes compelling the participation of a health care provider who experiences a difference in the withholding or withdrawal of artificial hydration and nutrition, it does not justify a position that precludes respecting patients' refusals of such treatment.

Furthermore, conceptually, no significant distinction can be sustained between artificial respiration and artificial hydration and nutrition. In both, artificial means are performing a natural function of the body.

The related argument from suffering (i.e., that patients who have artificial hydration and nutrition withheld or withdrawn suffer as they die and therefore artificial hydration and nutrition must not be withheld or withdrawn) is untenable for at least two reasons. First, the premise that patients suffer when artificial hydration and nutrition is withheld or withdrawn is not necessarily true. Measures can be taken to ensure comfort during the dying process following removal of artificial hydration and nutrition. Indeed, some patients will be more comfortable without artificial hydration and nutrition than with it.[27] Second, as was argued earlier, respect for autonomy requires that autonomous decisions be respected even if the consequence of the decision will be suffering for that individual. Thus, so long as the refusal is autonomous, withholding or withdrawal is acceptable.

Finally, and most importantly, if respect for refusals is grounded in respect for autonomy and dignity, then the nature of the treatment is irrelevant. What matters is whether the individual believes his or her life to be no longer worth living, whether the treatment that might prolong life is ordinary versus extraordinary or artificial hydration versus respiration. Therefore, respect for refusals of potentially life-sustaining treatment should not be limited to particular types of treatment.

Presence of Unrelievable Physical Pain

It has been suggested that refusals of potentially life-sustaining treatment should be limited to those situations involving unrelievable physical pain. However, I take exception to each of the three limits implicit in the expression 'unrelievable physical pain.'

First, consider 'unrelievable.' Some patients have physical pain that is relievable but they may find the side-effects of relief intolerable.[28] For example, morphine can cause severe nausea. Furthermore, in order to relieve pain in a number of patients, they must be medicated to the point where they can have no meaningful interaction with others.[29] Such cognitive and communicative side-effects are intolerable to some patients.

Second, consider 'physical.' Some patients have their physical pain controlled but nonetheless suffer from unrelievable psychological pain. Consider the following example:

> I have a 66-year-old female patient now. She will likely die in the next two months or so. I know her well. I have cared for her for nearly two years. We are very friendly, as physicians and patients can become in these very intimate situations. She has bowel and rectal cancer. Months ago, it invaded through her bladder and vagina. For all kinds of medical details that there is no point going into, 24 hours a day she has what is to her the utmost indignity. She has bladder leak through the vagina and bowel movement and so on and so forth. It gives terrible odour. You walk in the house and it catches you at the throat. She is well aware of it. She was an absolutely meticulous, clean lady. She has pain which is 90 per cent controlled. The pain is not the problem. The problem for her is this total indignity. She has been asking me to send her to heaven for weeks ...
>
> Her pain right now is being alive. If she had pain I would give her morphine. Her pain now is in her soul.[30]

Third, consider 'pain.' Some patients suffer from physical discomfort (like extreme breathlessness or unrelenting nausea) that is just as traumatic as physical pain: 'Shortness of breath is the best example. In the palliative care field it is very often the paradigm of a difficult death – running after and catching each breath, 40, 50 times per minute. We can administer drugs that will relieve this. We can very often relieve 100 per cent of the pain, but rarely can we relieve 100 per cent of severe shortness of breath except by severe sedation.'[31] Nothing in the core values of the legal system or in the approach taken to resolving conflicts among values identified earlier grounds this limit.

Therefore, respect for refusals of potentially life-sustaining treatment should not be limited to unrelievable physical pain and should extend to suffering which the individual, after going through a thorough informed choice process, considers to be worse than death.

Absence of Any Reasonable Alternative

In the Netherlands, one requirement for access to euthanasia and assisted suicide is that the physician must 'have come to the conclusion, together with the patient, that there is no reasonable alternative in light of the patient's situation.'[32] It might be suggested that such a requirement also be imposed upon respect for refusals of potentially life-sustaining treatment in Canada.

Indeed, I would argue that the value of autonomy is promoted by ensuring that alternatives are discussed with individuals refusing treatment to be sure that they know about the alternatives that are available to them (thus enhancing the informed nature of the refusal) and by encouraging society to make as many alternatives available as possible (thus enhancing the voluntariness of the refusal). The importance of doing so is powerfully illustrated by the case of Larry McAfee:

> Larry McAfee was twenty-nine years old when he became quadriplegic from injuries incurred in a motorcycle crash. From the beginning, McAfee required continuous ventilatory support. ... McAfee lived in nursing homes, as adequate funding to support him in his own home in the community was not offered in Georgia. In fact, he was transferred to a nursing home in Ohio for a time because Georgia did not have a nursing home capable of managing ventilator care. For seven months, he lived in a hospital intensive care unit. After four years, McAfee ... tired of institutional existence and developed the idea of having an 'off' switch placed in the ventilator circuit that he could activate with his mouth. He petitioned the courts to have a physician supply him with adequate sedation to minimize his discomfort when he chose to activate the switch and disconnect the ventilator. The Georgia Supreme Court decided that McAfee had the right as a competent adult to refuse life-sustaining treatment and supported his decision based upon the severity of his disabling condition. They further held that 'Mr McAfee's right to be free from pain at the time the ventilator is disconnected is inseparable from his right to refuse medical treatment' and that sedation 'in no way causes or accelerates death,' thus indirectly absolving his physicians from a role in assisting in his death.

Yet, after winning his court battle and having the necessary mechanism in place to effect his death, McAfee ultimately chose not to exercise this right. Why? When his case came to public attention, there was an outpouring of assistance for McAfee, including a special arrangement from Georgia Medicaid. He was eventually able to move into a group home in the community with twenty-four-hour personal assistance. Specialists in computer technology also worked with him to develop a system allowing the use of his skills as an engineer, and he was once again able to work. In short, when McAfee was presented with more options, he chose to live – despite the ongoing nature of his extensive disabling condition.[33]

As illustrated by this case, having and knowing about alternatives may well affect an individual's decision whether to refuse treatment.

However, in response to those who would make the absence of any reasonable alternative a requirement for respecting refusals of treatment, I would argue that the value of autonomy is not respected by allowing a third party to determine (even if in concert with the individual) whether an alternative to the withholding or withdrawal of potentially life-sustaining treatment is 'reasonable.' If respect for refusals is grounded in respect for autonomy and dignity (as has been previously argued), then whether a third party believes there to be a 'reasonable alternative' is irrelevant. What matters is whether the individual believes there to be a 'reasonable alternative.' Therefore, respect for refusals should not be limited to situations in which individuals other than the person refusing treatment believe there to be 'reasonable alternatives' to the refusal.

We should indeed make reasonable efforts to maximize options, and we should be sure that individuals are fully informed about their options, but we should not make the absence of any 'reasonable alternative' a condition of access to respect for refusals of potentially life-sustaining treatment.

Age

Some have suggested that the response to a refusal should depend upon the age of the individual refusing treatment. Thus, refusals made by competent adults should be respected but refusals made by immature minors should not. Refusals made by mature minors should be respected if non-treatment is in the minor's best interests.[34] I disagree with this argument because it accords less respect for the autonomy of an 18-year-old than it does for the autonomy of a 19-year-old. Such disrespect requires justification.

The *parens patriae* jurisdiction of the courts in equity has on occasion been offered as a justification for this supplemental best interests requirement for mature minors.[35] Some have argued that the *parens patriae* jurisdiction applies to minors and justifies requiring a finding by the court that non-treatment is in the minor's best interests prior to respecting a mature minor's refusal of treatment. As Justice Huddart of the British Columbia Supreme Court wrote in *Ney v. Canada (Attorney General)*, 'neither the common law nor the statute interferes with the *parens patriae* jurisdiction of the court, which may override a minor's refusal to consent to treatment that is in the minor's best interests.' However, others have argued that this position overstates the *parens patriae* jurisdiction and, as noted by Chief Justice Hoyt writing for the majority of the New Brunswick Court of Appeal in *Walker*, 'when a minor is found to be mature, I see no room for the operation of the court's *parens patriae* jurisdiction.'[36] The lower courts appear to be conflicted on the role of *parens patriae* in cases involving mature minors, and the Supreme Court of Canada has not addressed the issue.[37] We must therefore ask what the Supreme Court of Canada should do if confronted with a mature minor case in which the *parens patriae* jurisdiction might be invoked. Below, I will argue that the *parens patriae* jurisdiction does not support a best interests limit on the mature minor rule and that, confronted with a mature minor case, the Supreme Court of Canada should embrace an unlimited mature minor rule. I will therefore conclude that the response to a refusal should not depend on the age of the individual refusing treatment.

The *parens patriae* jurisdiction is broad but not unlimited: it applies to incompetent adults;[38] it applies to immature minors;[39] it cannot be exercised for the benefit of others;[40] for never competent persons, it must be exercised according to a best interest rather than a substituted judgment standard;[41] for previously competent persons, it must be exercised according to a substituted judgment standard;[42] and it may be used to order medical procedures.[43] What remains unclear is whether the *parens patriae* jurisdiction applies to mature minors. I would argue that it does not.

First, I would argue that the original *parens patriae* jurisdiction never applied to mature minors. The historical origin of the *parens patriae* jurisdiction in general is, as Justice La Forest noted, 'lost in the mists of antiquity.' Unfortunately, the origin of the jurisdiction with respect to minors is lost even deeper in the mists. However, we do know that the *parens patriae* jurisdiction originally arose as a manifestation of the King's right and responsibility to care for those who cannot take care of themselves. This was first expressed as a jurisdiction to care for lunatics and idiots. Connections were then drawn between lunatics and idiots and at least some children:

> [T]he Crown has also another jurisdiction as *pater patriae*, as a father over his children. The King has a right to take care of lunatics and infants who cannot take care of themselves.[44]

> The King has the protection of all his subjects, and of all their goods, lands, and tenements; and so of such as cannot govern themselves, nor order their land and tenements, his grace, as a father, must take upon him to provide for them, that they themselves and their things may be preserved, quoting Fiz. N.B. 232. That the King is bound, of common right, to defend his subjects, their goods and chattels, and every loyal subject is taken to be within the King's protection, for which reason it is (p), that idiots and lunatics who are incapable of taking care of themselves, are provided for by the King as *pater patriae*, and there is the same reason to extend this care to infants.[45]

> The King is protector of all his subjects (Bracton, iii.c.9; Fleta, c. 2 and Stamford fo.37): he is more particularly to take care of those who are not able to take care of themselves – consequently of infants.[46]

The original jurisdiction was therefore over those incapable of taking care of themselves. It was assumed that all minors were incapable of taking care of themselves. Therefore, it came to be believed that the *parens patriae* jurisdiction applied to all minors (*en ventre sa mere* until the age of 21).[47]

I would argue, however, that the actual jurisdiction was always narrower than the expressed jurisdiction because the expression of the jurisdiction was based on the false assumption that all minors were incapable of taking care of themselves. The actual jurisdiction was over those incapable of taking care of themselves. Now that we believe that some minors are capable of taking care of themselves, it can be concluded that the expressed jurisdiction should have referred to immature minors.

Now it might be argued, in response, that the contemporary courts' protective jurisdiction over minors stems from the wardship jurisdiction and that that jurisdiction clearly captured all minors. However, as noted by Justice La Forest, in the passage from *Eve* quoted previously, wardship only survived the abolition of the Court of Wards as a *device* for the exercise of the *parens patriae* jurisdiction rather than as a *distinct jurisdiction*.[48] As a device, it could not expand the ambit of the *parens patriae* jurisdiction. Thus, while the original wardship jurisdiction may well have encompassed all minors, the *parens patriae* jurisdiction did not.

It might also be argued, counter to my historical reconstruction of the jurisdiction, that regardless of the ambit of the original jurisdiction, the expressed jurisdiction captured all minors and, through use, the actual jurisdiction was broadened. However, to this I would respond that if it was broadened by the courts, the courts can narrow it again. If the Court was confronted with a case raising the question of whether the *parens patriae* jurisdiction was and ought to have been broadened to extend to mature minors, it should refer to Justice La Forest's approach to resolving the question of whether the jurisdiction applied in the situation before the Court in *Eve*: 'Though the scope or sphere of operation of the *parens patriae* jurisdiction may be unlimited, it by no means follows that the discretion to exercise it is unlimited. It must be exercised in accordance with its underlying principle.'[49] The underlying principle for the jurisdiction identified frequently by Justice La Forest in *Eve* is 'to act for the protection of those who cannot care for themselves.'[50] It should also reflect on the fact that 'capable of taking care of themselves' has been interpreted as 'competent' in the Court's jurisprudence with respect to the mentally ill (previously referred to as 'idiots and lunatics').[51] Looking to the underlying principle and to the clear connection between 'capable of taking care of themselves' with 'competency,' the Court should recognize that mature (i.e., competent) minors are capable of taking care of themselves, and the Court should conclude that the jurisdiction does not extend to mature minors.

I maintain that the *parens patriae* jurisdiction never did encompass all minors and that, even if it somehow came to encompass all minors, that broader reading should either be narrowed to correct for the earlier misunderstanding of the breadth of the ambit or to respond to the more sophisticated contemporary sense of what constitutes 'incapable of caring for themselves.' I would argue that the court's *parens patriae* jurisdiction over minors is an aspect of its general *parens patriae* jurisdiction, that is, a jurisdiction to protect those who cannot take care of themselves. The *parens patriae* jurisdiction applies to all and only incompetent persons and thus, by definition, not to mature minors.

The argument about the scope of the *parens patriae* jurisdiction can be applied to the question of the respect for refusals of treatment made by minors. Mature minors are, by definition, capable of understanding the nature and consequences of the decision before them and so do not fall within the ambit of the *parens patriae* jurisdiction. The jurisdiction, then, does not provide a basis on which a court can override a mature minor's wishes and cannot be used as a justification for requiring that a mature minor's decision be in his or her best interest. Therefore, age should not be used as an element in the test for respect for refusals of potentially life-sustaining treatment.

Before moving on, it should be recognized that it may be more difficult to assess a mature minor on the elements of the test that I put forward earlier. It may be more difficult to assess, for example, the competence of a minor[52] or the voluntariness of a minor's decision.[53] However, such challenges go to the application of the test rather than the identification of the elements of the test.

CONCLUSION

The test derived from the core values and guiding principle is that refusals of potentially life-sustaining treatment should be respected if: (1) the individual is capable of understanding the nature and consequences of the decision to be made; (2) the decision is voluntary; and (3) the decision is informed, where (a) there has been accurate and adequate disclosure of information and (b) the individual understands the information that has been disclosed. This test should be clearly and comprehensively set out in legislation and a regime to ensure observance of the test should be put in place. Furthermore, more research should be conducted to improve our ability to assess the elements of the test. Education programs should be established to ensure that health care providers are taught how to assess the elements of the test or, in particularly complex cases, to know when to consult experts in the field for assistance with the assessment.

In the end, I expect that this regime will be less permissive than the current regime. In particular, those who now would not pass the test but are not being adequately assessed, will cease to fall through the cracks. Thus, the vulnerable will be better protected by having corrective measures taken (e.g., more information or alternatives provided) or being diverted to a regime specifically designed to protect them if no corrective measures can render them competent and their decisions free and informed. This will be achieved without compromising the autonomy of competent individuals making free and informed refusals of treatment.

PART THREE

What the Law Should Be for
Assisted Suicide and
Voluntary Euthanasia

OVERVIEW

In this part, I argue for the decriminalization of assisted suicide and voluntary euthanasia in Canada. First, I argue that the distinctions commonly drawn in attempts to distinguish between the withholding and withdrawal of potentially life-sustaining treatment, on the one hand, and assisted suicide and euthanasia, on the other, are not sustainable distinctions. The distinctions considered here relate to the nature of the conduct (act vs omission), the cause of death (unnatural vs natural), the probability of death (certain vs possible), the intention (to end life vs to alleviate suffering), and the nature of the effect of the prohibition (violation of bodily integrity vs no violation).

Second, I argue that three of the concerns commonly expressed about decriminalizing assisted suicide and voluntary euthanasia, while very serious and legitimate, apply just as much to the withholding and withdrawal of potentially life-sustaining treatment as they do to assisted suicide and voluntary euthanasia. So long as the concerns do not preclude a permissive regime with respect to the former, they cannot preclude a permissive regime with respect to the latter. It is here that I explore concerns about freedom, competence, and inequality.

Third, I address criticisms launched against decriminalizing assisted suicide and voluntary euthanasia that escape from the unsustainable distinction problems identified above but nevertheless fail for other reasons. It is here that I explore arguments grounded in beliefs about the sanctity of life, the value of suffering, and the power of pain control and palliative care.[1]

Fourth, I consider the slippery slope argument against the decriminalization of assisted suicide and voluntary euthanasia. Although the slippery slope argument could fit into one or more of the other three categories of argument, I give it separate and extended consideration for two reasons: first, because so many people find it compelling; and second, because, while I ultimately conclude that it is not a persuasive argument against decriminalization of assisted suicide and voluntary euthanasia, I also conclude that it raises serious concerns that must be taken into account in regulating a permissive regime.

Finally, I argue that the *Canadian Charter of Rights and Freedoms*[2] prohibits permitting the withholding and withdrawal of potentially life-sustaining treatment and not permitting assisted suicide and voluntary euthanasia. It is important to stress here that I do not argue that there is a constitutional right to assisted suicide or voluntary euthanasia but rather that there is a constitutional right to non-interference by the state in an individual's assisted death.

I conclude that a regime that permits withholding and withdrawal of potentially life-sustaining treatment has no persuasive basis on which to prohibit assisted suicide and voluntary euthanasia. Therefore, so long as withholding and withdrawal of potentially life-sustaining treatment are legal in Canada, so too, should be assisted suicide and voluntary euthanasia.

As noted in the Introduction, some of the arguments made here will not persuade those who are not committed to respecting free and informed refusals of potentially life-sustaining treatment made by competent individuals. My arguments will not persuade readers willing to conclude, even after the discussion in Part II, that the law with respect to these practices should be made prohibitive rather than remain permissive. However, I am not trying to reach those (few) readers. Rather, I am trying to reach those who, at least after if not before reading Part II, believe that respect for competent individuals' free and informed refusals of potentially life-sustaining treatment should remain legal in Canada.

CHAPTER EIGHT

Unsustainable Distinctions

NATURE OF CONDUCT (ACT VS OMISSION)[1]

The acts/omissions distinction argument generally takes the following form: (1) to omit to save a life is acceptable whereas to act to end life is unacceptable; (2) the withholding and withdrawal of potentially life-sustaining treatment are omissions, but assisted suicide and euthanasia are acts; (3) therefore, the withholding and withdrawal of potentially life-sustaining treatment are acceptable but assisted suicide and voluntary euthanasia are not.[2]

There are at least two bases on which to lay a claim that the distinction between acts and omissions is not a sustainable distinction upon which to ground public policy with respect to assisted death. First, the withdrawal of potentially life-sustaining treatment is as much an act as assisted suicide and euthanasia are acts. Second, there is no moral significance to the distinction between acts and omissions.

First, consider my claim that the withdrawal of potentially life-sustaining treatment is an act. In the context of assisted death, something is an act when you *do* something knowing that, but for your action, the person would not die. Something is an omission when you *do not do* something knowing that, but for your omission, the person would not die.[3] When you withhold a necessary blood transfusion you are *not doing* something knowing that, but for your inaction, the person would not die. Therefore, withholding treatment is an omission. When you withdraw a respirator you are *doing* something knowing that, but for your act, the person would not die. Therefore, withdrawing treatment is an act. When you give a person a lethal injection you are *doing* something knowing that but for your act the person would not die.

Therefore, euthanasia is an act. Therefore, it cannot be concluded that the withholding and withdrawal of potentially life-sustaining treatment are acceptable because they are omissions, and assisted suicide and euthanasia are unacceptable because they are acts. Withholding is an omission, while withdrawal, assisted suicide, and euthanasia are acts.

This is not to say that one cannot draw a distinction between the withholding and withdrawal of potentially life-sustaining treatment, on the one hand, and assisted suicide and euthanasia, on the other, and find significance in the distinction. It is simply to say that this distinction does not map onto the distinction between acts and omissions and that therefore one cannot hang the assessment of the withholding and withdrawal of potentially life-sustaining treatment versus assisted suicide and voluntary euthanasia on the distinction between acts and omissions.

Second, consider my claim that there is no significance to the distinction between acts and omissions.[4] James Rachels makes this argument through the following well-known, oft-repeated, and hotly contested illustration:

1 Smith stands to gain a large inheritance if anything should happen to his six-year-old cousin. One evening while the child is taking his bath, Smith sneaks into the bathroom and drowns the child, and then arranges things so that it will look like an accident.
2 Jones also stands to gain if anything should happen to his six-year-old cousin. Like Smith, Jones sneaks in planning to drown the child in his bath. However, just as he enters the bathroom Jones sees the child slip, hit his head, and fall face down in the water. Jones is delighted; he stands by, ready to push the child's head back under if it is necessary, but it is not necessary. With only a little thrashing about, the child drowns all by himself, 'accidentally,' as Jones watches and does nothing.[5]

To give a related example, suppose that we have the same Smith and Jones as above. The cousin is in hospital following a car accident. He is on a respirator but is expected to recover fully. In the first scenario, Smith enters the hospital room surreptitiously and disconnects the respirator. In the second scenario, Jones visits his cousin and watches as he has a violent seizure and accidentally disconnects the power supply to the respirator. In both scenarios, the young cousin dies. Although Smith acts and Jones omits to act, both the act and the omission are reprehensible but the distinction between acts and omissions plays no role in Smith's and Jones's culpability.

A number of arguments have been made in response to the conclusion that there is no morally significant distinction between acts and omissions.[6] These arguments all share a fatal flaw: they all end up relying upon a feature *in addition to* the acts and omissions feature. The feature itself may vary between the arguments (it might be intentionality, causation, or probability of death) but the addition of a feature is shared. The addition of a feature means that something other than the distinction between acts and omissions itself is critical. For example, it might be argued in response to these examples that both Smith and Jones are culpable but that while Jones is bad, Smith is worse. The distinction between acts and omissions therefore retains moral significance. However, this response only shows that, if anything, the distinction between acts and omissions is relevant to relative culpability. It does not establish that the distinction distinguishes morally acceptable from morally unacceptable conduct. The distinction between acts and omissions alone does not do the work desired of it. An additional element is required. Potential additional elements will be considered, and rejected, in the subsequent sections of this chapter (e.g., cause of death, probability of death, and the intention to end life).

The distinction between acts and omissions has been widely relied upon to justify distinguishing between the withholding and withdrawal of potentially life-sustaining treatment and assisted suicide and voluntary euthanasia. However, for the reasons given above, it has been fairly described as 'backed by tradition but not by reason'[7] and as 'both morally and intellectually misshapen.'[8] I too conclude that the distinction between acts and omissions must not be permitted to shape the legal regime dealing with assisted death.

CAUSE OF DEATH
(DISEASE / 'NATURAL' VS ACTION / 'UNNATURAL')

The argument frequently made with respect to cause of death is that when a health care provider withholds or withdraws treatment, the disease kills the patient, whereas when a health care provider performs euthanasia, a drug kills the patient. Framed another way, in the former, death results from 'natural causes,' whereas in the latter, it results from 'unnatural causes.'[9] So, for example, Yale Kamisar argues, 'in letting die, the cause of death is seen as the underlying disease process or trauma. In assisted suicide/euthanasia, the cause of death is seen as the inherently lethal action itself.'[10] However, this distinction does not map at all onto the line between the withholding and withdrawal of potentially life-sustaining treatment, on the one side, and assisted suicide and voluntary euthanasia, on the other.

As with assisted suicide and euthanasia, an 'unnatural cause' (the removal of a respirator) rather than a 'natural cause' (the underlying disease) can cause death in a case involving withdrawal of potentially life-sustaining treatment. An example should help to illustrate this point. Consider someone who had polio as a child and requires a respirator for daily living. If a thief removed the respirator from that person, few would say that the polio killed the person or that the person died of 'natural causes.' Most, if not all, would say that the removal of the respirator killed the person and the person died of 'unnatural causes.' Consider also a person with a pacemaker. Someone intentionally releases a strong electromagnetic pulse when she enters a room, the pulse causes her pacemaker to stop working, and she dies. Did she die of natural causes? Was the agent of her death the underlying heart disease that required that she have a pacemaker or was it the electromagnetic pulse? Most, if not all, would say that the pulse killed the woman and that she died of 'unnatural causes,' and yet, this is ultimately an example of withdrawal of treatment.[11]

One could respond to these examples by denying the intuition that the person who took the respirator or released the electromagnetic pulse caused the death. One could claim that the person did not cause the death but was nonetheless culpable in the death. However, this manoeuvre will not rescue this distinction for the purposes of sustaining differential treatment of withholding and withdrawing life-sustaining treatment, on the one hand, and assisted suicide and euthanasia, on the other, because on this manoeuvre a person who withdraws treatment is culpable. Both culpable and nonculpable conduct will be found on both sides of the line drawn by causation.[12] Thus, even by denying the causal intuition, the distinction fails to do the work required of it. Again, something else is required to sustain the differential treatment.

PROBABILITY OF DEATH (CERTAINTY VS POSSIBILITY)

It might be argued that a distinction can be drawn between acts and omissions with a certainty of causing death and acts and omissions with just a possibility of causing death. This distinction might then be linked to the withholding and withdrawal of potentially life-sustaining treatment, on the one hand, and assisted suicide and euthanasia, on the other. However, again, there can be as much certainty of death in a case involving the withdrawal of potentially life-sustaining treatment as there can be in a case of euthanasia. For example, when artificial hydration and nutrition are withdrawn from a patient in a persistent vegetative state, death is certain. Similarly, when a lethal dose of potassium chloride is given to a patient, death is certain. Again, this distinction fails to do the work expected or desired of it.

INTENTION (TO END LIFE VS TO ALLEVIATE SUFFERING)

Intention is frequently cited in an attempt to draw a distinction between the withholding and withdrawal of potentially life-sustaining treatment, on the one hand, and euthanasia, on the other. Some argue that the intention of withholding and withdrawal of potentially life-sustaining treatment is to alleviate suffering while the intention of assisted suicide and euthanasia is to end life. Hastening death with the intention of alleviating suffering is considered acceptable and hastening death with the intention of ending life is considered unacceptable. Therefore, they conclude, the withholding and withdrawal of potentially life-sustaining treatment are acceptable and assisted suicide and euthanasia are not.

One must, however, distinguish between two senses of intention: subjective foresight and motive or goal. Death is frequently a known consequence of the withholding and withdrawal of potentially life-sustaining treatment. Therefore, on this meaning of intention, the argument dissolves. Similarly, the motive or goal of all forms of assisted death is to alleviate suffering. Therefore, on this meaning of intention, the argument also dissolves. Consider each of these rejoinders in greater detail.

First, consider the issue of foresight. Just as when a health care provider injects a lethal dose of potassium chloride, when a health care provider withdraws artificial hydration and nutrition, he or she knows that a consequence of that action will be death. The subjective foresight test can be met by categories of assisted death on either side of the line between withholding and withdrawal of potentially life-sustaining treatment and assisted suicide and euthanasia.

Second, consider the issue of motive or goal. When a health care provider withdraws artificial hydration and nutrition, his or her motive is to alleviate suffering. When a health care provider injects a lethal dose of potassium chloride, his or her motive is to alleviate suffering. Again, the motive test can be met by categories of assisted death on either side of the line.

It is here that the principle of double effect must be considered. On this principle, 'it is sometimes permissible to bring about by oblique intention what one may not directly intend.'[13] However, this principle cannot ground a distinction between the categories of assisted death because it, too, captures some events on both sides of the line. Just as when a health care provider injects a lethal dose of potassium chloride, when he or she withdraws artificial hydration and nutrition at the request of a patient, no primary effect excuses the secondary effect. No effect of alleviating suffering exists apart from the effect of ending life. The intention to end life is direct rather than 'oblique,' and hence, on the principle of double effect, impermissible. And yet, as shown previously, the withdrawal of artificial hydration and nutrition from a patient is legally permissible. Therefore, the principle of double effect cannot be used to ground the distinction between the withholding and withdrawal of potentially life-sustaining treatment, on the one hand, and assisted suicide and voluntary euthanasia, on the other.

NATURE OF THE EFFECT OF THE PROHIBITION
(VIOLATION OF BODILY INTEGRITY VS NO VIOLATION)

It might be argued that, in its effort to preserve individuals' lives, the state is willing to override autonomy unless that would require violating the patients' bodily integrity. On this view, treating competent individuals against their will violates bodily integrity and would therefore be unacceptable, but preventing third parties from assisting with a suicide or committing euthanasia does not violate the individual's bodily integrity and would therefore be acceptable. In the first type of case, by allowing third parties to treat patients against their wishes, the state would allow third parties to violate the patients' bodily integrity (evoking images of strapping an unwilling patient to an operating table). Whereas, in the second type of case, by not permitting third parties to provide patients with assisted suicide or euthanasia, the state is merely preventing third parties from doing something to the patients and is not allowing any violation of bodily integrity. Thus, it might be claimed, a bright line is drawn between the withholding and withdrawal of potentially life-sustaining treatment, on the one side, and euthanasia and assisted suicide, on the other.

This distinction does not, however, do the work required of it. Suicide and attempted suicide are legal and the state could prevent them without violating bodily integrity (e.g., by confining suicidal individuals). Potentially life-shortening palliative treatment is legal and the deaths caused by it could be prevented without violations of bodily integrity (by simply not allowing the provision of potentially life-shortening palliative treatment). These are two examples of situations in which the state could preserve individuals' lives without violating the individuals' bodily integrity – yet chooses not to.

Therefore, it can be concluded that the distinction based on violation of bodily integrity does not support permitting the provision of potentially life-shortening palliative treatment and the withholding and withdrawal of potentially life-sustaining treatment, on the one hand, and prohibiting assisted suicide and euthanasia, on the other.

OTHER AREAS OF LAW

It should be noted that these five distinctions are not uniformly applied in other areas of law to distinguish between culpable and non-culpable conduct. Acts that cause death are sometimes regarded as non-culpable conduct (e.g., shooting a person in self-defence or war) and omissions that cause death are sometimes regarded as culpable conduct (e.g., a lifeguard leaving a child to drown in a pool). Naturally caused death sometimes generates ascriptions of culpability (e.g., not taking a child with pneumonia to a physician for treatment) and unnaturally caused death sometimes fails to generate ascriptions of culpability (e.g., shooting a home invader who is trying to kill your child). Causing a certain death is sometimes regarded as non-culpable conduct (e.g., shooting a person who is threatening you with a gun). Causing an uncertain death is sometimes regarded as culpable conduct (shooting someone in the abdomen such that it is possible but not certain that he will die). Intending to end life (on both senses of intention) is not always culpable (e.g., shooting a person in self-defence). Ending life unintentionally is sometimes culpable (e.g., manslaughter). Violating bodily integrity is sometimes non-culpable (e.g., shooting in self-defence or war). Not violating bodily integrity is sometimes culpable (e.g., a lifeguard not saving a drowning swimmer or a parent not taking his child with pneumonia to a doctor). Clearly, these distinctions are not used on their own in the law to distinguish between culpable and non-culpable conduct. Something more is needed.

CHAPTER NINE

Inconsistencies across Categories of Assisted Death

FREEDOM

The concern most frequently expressed with respect to freedom and assisted death is that individuals may not always be acting voluntarily when they make requests for assisted death.[1] Some argue that many individuals will see themselves as a burden on their loved ones or on society in general and they may feel pressured into choosing an earlier death. Others may be vulnerable to financial or other sorts of pressures that virtually coerce them into consenting to assisted death. Such circumstances, some conclude, suggest that these requests for assisted death are not fully free.

At least three sorts of limits on freedom can be identified. First, pressure to seek assisted death might come from within the individual because that individual has internalized societal attitudes against being a burden on others. Second, explicit external pressures might come from others telling the individual not to be a burden. Third, implicit external pressures might come from society having made assisted death available; individuals might feel compelled to seek out assisted death because society has made it available.

Although concerns about voluntariness in the context of assisted death are legitimate, they are not being raised consistently. A competent woman who is severely disabled and completely dependent upon her family might refuse antibiotics to treat a simple pneumonia in order not to burden her family. In one actual case, a 76-year-old diabetic man told his health care team that he had decided to stop dialysis. Since the man's health did not seem to warrant stopping, the health care team probed further. They discovered that he wished to stop his dialysis because he felt he was becoming an increasing burden on his wife and was overtaxing her resources.[2] It is indeed true that some competent individuals may see themselves as a burden on their loved ones or society and refuse potentially life-sustaining treatment. However, that has not led to calls for prohibiting respect for requests to withhold treatment. Assisted suicide and voluntary euthanasia should not be treated differently.

The freedom argument applies as much to individuals consenting to the withholding or withdrawal of life-sustaining treatment as it does to assisted suicide and voluntary euthanasia. As long as it does not block accepting the former, it cannot block accepting the latter.

It must be emphasized that, in rejecting the freedom argument frequently made against decriminalizing assisted suicide and voluntary euthanasia, I accept that freedom is a matter for serious concern in the context of assisted death. Indeed, an assessment of the voluntariness of a decision is a central feature of my alternative approach (as laid out in Chapter 5). However, I am saying that concerns about freedom cannot serve as the basis to keep assisted suicide and voluntary euthanasia illegal in a regime that permits the withholding and withdrawal of potentially life-sustaining treatment. Voluntariness is a matter for serious concern but it is a matter for concern across all of the categories of assisted death. It cannot ground a distinction between the categories.

COMPETENCE

It is often argued that the capacity of dying patients to make autonomous decisions can be compromised by grief, fear of dying, illness, or by the treatments they are receiving for their illness. Proponents of this argument generally suggest that some (if not all) of the individuals who express a wish for assisted suicide or euthanasia are incompetent because individuals who are sufficiently ill to qualify for assisted suicide or euthanasia are likely to have had their competence eroded by pain, disease, or drugs.[3] Now it is indeed true that pain, drugs, and disease can impair competence. However, the competence argument applies as much to individuals consenting to the withholding or withdrawal of life-sustaining treatment as it does to assisted suicide and voluntary euthanasia. As long as it does not block accepting the former, it cannot block accepting the latter. The same pressures on competence are present in situations in which individuals request the withholding or withdrawal of life-sustaining treatment as in situations in which individuals request assisted suicide or euthanasia.

In addition, the fact that pain, drugs, or disease have rendered some individuals incompetent does not imply that all individuals with similar pain, drugs, or disease are incompetent. Even if some are incompetent, not all will be. In this book, I argue for access to assisted suicide and euthanasia for those who have not been rendered incompetent by pain, drugs, or disease.

It is important to stress here that I am not ignoring the complexity of the assessment of competency. The reader is referred back to the discussion of competency in Chapter 7. I am simply arguing here that as long as the complexity does not ground limits on respecting refusals of treatment, it cannot ground limits on access to assisted suicide or euthanasia.

INEQUALITY

In 1994, the New York State Task Force on Life and the Law expressed concern about the dangers of a permissive regime for the most vulnerable in society: 'It must be recognized that assisted suicide and euthanasia will be practised through the prism of social inequality and prejudice that characterizes the delivery of services in all segments of society, including health care. Those who will be most vulnerable to abuse, error or indifference are the poor, minorities, and those who are least educated and least empowered.'[4]

In a similar vein, John Pickering, Chair of the American Bar Association's Commission on Legal Problems of the Elderly, argued against the decriminalization of assisted suicide and voluntary euthanasia: 'Before there can be such truly voluntary choice to terminate life, there must be universal access to affordable health care. The lack of access to or the financial burdens of health care hardly permit voluntary choice for many. What may be voluntary in Beverly Hills is not likely to be voluntary in Watts.'[5]

These concerns about implications for the vulnerable of a permissive regime with respect to assisted suicide and voluntary euthanasia must be taken seriously. However, again, they apply as much to the withholding and withdrawal of potentially life-sustaining treatment as to assisted suicide and voluntary euthanasia.

The financial burdens of health care are indeed far more likely to compromise the voluntariness of choice of the poor than the rich.

Therefore, while a request for assisted suicide may be voluntary for the rich, it is less likely to be voluntary for the poor. However, a refusal of treatment that is voluntary for the rich is also less likely to be voluntary for the poor. A permissive regime with respect to respecting refusals of treatment also threatens the vulnerable in society. And yet, there are no calls to criminalize respect for refusals of potentially life-sustaining treatment. Rather, there are calls to put protective mechanisms into the permissive regime. The same response is due to a permissive regime with respect to assisted suicide and euthanasia.

Concerns about the vulnerable must be taken into account when building protections into the permissive regime to regulate all forms of assisted death.[6] However, the concerns do not provide grounds for distinguishing between categories of assisted death and permitting some while prohibiting others.

CHAPTER TEN

Invalid Arguments

SANCTITY OF LIFE

Sanctity of life arguments can be divided into two categories: religious and secular. The religious arguments tend to be based on the view that life is sacred and on divine commandments (e.g., in Christianity, the Sixth Commandment, 'Thou shalt not kill'). The secular arguments tend to be based on deontological arguments positing a rule: Do not kill. This rule can be derived from a moral theory such as that of Immanuel Kant.[1] The secular arguments are also frequently grounded in the following argument: the principle that 'killing is wrong' is widely recognized as a foundational principle in our society; euthanasia and assisted suicide violate this principle; therefore they ought not to be permitted.

With respect to the religious sanctity of life arguments, it should first be noted that some religious groups support the decriminalization of assisted suicide and euthanasia. Not all religious groups accept the claim that the sanctity of life principle demands a prohibitive regime.[2] Second, while many Canadians believe in a Christian commandment, many others do not. The existence of a Christian commandment alone is neither necessary nor sufficient to ground a legal response.[3] It is not necessary – fishing without a licence is illegal even though it is not contrary to any religious principle. It is not sufficient – commandments prohibit adultery, taking the Lord's name in vain, and coveting a neighbour's house but none of these activities is illegal in Canada.[4] While religions and legal principles sometimes overlap, congruence is not universal. The mere fact that a particular religious group holds a particular belief is in itself neither a reason to keep it out of the law nor a reason to put it in the law. The religious principle of sanctity of life is therefore not grounds for prohibiting assisted suicide and voluntary euthanasia in Canada.[5]

With respect to the secular sanctity of life argument based on the view that 'killing is wrong' is a foundational principle in our society, the following responses can be made. First, as demonstrated in Part II, 'killing is wrong' is not an absolute principle in our society. For example, self-defence is an absolute defence to a charge of murder. Killing is permitted (indeed ordered) by the state in times of war. Suicide is legal. Therefore, it will take more than a simple recitation of the principle 'killing is wrong' to ground a prohibition of assisted suicide and voluntary euthanasia.

A further response to the secular sanctity of life argument is available. One consequence of Chapter 8 is that it is impossible to construct a definition of 'killing' such that:

- Withdrawal of potentially life-sustaining treatment is not killing while euthanasia and assisted suicide are killing, and
- Killing is morally wrong.

In other words, a definition of 'killing' that maps onto the desired distinction has no moral plausibility and a definition of 'killing' with moral plausibility does not map onto the desired distinction. Therefore, the principle 'killing is wrong' does not effectively distinguish between the withdrawal of potentially life-sustaining treatment, on the one hand, and euthanasia and assisted suicide, on the other.

SUFFERING AS A SOURCE OF MEANING AND UNDERSTANDING

It is frequently argued that suffering has value as a source of meaning and understanding and that assisted suicide and voluntary euthanasia, in cutting short suffering, deny the realization of this value.[6] However, not all people find value in suffering. The Judeo-Christian tradition, to which the view of suffering as valuable can be traced, should not be imposed upon non-believers. As discussed earlier, it is indefensible to ground a prohibition in the beliefs of a particular religious group. Obviously those who find value in suffering should be free to suffer. However, those that do not, should not be forced to endure suffering in which they do not find value.

Furthermore, to accept the argument from suffering could take us to a prohibition on anesthesia and other medical interventions aimed at the alleviation of suffering. If it is wrong to cut short suffering and thus deny the realization of the value of suffering, then it is wrong to provide analgesia, anesthesia, and surgical interventions directed at pain relief. These activities are and ought to be permitted in our society. Therefore, the argument from suffering against assisted suicide and euthanasia fails.

Finally, this invalid argument is applied inconsistently across categories. If the value of suffering precludes permitting assisted suicide and euthanasia, then it also precludes withholding and withdrawal of potentially life-sustaining treatment. These latter forms of assisted death also cut short suffering and thus deny the realization of the value. So long as the withholding and withdrawal of treatment are permitted, so too should be assisted suicide and euthanasia.

FAMILIAL RECONCILIATION

It is frequently argued that valuable familial reconciliation can occur in the last days of living. If these days are cut short through assisted suicide or voluntary euthanasia, then the reconciliation will never be achieved.[7] However, this argument ignores a number of basic facts about the world. First, some people have no family or friends with whom to reconcile. Second, many people are on good terms with their family and friends and have no need of reconciliation. Third, reconciliation with family and friends is sometimes impossible. Fourth, some people do not wish to reconcile with their family and friends. In other words: reconciliation may not be necessary; even if necessary, it may not be possible; even if possible, it may not be desired. Reconciliation, like suffering, should not be mandatory.

Furthermore, it is not necessarily the case that assisted death presents any less opportunity for reconciliation and growth than an uninterrupted dying process. In planning and carrying out an assisted death, an individual may well decide to first attempt to reconcile with estranged family and friends. Indeed, knowing that death will definitely come soon may spur attempts at reconciliation as part of the preparation process. In addition, growth may be possible for those involved in planning and carrying out an assisted death. If assisted death is not permitted, then family and friends risk legal liability if they help plan and carry out the death and as a result they are often neither informed in advance nor present at the death. This can leave them with intense feelings of estrangement, exclusion, and/or guilt. If assisted death is permitted, then family and friends can help with the decision-making, planning, and carrying out of the assisted death. This might be a time of profound communication and support which might lead to as much growth and reconciliation as a lengthy undesired dying process.[8]

Finally, the (invalid) familial reconciliation argument needs to be applied consistently across categories. It either works to prohibit all forms of assisted death or none.

LACK OF NECESSITY

Two related arguments should be considered under the heading 'lack of necessity':[9] first, the argument that the decriminalization of assisted suicide and voluntary euthanasia would not be necessary if adequate pain control were made available to everyone; and second, the argument that the decriminalization of assisted suicide and voluntary euthanasia would not be necessary if adequate palliative care were made available to everyone.[10]

These related arguments are grounded in false premises. First, they assume that people seek assisted suicide or euthanasia because of uncontrolled pain or lack of access to palliative care. However, a close review of the empirical data on the factors that lead to requests for assisted suicide and euthanasia reveals that uncontrolled pain or lack of access to palliative care is not the only, or even the most common, reason people seek assisted suicide or euthanasia.[11] Access to adequate pain control and palliative care will reduce – but not eliminate – the number of requests for assisted suicide or euthanasia.

Second, adequate pain control and palliative care is unavailable to many people and will remain so for the foreseeable future.[12] The problem with the argument from necessity is revealed in the statement that its advocates would have to make to people who are dying in pain now: 'We are not going to make assisted suicide or voluntary euthanasia available to you because you would not want it if proper pain control or palliative care were available to you. But we are not able to make proper pain control or palliative care available to you.' It has been argued that decriminalizing euthanasia and assisted suicide would dissipate the political pressure needed to ensure that, as a matter of national policy, every Canadian has access to adequate pain control and palliative care. On this view, the end of universal access to adequate pain control and palliative care justifies the means of denying access to euthanasia and assisted suicide. Against this view, my most persuasive counterargument would be the observation that such reasoning would justify overriding patients' refusals of treatment as well, as I discuss below.

Third, not all physical pain can be controlled. Some of the leading physicians in Canada testified before the Senate Committee on Euthanasia and Assisted Suicide that, even with the best palliative care, some physical pain cannot be controlled.[13] Assisted suicide and voluntary euthanasia will not be rendered completely unnecessary by making pain control and palliative care more widely available.

Fourth, the alleviation of physical pain is not necessarily congruent with the alleviation of suffering. For example, individuals whose physical pain is controlled by morphine may suffer from incessant vomiting and other forms of serious physical discomfort. Consider the following example from palliative care physician Marcel Boisvert: 'Shortness of breath is the best example [of suffering that is not physical pain]. In the palliative care field it is very often the paradigm of a difficult death – running after and catching each breath, 40, 50 times per minute. We can administer drugs that will relieve this. We can very often relieve 100 per cent of the pain, but rarely can we relieve 100 per cent of severe shortness of breath except by severe sedation.'[14]

Individuals may also suffer from mental anguish such as grief and fear. Such non-physical suffering cannot always be controlled by pain control or palliative care. Thus, proper pain control and palliative care will reduce – but not eliminate – the number of requests for euthanasia and assisted suicide.

Fifth, pain control and palliative care are not attractive options to some individuals. Some consider the means of controlling the pain unacceptable. For example, total sedation[15] might be required to control pain and yet some individuals would find total sedation to be worse than death and/or equivalent to euthanasia. For some, the religious overtones of much palliative care render it unacceptable.[16]

Sixth, the argument could just as easily be applied to the withholding and withdrawal of potentially life-sustaining treatment as to assisted suicide and euthanasia. If adequate pain control and palliative care were made available to all, refusals of treatment would drop. Therefore, until pain control and palliative care are available to all, refusals of treatment should not be respected. However, so long as this argument is not used to restrict respect for refusals of treatment, it cannot be used to restrict access to assisted suicide and euthanasia.

Before leaving this discussion of palliative care, I should note that nothing I have said goes against vigorous expansion of access to better pain control and symptom management for all Canadians. Indeed, such expansion is critical for appropriate care of patients as it increases the options available to patients and thereby contributes to respect for autonomy and dignity. Nonetheless, palliative care and other forms of pain control and symptom management must remain options to be chosed or rejected by patients. The availability or unavailability of these options must not be used to deny the selection of other options, such as assisted death.

CHAPTER ELEVEN

Slippery Slope Arguments

The slippery slope argument is commonly expressed in the following terms. If society allows assisted suicide and voluntary euthanasia, then there will be a slide towards the bottom of a slippery slope and many clearly unacceptable practices will become prevalent.[1] For example, it is feared that we will soon find ourselves unable to prevent involuntary euthanasia of the elderly, the disabled, and other vulnerable individuals.[2] Once it is accepted that one particular life is not worth living and can be deliberately terminated, then there will be no good (or persuasive) reason to claim that the lives of the disabled, the elderly, and other vulnerable people are worth living. To prevent such an undesirable result, all lives must be valued and assisted suicide and voluntary euthanasia must not be permitted.

There are two forms of slippery slopes: logical; and empirical.[3] In the interest of analytical clarity, I examine each type independently.

THE LOGICAL SLIPPERY SLOPE

The logical slippery slope argument takes the following form: if we allow assisted suicide and voluntary euthanasia, we will not be able to draw any logical distinction between acceptable and unacceptable killings, and, hence, we will slide towards the bottom of the slope (i.e., towards allowing involuntary euthanasia and thus the killing of demented, mentally handicapped, and indigent persons as well as any other group deemed 'unfit' for continued existence).

However, if a logically sustainable distinction can be drawn between the evaluation of life at the top of the slope and the evaluation of life at the bottom of the slope, then we have sufficient materials to erect a barrier on the slope. In other words, if reasons for allowing the activities at the top do not logically entail reasons for allowing activities at the bottom, then the descent is not logically necessary. Since we can distinguish between different evaluations (e.g., evaluations of the value of life made by the subject and evaluations of the value of life made by another person), we can avoid the logical slippery slope even if we allow assisted suicide and voluntary euthanasia. So long as we retain a firm criterion of free and informed consent, the logical slide to involuntary assisted death will not be a problem.

THE EMPIRICAL SLIPPERY SLOPE

The empirical slippery slope argument is not so easily addressed. The argument here is that 'once certain practices are accepted, people shall in fact go on to accept other practices as well. This is simply a claim about what people will do, and not a claim about what they are logically committed to.'[4] Clearly, this version of the slippery slope argument is more difficult for advocates of assisted suicide and voluntary euthanasia.

Obviously, we have no direct empirical data on whether people in Canada would in fact over the next five, ten, or twenty years move from accepting assisted suicide and voluntary euthanasia to accepting involuntary euthanasia. Indeed, it is doubtful that any study could be designed to gather that data without tracking practice in a trial period of regulated but decriminalized assisted suicide and voluntary euthanasia. In the absence of such specific data, many turn to history and to other countries in search of evidence as to whether slippage would in fact follow decriminalization. This is where a careful analysis of the historical experience of the Nazis and the contemporary experience of the Netherlands becomes relevant.

The Nazis

The notorious death camps of Nazi Germany are frequently offered as evidence of human inability to avoid descent down the empirical slippery slope.[5] Indeed, there is no denying that the Nazi regime established a horrific program of murder and genocide under the banner of euthanasia. However, caution must be exercised in drawing conclusions from the Nazi experience about what people in Canada in the beginning of the twenty-first century will in fact do if assisted suicide and voluntary euthanasia are decriminalized. There are a number of significant differences between the Nazi experience and the contemporary Canadian movement to decriminalize assisted suicide and voluntary euthanasia.

First, the Nazi program did not slide from voluntary to involuntary. It was, from the beginning, involuntary. The Nazi program illustrates only that, although Canada is currently a society that does not permit involuntary euthanasia, it might be transformed into a society that kills millions of people for political ends. Second, the Nazi program was motivated by jingoism, racism, and a fascist political ideology. By contrast, the movement to decriminalize assisted suicide and voluntary euthanasia is motivated by a desire to alleviate suffering and respect individual autonomy.[6] Third, pre-Nazi Germany did not have as a part of its collective consciousness an awareness of the horrors of the Holocaust. The example of Nazi Germany could actually deter the very slippage it is taken to indicate is possible.

In addition, one can apply the technique of *retorqueo argumentum* (turning the argument back on the one who uses it) on the Nazi analogy.[7] For if the Nazi practice of involuntary euthanasia precludes voluntary euthanasia, then the Nazi practice of involuntary research involving humans precludes voluntary research involving humans. Absent from discussions of euthanasia relying on the Nazi analogy is a recognition of the fact that the Nazi regime conducted horrific experiments on non-consenting humans. These experiments included:

(1) immersion in tanks of cold water of varying temperatures for periods up to fourteen hours to develop techniques for rapid and complete resuscitation of German pilots downed at sea; (2) simulation of high altitude atmospheric conditions in decompression chambers, with autopsies then performed to study the effect of sudden pressure changes on the body; (3) attempted mass sterilization through castration doses of x-rays, treated diet and intrauterine injections apparently of silver nitrate; (4) mutilation of prisoners as experimental surgical subjects for the training of German surgical students; (5) injection of virulent typhus into prisoners to ensure a ready supply of virus for typhus experiments; (6) infliction of bullet wounds and incisions and introduction of bacteria into the wounds to study and treat infections; (7) shooting of prisoners with poisonous aconite bullets to study the effects of aconite poisoning; (8) forced ingestion of seawater into prisoners to test desalinization processes; (9) experimental bone

transplantation; (10) execution and dismemberment of prisoners to furnish 'subhuman' skeletal specimens for an anthropological museum; and (11) injection of malaria to test malaria immunity.[8]

The Nazi experience with research involving humans is rightly advanced as a chilling reminder of the need to be vigilant with respect to the regulation of research involving humans, but it is not advanced as grounds to prohibit voluntary human experimentation. Unless one is willing to accept a prohibition on all research involving humans, one cannot consistently use the Nazi experience with involuntary euthanasia as grounds to prohibit assisted suicide or voluntary euthanasia.

One response to this *retorqueo* might be to say that we are simply as a matter of fact less likely to slide from voluntary experimentation to involuntary experimentation than we are to slide from voluntary euthanasia to involuntary euthanasia. Therefore, the Nazi experience with involuntary experimentation need serve only as a caveat but the Nazi experience with involuntary euthanasia can serve as an absolute block. However, there is evidence that we are capable of sliding from voluntary experimentation to involuntary experimentation. The experiences of the Tuskegee Syphilis study[9] and the Allan Memorial Hospital 'brainwashing' studies,[10] for example, vividly illustrate our capacity to slide down the Nazi slope.[11]

This *retorqueo argumentum* does not disprove the claim that the Nazi experience is evidence of the empirical slippery slope. However, the argument does raise serious questions about the application and force of the proposed analogy between the Nazi experience and decriminalization of assisted suicide and euthanasia in Canada.

The Netherlands

Another analogy is frequently drawn to current practice in the Netherlands. Some argue the Netherlands moved to a permissive regime regarding assisted suicide and voluntary euthanasia and then slid down the slope to involuntary euthanasia.[12] Hendin et al. claim that 'during the past 2 decades, the Netherlands has moved from considering assisted suicide (preferred over euthanasia by the Dutch Voluntary Euthanasia Society) to giving legal sanction to both physician-assisted suicide and euthanasia, from euthanasia for terminally ill patients to euthanasia for those who are chronically ill, from euthanasia for physical illness to euthanasia for psychological distress, and from voluntary euthanasia to nonvoluntary and involuntary euthanasia.'[13] Expressed more graphically,

> The lesson we can pass on to the world is that when you start to admit that killing is a solution to one problem, you will have many more problems tomorrow for which killing may also be a solution. Once you take away the dike that protects us, and if you have only one hold in the dike – and we have some experience with dikes in Holland – there will be a big flood, the dike will break, and the land will be flooded. That is exactly what is happening now in Holland.
>
> We talk about the slippery slope. Holland is no longer on the slippery slope; it has turned into Niagara Falls, which we will go down quickly.[14]

The implication is that Canada, too, would slide to the objectionable bottom of the empirical slippery slope if we decriminalize assisted suicide and voluntary euthanasia.

While the Dutch experience should give us some concern about an empirical slippery slope, it should not give us the level of concern suggested by these commentators. In this section, I will endeavour to show that the Dutch experience does not provide a basis on which to conclude that assisted suicide and voluntary euthanasia should not be decriminalized in Canada.

It should be emphasized here that I am not claiming that the Dutch experience provides a positive basis for decriminalizing assisted suicide and euthanasia. That is, I am not arguing that 'the Netherlands has not slid down the slope and so Canada would not slide down the slope were it to decriminalize assisted suicide and euthanasia.' That would be a complicated argument to make and a difficult argument to sustain because of significant differences between Canada and the Netherlands. For example, at least *prima facie*, the exercise of autonomy, even in the face of potential harm to self, is given greater latitude in the Netherlands than in Canada.[15] The role of the doctrine of necessity (*overmacht* in the Netherlands and 'the defence of necessity' in Canada) is also significantly different between Canada and the Netherlands, and it has played a crucial role in the establishment of the status of assisted suicide and euthanasia in the Netherlands.[16] These kinds of differences would need to be articulated and analysed for their relevance to the positive argument if one were to try to make the positive argument. Indeed, if my argument about the Netherlands was 'the

Netherlands has permitted assisted suicide and euthanasia and there-fore so should Canada' or 'the Netherlands has not slid down the slip-pery slope and so Canada would not slide down the slope were it to decriminalize assisted suicide and euthanasia,' then I would need to account for these differences and, if unable to do so, would see the validity of my argument undermined.

However, these are not my arguments. Rather, I am making a nega-tive rather than a positive claim. The argument that opponents of decriminalization frequently make is 'the Netherlands have slid down the slippery slope and so Canada would slide down the slope were it to decriminalize assisted suicide and euthanasia.' I am denying the first premise of this argument, that is, that the Netherlands has slid down the slippery slope. My discussion of the Netherlands experience has the narrow purpose of assessing the validity of the use of the Neth-erlands experience with assisted death as evidence of the force of the slippery slope argument against decriminalization.

Much has been written about the Dutch experience with respect to assisted death. Unfortunately, a lot of what has been written has either misinterpreted or misrepresented the Dutch situation, and this has greatly clouded the debate about the significance of the Dutch experi-ence for Canadian public policy. John Griffiths et al. are blunt in their assessment of much of the literature: 'Imprecision, exaggeration, sug-gestion and innuendo, misinterpretation and misrepresentation, ideo-logical *ipse dixitism*, and downright lying and slander (not to speak of bad manners) have taken the place of careful analysis of the problem and consideration of the Dutch evidence.'[17]

To accurately assess the force of the slippery slope argument grounded in the Dutch experience, I first address a number of the most common and/or egregious misinterpretations and misrepresentations found in the literature. Then I give what I take to be a fair and accurate depiction of Dutch practices and policies with respect to assisted death. Finally, I assess the force for Canadian policy-making of the slip-pery slope argument that might be made on the basis of the Dutch experience.

Misinterpretations and Misrepresentations

Euthanasia Is Widespread
Some proponents of the empirical slippery slope argument claim that euthanasia is widespread in the Netherlands. Richard Fenigsen, for

example, claims: 'The findings published in the report indicate that annually 25,306 cases of euthanasia (as defined by Fletcher) occur in the Netherlands ... The 25,306 cases of euthanasia constitute 19.4% of the 130,000 deaths that occur in the Netherlands each year.'[18] Hendin et al. claim: 'Given legal sanction, euthanasia, intended originally for the exceptional case, has become an accepted way of dealing with serious or terminal illness in the Netherlands.'[19]

Such claims about the incidence of euthanasia in the Netherlands demand two cautions. First, a great deal of confusion and equivocation surrounds the term 'euthanasia.' The authors of the report referred to by Fenigsen include only voluntary active euthanasia in the term 'euthanasia,' while Fenigsen and many other opponents of a permissive regime with respect to assisted death include the withholding and withdrawal of potentially life-sustaining treatment and the provision of potentially life-shortening palliative treatment in the term. Thus, on the basis of the same data, one group concludes that there are 2,300 cases per year of euthanasia and the other concludes that there are 25,306. On the latter definition, euthanasia is obviously far more widespread than on the former. However, on the latter, euthanasia is also far less morally problematic and controversial than on the former.

Second, the claim that euthanasia (defined narrowly) is widespread is simply not supported by the data. Two major studies have been commissioned by the Dutch government; one in 1990[20] and one in 1995.[21] In 1990, 1.8 per cent of deaths resulted from euthanasia and 0.3 per cent resulted from assisted suicide. In 1995, 2.4 per cent resulted from euthanasia and 0.3 per cent resulted from assisted suicide.[22]

Euthanasia Is Available on Demand

The claim that euthanasia is available on demand can mean, first, that all requests for euthanasia are granted and, second, that euthanasia will be performed almost immediately upon request. Neither claim is true. Consider each in turn.

The 1995 study mentioned above revealed that there are approximately 10,000 concrete requests for euthanasia and assisted suicide each year and that approximately 6,000 are not carried out (because the physician refuses in approximately 3,000 cases and the patient dies before the request can be honoured in most of the other cases).[23] Thus, only about one-third of requests for euthanasia or assisted suicide actually result in a death by euthanasia or assisted suicide.

With respect to the immediacy of availability, the Canadian Senate

Committee on Euthanasia and Assisted Suicide was told that 59 per cent of patients undergoing euthanasia died on the same day that they requested euthanasia and that in 11 per cent of cases, patients died in the same hour.[24] Dr van der Wal, the author of the paper cited as the source of these statistics, was shown the prior witness statements and, in turn, he explained what they actually represented:

> Yes, [the patients] did die on the same day that they requested euthanasia for the last time. Do you understand the difference? The patients had discussed the subject and had explicitly requested euthanasia many times before, but the day on which they died was the last time that they requested it.
>
> The next sentence says that in 11 per cent of cases, patients died in the same hour that the first request was made. It was not the first request; it was the last request. If you would like to verify this, you should read my paper in *Family Practice* which has been mentioned today ...
>
> The facts are completely distorted.[25]

Quite clearly, the data do not support the claim that euthanasia is available 'on demand.'

Palliative Care Is Absent

A number of commentators on the Dutch situation claim that there is no (or grossly inadequate) palliative care in the Netherlands and, as a result, people seek euthanasia. If there were (better) palliative care, they argue, the incidence of euthanasia requests would decrease.[26] However, the claim of the absence or gross inadequacy of palliative care shows a misunderstanding of the Dutch health care system. The following corrective explanation was offered to the Canadian Senate Committee on Euthanasia and Assisted Suicide by two panels of Dutch experts.

> Dr Van Delden: We do not have separate palliative care facilities in general. There are some facilities, but that is not the major way in which we deal with this. Palliative care is integrated into other existing forms of health care. Hence, it is integrated into the hospital. A central part is played by our nursing homes. Also, the general physician plays a central role in palliative care.
>
> You must understand that we do not have a separate facility where we bring in people who need palliative care. Instead, we bring the care to where the needy are located.

Dr Heintz: In the Netherlands, we also have a system of Comprehensive Cancer Centres, an administrative body that covers a certain area of the country. The whole country is covered by those centres. Within those comprehensive cancer centres, all the health care organizations, hospitals, GPs, and nursing homes can obtain advice or consultation from all the cancer specialists, including the palliative care specialists.

Dr Dillmann: In order to get a good picture of palliative care in the Netherlands you must understand some important elements of the situation in the Netherlands. Palliative care is in operation in the general hospitals. In many hospitals, pain teams are in operation. If it is discovered that more treatment is impossible or patients want to go home, then they will usually be transferred to their home situation, provided substantial care is present there. The nursing home system could also play a role there in offering day care, which is important for demented patients.

If patients are too sick to be in their homes, they can go to a nursing home.

I will take this opportunity to give you more details about the nursing home system in the Netherlands. Many of your concerns about palliative care could be removed by taking a closer look at that particular system. In the Netherlands, there are approximately 50,000 hospital beds and 45,000 nursing home beds. It is approximately a 1:1 ratio.

A nursing home physician is a distinct medical specialty with its own curriculum and licensing authorities. Each nursing home has a staff of trained nursing home physicians. Moreover, nursing home medicine is covered by the state. It is a state expenditure based on social insurance. Nursing home patients do not pay for the treatment out of their own pockets. Generally, this is the case for health care facilities in the Netherlands, since 99.4 per cent of the population has proper health care insurance. Even if they do not have insurance, the state will cover their nursing home expenses.

When you take into account facilities such as nursing homes, the GP system – which is strongly developed in the Netherlands as has and [sic] a strong curriculum – hospitals, and cancer centres, you will understand why the label 'palliative care' cannot easily be distinguished in the Netherlands. We feel that that is the case because many facilities are taken in by existing facilities.[27]

The Dutch will agree that there is room for improvement (especially moving beyond pain control). However, palliative care is widely available in the Netherlands and claims to the contrary are not supported by the data.[28]

Non-Voluntary Euthanasia Is Widespread

Prior to the publication of the Remmelink Report, claims were made that non-voluntary euthanasia was widespread in the Netherlands. For example, Fenigsen stated that '[t]here is now ample evidence that 'voluntary' euthanasia is accompanied by the practice of crypthanasia (active euthanasia on sick people without their knowledge).'[29]

Following the publication of the report, these claims were reiterated with what was taken to be proof found in the report; the report is frequently cited as revealing that there are 1,000 cases of non-voluntary euthanasia every year in the Netherlands.

At least two responses can be made to this charge. First, care must be taken with the definition of the term 'non-voluntary euthanasia' (or Fenigsen's 'crypthanasia'). In assessing the truth and moral weight of an empirical claim about the incidence of non-voluntary euthanasia, the reader must be sure whether or not the claimant includes within euthanasia the withholding and withdrawal of potentially life-sustaining treatment and the provision of potentially life-shortening palliative treatment.

Second, an analysis of the data shows that non-voluntary euthanasia (as defined by the Remmelink Report, the Senate Committee on Euthanasia and Assisted Suicide, and this book, e.g., lethal injection of potassium chloride where the wishes of the individual are not known) is not widespread. The oft-cited 1,000 figure comes from a study that concluded that 0.8 per cent of deaths resulted from LAWER (life-terminating acts without explicit request of patient)[30] where the authors offered the following explanation of their statistics:

> In 59% of all LAWER the physician had information about the patient's wishes (discussion with the patient and/or a previously expressed wish) short of an explicit request. In all other cases discussion with the patient was no longer possible. In 56% of cases the patient was thought to be no longer able to assess his situation and to make a clear decision. In 41% of cases where the decision had not been discussed with the patient (because that was not possible) and the patient had not expressed a wish previously, the family had asked for hastening of the end of the patient's life. In 70% of all cases the decision had been discussed with a colleague and in 83% there had been discussion with relatives. In 2% a physician had made

the decision without discussing it with anybody. In 86% of cases life was shortened by a few hours or days at most. The physician knew his patient on the average 2.4 years (specialist) and 7.2 years (general practitioner). 2.3% of the general practitioners and 31% of the specialists knew their patient less than one month (interview study).[31]

Thus, in 600 of the 1,000 cases, something about the patient's wishes was known although explicit consent according to the legal guidelines had not been given. In only 400 cases were the wishes not known at all. Quite clearly, the data on the incidence of LAWER in the Netherlands do not support a claim of widespread non-voluntary euthanasia. They do support a claim of some non-voluntary euthanasia but arguably considerably less than the projected 1,000 cases per year.

Non-Voluntary Euthanasia Is Increasingly Accepted

Richard Fenigsen has claimed that 'crypthanasia is not an "abuse" of the practice of voluntary euthanasia; it is widely accepted, openly supported, and praised as a charitable deed.'[32] John Keown has reported 'growing condonation'[33] and 'growing support for'[34] non-voluntary euthanasia in the Netherlands. However, no empirical data support the claim that non-voluntary euthanasia is increasingly accepted. The incidence did not increase between 1990 and 1995.[35] If incidence reflects acceptance, then there is no evidence of increasing acceptance. More significantly, the incidence of non-voluntary euthanasia uncovered by the 1990 study was a source of both concern and action on the part of the Dutch authorities as well as many proponents of the Dutch regime.[36]

Involuntary Euthanasia Is Being Performed

Richard Fenigsen, Herbert Hendin, and others have claimed that involuntary euthanasia is being performed in the Netherlands.[37]

The figures published in the [Remmelink] report indicate that 14,691 cases of involuntary euthanasia occur annually in the Netherlands. This is 11.3% of the total number of deaths in the country. The number 14,691 includes 1,000 cases of active involuntary euthanasia; 8,100 cases in which morphine was given in excessive doses with the intent to terminate life, of which 4,941 cases, or 61% were done without the patient's consent; and 8,750 cases in which life-prolonging treatment was stopped or withheld with the intent to cause death without the patient's consent. This estimate should be supplemented with the cases of involuntary euthanasia on newborns with disabilities, children with life-threatening diseases, and psychiatric patients.[38]

However, contrary to these claims, there were no cases of involuntary euthanasia in either the 1990 or 1995 studies. What Fenigsen and others call 'involuntary euthanasia' is in fact non-voluntary euthanasia or cessation of treatment.

Involuntary Euthanasia Is Increasingly Accepted

Implicit in the claims made by Fenigsen and Hendin and others is the claim that involuntary euthanasia is increasingly accepted in the Netherlands. However, there is no reputable evidence that involuntary euthanasia is happening, let alone increasingly accepted.

Abuses Are Widespread

Many authors refer to specific cases which they feel indicate that abuses are widespread in the Netherlands. However, there is reason to be suspicious of these references. Consider the major sources of the claims of abuse. With respect to the cases described by Richard Fenigsen in his oft-cited article 'A Case Against Dutch Euthanasia,' John Griffiths reports: '[W]hen these specific charges were investigated by the Medical Inspectorate at the request of the Dutch prosecutorial authorities (who were alerted by the NVVE to the fact that a number of cases of murder or manslaughter seemed to be involved), it appeared that the 6 cases Fenigsen referred to as based on his own personal knowledge had taken place a decade earlier. One had taken place in Denmark. Of the remaining 5, 4 involved abstinence and one termination of life without an explicit request (apparently a case of "help in dying"). There seems in several of the cases to have been some carelessness on the part of the doctors involved. Fenigsen himself agreed with these conclusions of the Inspectorate.'[39] With respect to the cases described by Herbert Hendin in his article 'Seduced by Death: Doctors, Patients, and the Dutch Cure,' Ronald Dworkin reports:

> Five doctors, four of whom Hendin describes as 'major sources' of his research, wrote a joint letter to the journal that published his initial article, which had the same title as the later book. The letter read, in part, 'The following persons interviewed by dr [sic] Herbert Hendin ... wish to declare that the texts of the interviews ... do not contain a truthful descrip-

tion of the interviews. The text contains several errors and flawed inter-
pretations.' They asked that their letter be published with the article. It
was not, and though Hendin made some changes in the article before
publication, these changes, according to the Groningen scholars and three
of the doctors, with whom I spoke on the telephone, did not correct the
misinterpretations, which, in their opinion, are perpetuated in Hendin's
later writings.[40]

With respect to the cases described by Carlos Gomez in his book *Regulating Death: Euthanasia and the Case of the Netherlands*, John Griffiths
offers the following critique:

> Gomez' description of the interaction between doctor and patient is
> based on information concerning 24 cases, collected long after the fact by
> a person (himself) whose grasp of the context was limited and who
> apparently did not speak Dutch, by means of interviews with a highly
> unrepresentative group of doctors who themselves were operating on the
> basis of memory and trying to describe subtle and complex interactions
> that had taken place as long as 5 years earlier, and whose English proba-
> bly was not muscular enough for the task. That Gomez draws firm con-
> clusions about the influence of the doctor on the patient's decision on the
> basis of this sort of information can only be described as scientifically
> irresponsible.[41]

Like Dworkin, I am not able to assess these critiques of the claims of
abuses,[42] and I do not offer these critiques as proof that abuses do not
occur. Rather, I reproduce them here to cast doubt on the 'evidence' of
abuse that has been produced to date and to suggest we should read
these frequently cited narratives of abuses with a healthy degree of
scepticism. Clearly, the possibility that there is abuse cannot be dis-
counted, but neither can it be regarded as proven to be more than a
possibility.

The Dutch Experience

Incidence of Assisted Death

Based on the 1995 data, the following conclusions about the incidence
of the various kinds of assisted death (using the definitions set out at
the beginning of this book) can be drawn (all figures are expressed as a
percentage of total deaths)[43]:

- Euthanasia, 3.1
  - Voluntary 2.76[44]
  - Non-voluntary 0.34[45]
- Assisted suicide, 0.2
- Withholding and withdrawal, 20
  - Voluntary, 9[46]
  - Non-voluntary, 10.2[47]
  - Unknown, 1[48]
- Life-shortening palliative treatment, 19
  - Voluntary, 8.17[49]
  - Non-voluntary, 7.98[50]
  - Unknown, 2.85[51]
- Involuntary assisted death, 0

Reporting Rates

Accurate data on reporting rates are, for obvious reasons, difficult to gather. However, a recent article published in the *Journal of Medical Ethics* concluded that almost two-thirds of all cases of assisted suicide and euthanasia in the Netherlands in 1995 were not reported.[52] Van der Wal and Van der Maas conducted a number of well-respected empirical studies and concluded that, in 1990, the reporting rate was 18 per cent and by 1995 it had risen to 41 per cent.[53] As a result of the 1995 Van der Wal and Van der Maas report, reporting procedures were reformed and review committees were introduced. Reporting requirements were also featured in the new legislation.[54] According to the Ministry of Justice, in 2000, there were 2,123 notifications of cases of euthanasia (compared with 1,466 in 1995 and 486 in 1990).[55] Clearly, notification rates are improving.

The Case Law

Euthanasia and assisted suicide are illegal in the Netherlands; they are prohibited under Articles 293[56] and 294[57] of the *Criminal Code* respectively. Dutch courts have held that Article 40 of the *Criminal Code* (which states that 'a person who commits an offense as a result of a force he could not be expected to resist [*overmacht*] is not criminally liable')[58] could provide a defence (as excuse or justification) to a charge under Article 293. This understanding of the stark wording of Article 40 can be explained by a review of the historical development of the case law on this point as well as by a description of a very recent piece of legislation. I will begin with the former, wherein, the Dutch courts have explored the role of, and limits on, the application of *overmacht* as a defence in cases of euthanasia.[59]

Eindhoven, 1952[60] – First Euthanasia Case

The first case of euthanasia to come before the courts[61] involved a physician who, on request, killed his brother who was suffering from advanced tuberculosis. The physician claimed 'it was impossible for him and he could not be expected, to ignore the claims of his conscience, which compelled him to comply with the explicit wish of his brother.'[62] The District Court convicted the physician but only sentenced him to one year probation.

Postma, 1973[63] – Life-Shortening Palliative Treatment Guidelines

Guidelines with respect to assisted death began to emerge in the case law when a physician, on request, gave her mother a lethal injection of morphine and was prosecuted for doing so. In this case, the District Court quoted the Medical Inspector's testimony:

According to the expert witness, a doctor and medical inspector of national health, the average physician in the Netherlands no longer considers it right that the life of a patient be stretched to the bitter end when the following conditions are present:

A [When] it concerns a patient who is incurable because of illness or accident – which may or may not be coupled with shorter or longer periods of improvement or decline – or who must be regarded as incurably ill from a medical standpoint.

B Subjectively, his physical or spiritual suffering is unbearable and serious to the patient.

C The patient has indicated in writing, it could even be beforehand, that he desires to terminate his life, in any case that he wants to be delivered from his suffering.

D According to medical opinion, the dying phase has begun for the patient or is indicated.

E Action is taken by the doctor, that is, the attending physician or medical specialist, or in consultation with that physician.

[When all of the above conditions are present] it is widely accepted in medical circles in our country and also by the expert witness, that in order to relieve the suffering of the patient completely, or as much as possible, ever larger doses of medicine are administered ... and that the administering physician then is fully aware and accepts that the good intended, namely the alleviation of suffering, brings with it the shortening of the patient's life.[64]

The Court accepted all but the 'dying phase' condition. The Court then found that the physician had not met the conditions of accepted medical practice because she had given her mother an immediately lethal injection of morphine aimed at killing her rather than ever-escalating levels of morphine aimed at alleviating her suffering. Ms Postma was convicted but, because of 'the perfect purity of [the defendant's] motives beyond doubt,'[65] she was only given a suspended sentence of one week in prison.

Wertheim, 1981[66] – Assisted Suicide Guidelines

In this case, Ms Wertheim, an assisted death activist, helped a 67-year-old woman to commit suicide. The woman, suffering from a number of mental and physical conditions, was referred to Ms Wertheim by her physician who had refused to assist in her suicide. Ms Wertheim was found to have failed to meet the requirements for justifiable assisted suicide set out by the Court in this case. However, she was given a very light sentence.[67]

This case is particularly significant because it provided the District Court an opportunity to set out the following conditions with respect to the person requesting assistance for justifiable violations of Article 294:

- The physical or mental suffering of the person was such that he experienced it as unbearable;
- This suffering as well as the desire to die were enduring;
- The decision to die was made voluntarily;
- The person was well informed about his situation and the available alternatives, was capable of weighing the relevant considerations, and had actually done so;
- There were no alternative means to improve the situation;
- The person's death did not cause others any unnecessary suffering.[68]

The Court also set out the following conditions with respect to the person providing the assistance:

- The decision to give assistance may not be made by one person alone;

- A doctor must be involved in the decision to give assistance and must determine the method to be used;
- The decision to give assistance and the assistance itself must exhibit the utmost care which includes: discussing the matter with other doctors if the patient's condition is in the terminal phase, or, if the patient has not yet reached this phase, consulting other experts such as a psychiatrist, psychologist or social worker.[69]

Following this case, the Committee of Procurators-General decided that decisions to prosecute cases of euthanasia and assisted suicide should be made by the committee and that it would use the guidelines set out in *Postma* and *Wertheim* to determine whether or not to proceed with a prosecution.[70] Test cases would then be taken when the guidelines were insufficient for determining whether the euthanasia or assisted suicide fell within the boundaries of acceptability.

Schoonheim, 1984[71] – Euthanasia at the Supreme Court of the Netherlands

This was the first case of euthanasia to come before the Supreme Court of the Netherlands. The following facts were set out by the Court of Appeals:

> From the beginning, she [Ms B] repeatedly made clear to the defendant and others that she was suffering seriously from the deterioration of her physical condition. She also repeatedly asked defendant to perform euthanasia.
>
> Her wish to have her life terminated was especially manifest on two occasions. The first was in April of 1980, when Ms B, at age 93, signed her living will. In this document she stated her wish that euthanasia be performed upon her in case her situation should develop into one in which no recovery to a tolerable and dignified condition of life was to be expected. The second occasion was after she had broken her hip on 16 September 1981, and surgery was being considered.
>
> Ms. B suffered terribly from the steady decline of her health, which manifested itself in deterioration of her hearing, eyesight and power of speech, although the last showed temporary improvements. She had dizzy spells, she was permanently handicapped and bedridden due to the above-mentioned hip fracture, and there was no prospect of any substantial improvement of her condition.
>
> In the weekend of the week preceding her death on Friday, 16 July 1982, Ms B was afflicted by a major deterioration in her condition. She

was no longer able to eat or drink and lost consciousness. On Monday, 12 July, her condition had improved a little; she had regained the power of speech and was in full possession of her faculties. However, she had suffered severely under the collapse, mentally as well as physically, and she made clear that she did not want to have to go through something like this again. Once again she urgently requested the defendant to perform euthanasia upon her.

The defendant discussed the situation several times in depth with his assistant-physician, who had also spoken with Ms B a number of times, and to whom she had also expressed her desire for euthanasia. After having spoken with Ms B's son more than once as well, the defendant finally decided on Friday, 16 July, with the approval of both his assistant and Ms B's son, to comply with her request. In defendant's opinion, Ms B experienced every day that she was still alive as a heavy burden under which she suffered unbearably. That same day, the defendant ended Ms B's life, applying a medically accepted method.

A few hours later, the defendant reported the euthanasia to the local police.[72]

The Supreme Court of the Netherlands reviewed a number of possible defences to a charge under Article 293 and fixed upon *overmacht*. The Court held that the Court of Appeals did not provide adequate justification for rejecting this defence in this case and referred the case back to another Court of Appeals which, ultimately, accepted Dr Schoonheim's defence of necessity.

Thus, the highest level of court established that euthanasia can be justifiable and that cases must be viewed through the lens of *overmacht*.

Admiraal, 1985[73] – Requirements of Careful Practice

Anesthetist Dr Peter Admiraal provided euthanasia upon the repeated request of a woman suffering from multiple sclerosis who felt that her life was no longer worth living as she was confined to a nursing home, in need of constant nursing care, and completely dependent on others. Dr Admiraal's acquittal confirmed that physicians who follow the 'Requirements of Careful Practice'[74] set out by the medical association would not be convicted. The Minister of Justice subsequently informed the medical association that physicians who follow these requirements will not be prosecuted.[75]

Chabot, 1994[76] – Psychological Suffering

Ms B was a 50-year-old woman suffering from 'an adjustment disorder consisting of a depressed mood, without psychotic signs, in the context of a complicated bereavement process.'[77] She had had two sons, Patrick and Rodney. In 1986, Patrick committed suicide. In late 1988, Ms B's father died and she left her husband. In 1990, she was divorced. In November 1990, Rodney was in a traffic accident and, in the course of being treated for his injuries, was diagnosed with cancer. After he died in May 1991, Ms B tried, unsuccessfully, to commit suicide. Later, through the Dutch Association of Voluntary Euthanasia, she was put in contact with Dr Chabot, a psychiatrist. He met with her repeatedly, met with her family, and consulted with seven professionals – 'four psychiatrists, a clinical psychologist, a GP and a well-known professor of ethics (of Protestant persuasion).'[78] Dr Chabot concluded that Ms B 'was experiencing intense, long-term psychic suffering that, for her, was unbearable and without prospect of improvement. Her request for assistance was well-considered: in letters and discussions with him she presented the reasons for her decision clearly and consistently and showed that she understood her situation and the consequences of her decision. In his judgment, her rejection of therapy was also well-considered.'[79]

The Supreme Court of the Netherlands drew several important conclusions from this case with respect to possible limits on justifiable euthanasia: (1) suffering need not be physical; (2) a patient need not be terminally ill; and (3) a patient may be a psychiatric patient. However, the Court also held that, in the case of non-physical suffering, consultation with another colleague is not sufficient – examination by an independent colleague is required. Although Dr Chabot had consulted widely, he was convicted because he had not arranged for an independent examination. Taking into account the circumstances of the case, however, the Supreme Court imposed no penalty.

Prins and Kadijk, 1996[80] – Non-voluntary Euthanasia

In 1996, the Dutch courts were confronted with two cases involving non-voluntary euthanasia – two severely defective newborn babies were euthanized with the consent of their parents.

In *Prins*, a baby was born with severe anomalies. The decision was made to withhold and withdraw all treatment except comfort care. The baby was suffering unbearable pain and, at the request of the parents, Dr Prins performed euthanasia. The District Court accepted the defence of necessity because: '(a) the baby's suffering had been unbearable and hopeless, and there had not been another medically responsible way to alleviate it; (b) both the decision-making leading to the

termination of life and the way in which it was carried out had satisfied the "requirements of careful practice"; (c) the doctor's behaviour
had been consistent with scientifically sound medical judgment and
the norms of medical ethics; (d) termination of life had taken place at
the express and repeated request of the parents as legal representatives
of the newborn baby.'[81]

In *Kadijk*, a baby was born with trisomy-13, which is a serious chro-
mosomal anomaly incompatible with survival. When told about her
condition and prognosis, her parents decided not to resuscitate or treat
beyond the provision of comfort care. When the baby developed very
painful complications and her condition deteriorated further, her parents requested euthanasia. The physician consulted with colleagues
and ultimately performed euthanasia.

In both cases, the District Court accepted the defence of necessity. In
Kadijk, the Court issued the following judgment:

> The Court concludes that the defendant's choice to bring about the girl's
> death in violation of article 289 of the Criminal Code, in the circumstances
> of this case, in which the girl – whose death was inevitable and who had
> been taken home so she could die there – was visibly in great pain and for
> whom an inhumane death, in a fashion strongly contrary to her parent's
> feelings, was imminent, was justified.
>
> Important for the Court's assessment of the decision-making and carry-
> ing out of the decision is
>
> - the fact that there was no doubt at all about the diagnosis and the prog-
>   nosis based on it, and that the parents as well as the defendant were
>   familiar with these;
> - the fact that there was no doubt at all as to the well-considered consent
>   of the parents to the termination of life;
> - the fact that the defendant secured the advice of an independent,
>   experienced doctor (GP) and consulted one of the responsible pedia-
>   tricians;
> - the fact that he brought about the baby's death in a conscientious and
>   careful manner, after having satisfied himself of the correctness of the
>   chosen method;
> - the fact that he has carefully given account of his conduct in this
>   matter.
>
> The Court comes to the conclusion that the situation in which the

defendant found himself can, according to scientifically responsible medical opinion and the norms of medical ethics, be considered a situation of necessity in which the choice made by the defendant is to be considered justified, so that he must be acquitted.[82]

It is clear, under the case law considered so far, if certain conditions are met, a defence of necessity for euthanasia will be available in the Netherlands. In other words, if a physician performs euthanasia following the 'Requirements of Careful Practice' he or she will not be prosecuted. If prosecuted, a physician who fails to follow those requirements but performs euthanasia in a situation which, according to scientifically responsible medical opinion and the norms of medical ethics, is a situation of necessity in which the choice made by the physician is considered justified, he or she will be acquitted. Ultimately, then, the basic boundaries with respect to justifiable euthanasia were drawn by the 'Requirements of Careful Practice,' and where those requirements did not provide adequate guidance with respect to the boundaries, the courts would provide additional guidance on a case-by-case basis with reference to scientifically responsible medical opinion and the norms of medical ethics.

Legislation

On 1 April 2002, new legislation was decreed in the Netherlands that, in effect, codifies much of the approach taken in cases previously described. The Act sets out 'Requirements for Due Care' for physicians to meet in cases of euthanasia and assisted suicide. If physicians comply with these requirements, then they will not be criminally liable for the deaths they assist in. The requirements are as follows:

Chapter II. Requirements for Due Care
Article 2

1. The requirements of due care, referred to in Article 293 second paragraph Penal Code mean that the physician:
   a. holds the conviction that the request by the patient was voluntary and well-considered,
   b. holds the conviction that the patient's suffering was lasting and unbearable,
   c. has informed the patient about the situation he was in and about his prospects,

d. and the patient hold the conviction that there was no other reasonable solution for the situation he was in,

e. has consulted at least one other, independent physician who has seen the patient and has given his written opinion on the requirements of due care, referred to in parts a–d, and

f. has terminated a life or assisted in a suicide with due care.[83]

The legislation also establishes that the request for assisted death may validly be made through advance directives by previously competent patients 16 years of age and older.[84] It also covers requests for assisted death by competent minors between 16 and 18 years of age (it permits respect for the request if the parent(s) and/or guardian(s) have been involved in the decision-making process) and requests for assisted death by competent minors between 12 and 16 years of age (it permits respect for the request if the guardian(s) agree with the request).[85] Finally, it sets out a comprehensive scheme for 'Regional Review Committees for Termination of Life on Request and Assisted Suicide.'[86]

Thus, it can be concluded that euthanasia and assisted suicide remain illegal in the Netherlands but there will be no offence if certain conditions are met (i.e., the due care criteria and the reporting requirements).

Responses to the Slippery Slope Argument Raised on the Basis of the Dutch Experience

It should first be noted that there is good reason to be concerned about the situation in the Netherlands. As we have already seen, non-voluntary euthanasia and non-voluntary withholding and withdrawal of potentially life-sustaining treatment are all occurring. Procedural guidelines are not always followed. For example, appropriate consultation and reporting do not always occur. The safeguards intended to protect the vulnerable do not appear, at least as currently implemented, to be sufficient. However, no conclusions follow about decriminalizing assisted suicide and euthanasia in Canada. At least the following responses to the Netherlands-based slippery slope argument can be made.

The Temporal Slippery Slope

A critical step in the slippery slope argument is that increased permissiveness caused the slide down the slippery slope; if that is not true, then the Netherlands-based empirical slippery slope argument against decriminalization loses its force. However, there is no evidence that the shift in policy and practice with respect to the state's response to euthanasia and assisted suicide in the Netherlands caused any slide down a slippery slope.

As Van Delden et al. note, in 'Dances with Data,' '[t]o demonstrate a slippery slope one would need to show that something changed after introducing a certain practice and for this at least two investigations would be required.'[87] When that article was published in 1993, there had been only one investigation (the 1990 study). Therefore, no slide attributable to change could be demonstrated. Subsequent to the 'Dances with Data' article, the 1995 study was conducted and it revealed a slight *decrease* in the number of instances of LAWER. Thus, as John Griffiths notes, 'In the end, a reasonable observer would have to conclude, we think, that there is no significant evidence that the frequency of termination of life without an explicit request is higher in the Netherlands than it used to be.'[88]

The Comparative International Slippery Slope

The slippery slope argument is also grounded in the assumption that the incidence of non-voluntary euthanasia is higher in the Netherlands than in those countries where it is illegal without grounds for immunity from prosecution. The truth of this assumption has not been empirically demonstrated and indeed there are now data to suggest that the assumption is false. The authors of a recent Australian study summarized their results as follows: 'The proportion of all Australian deaths that involved a medical end-of-life decision were: euthanasia, 1.8% (including physician-assisted suicide, 0.1%); ending of patient's life without patient's concurrent explicit request, 3.5%; withholding or withdrawing of potentially life-prolonging treatment, 28.6%; alleviation of pain with opioids in doses large enough that there was a probable life-shortening effect, 30.9%. In 30% of all Australian deaths, a medical end-of-life decision was made with the explicit intention of ending the patient's life, of which 4% were in response to a direct request from the patient. Overall, Australia had a higher rate of intentional ending of life without the patient's request than the Netherlands.'[89]

The authors concluded that 'Australian law has not prevented doctors from practising euthanasia or making medical end-of-life decisions explicitly intended to hasten the patient's death without the patient's request.'[90] J. Griffiths et al. also provide the following as support for their dismissal of the comparative international slippery slope argument: 'Recent research in the United States gives rates of assistance with suicide roughly comparable to the Dutch figure for euthanasia (see the sources cited in Dworkin et al. 1997). "Physician-negotiated death" is estimated at about 70% of all deaths in the United States (see Kass 1993: 34; cf. Quill 1996: 199).'[91] These facts cast even more doubt on the use of the Netherlands in the empirical slippery slope argument against decriminalization of assisted death.

Finally, it should also be noted, from a comparative international perspective, that there is evidence of societies decriminalizing assisted suicide and/or voluntary euthanasia and not sliding down the slippery slope to involuntary euthanasia. Indeed, examples point in the opposite direction. Infanticide has been practised in numerous cultures around the world without any of these cultures sliding to involuntary euthanasia.[92] Senicide was practised by Inuit cultures again without any slide to involuntary euthanasia.[93] Assisted suicide has not been illegal in Switzerland for many years without a slide.[94] Oregon decriminalized assisted suicide in 1997 and has not witnessed any precipitous slide down the slippery slope.[95] The comparative international empirical data are thus, for the proponents of the slippery slope argument, at best mixed and, at worst, counter to their argument.

The Current Canadian Location on the Slope

The slippery slope argument often implicitly assumes that Canada is currently at the very top of a slippery slope and must resist any reform that will put it onto the slope and take it inexorably down to the bottom. This assumption is incorrect, for Canada is already on the slope. The withholding and withdrawal of potentially life-sustaining treatment without explicit request is already widely practised in North America. No clear legislative safeguards are in place to ensure that refusals of life-sustaining treatment are truly free and informed and are not due, for example, to pressure from families or lack of access to pain management.

Furthermore, assisted suicide and euthanasia are already occurring in North America. For obvious reasons, it is difficult to gain accurate and complete data on the incidence of assisted suicide and euthanasia; they are illegal acts and health care providers are likely to under-report criminal activity. Nonetheless, studies provide some indication of the incidence of assisted suicide and euthanasia. Russel Ogden, a criminologist, testified before the Senate Committee: 'I discovered that here in British Columbia, euthanasia in the AIDS population occurs both with and without the assistance of physicians. Between 1980 and 1993, I learned of 34 cases of assisted suicide and euthanasia amongst the AIDS population. I also learned of other deaths outside of the AIDS population, but did not include those in my data. I have learned of many more deaths amongst patients with ALS, cancer and AIDS since the publication of these findings.'[96]

In a study of Manitoba physicians released in 1995, 72 per cent of those who responded to the survey said that they believe that euthanasia is performed by some physicians and 15 per cent said that they had participated in an assisted suicide or euthanasia.[97] The deputy chief coroner of Ontario was reported in the *Montreal Gazette* as believing that euthanasia is happening across Ontario: 'His office suspects many relatives administer drugs that hasten death in the last stages of life. But they're not likely to be caught unless they talk about it publicly.'[98]

Studies in the United States yield similar results. A 'National Survey of Physician-Assisted Suicide and Euthanasia in the United States' was published in the *New England Journal of Medicine* in April 1998. The authors concluded that 'a substantial proportion of physicians in the United States in the specialties surveyed report that they receive requests for physician-assisted suicide and euthanasia, and about 6 percent have complied with such requests at least once.'[99]

Clearly, assisted suicide and euthanasia are occurring in North America. How often, why, and under what conditions they are occurring remains unclear.

Slippery Slope Risks/Harms of the Status Quo

While there may be harms associated with decriminalizing assisted suicide and voluntary euthanasia (e.g., potential for slippage down the slope), there are also harms associated with maintaining the *status quo*. Arn Shilder of the British Columbia Persons with AIDS Society described the *status quo* as follows:

> What is the status quo? From my vantage point, the status quo is my friends dying from botched back-street euthanasias. Heroin from Hastings Street for lethal injections and plastic bags for suffocation are the order of the day. Guns and razor blades have also been used by those who do not have access to drugs ...
>
> The status quo regarding euthanasia in Canada is about people being

denied a sense of control over decisions regarding their final days. It is about people who care for each other being forced to lie and disregard the rule of the law.[100]

If we retain the *status quo*, we may see individuals refuse clearly life-sustaining treatment in order to ensure that they never end up in a situation in which they wish to die but are unable to commit suicide and have no access to an assisted suicide or voluntary euthanasia. We may see individuals attempt to commit suicide without the assistance of trained professionals, fail, and end up suffering even more. We may see an erosion of the criminal justice response to assisted death. Juries might refuse to convict because of the mandatory minimum life sentence attached to murder even if they disapprove of the accused person's conduct. Others may take this refusal to convict as decreasing the risk of penalty for non-voluntary euthanasia and we may see an increase in euthanasia of the vulnerable. As appears to be happening in Australia, we may see an incidence of non-voluntary euthanasia (and non-voluntary withholding and withdrawal of potentially life-sustaining treatment) that is greater than that in the Netherlands. There are clearly real slippery slope risks to the vulnerable in the *status quo*.

Conclusion

The Dutch experience with euthanasia does not provide convincing evidence to support the claim that if Canada decriminalizes assisted suicide and voluntary euthanasia, Canada will in fact slide to permitting involuntary euthanasia.

CONSISTENCY

The consistency argument raised several times earlier in this book can be made again here. If slippage from voluntary euthanasia to non-voluntary or involuntary euthanasia is possible, then slippage is also possible down the slope from voluntary to non-voluntary and involuntary withholding and withdrawal of potentially life-sustaining treatment. So long as the danger of the slippery slope does not preclude these latter sorts of assisted death practices, it cannot preclude assisted suicide and voluntary euthanasia.

The empirical slippery slope is a matter for serious concern. However, the solution to the concern must be the same for assisted suicide and voluntary euthanasia as for the withholding and withdrawal of potentially life-sustaining treatment. The solution is not to prohibit any particular form(s) of assisted death but rather to be vigilant with respect to the satisfaction of the necessary conditions for permissible assisted death.

CHAPTER TWELVE

The *Canadian Charter of Rights and Freedoms*

In this final chapter, I argue that a legislative regime that permits attempted suicide and the withholding and withdrawal of potentially life-sustaining treatment but prohibits assisted suicide and voluntary euthanasia is unconstitutional, that is, it is in breach of sections 7 and 15 of the *Charter* and cannot be saved by section 1.[1] To make this argument, I must challenge the reasoning and result of Justice Sopinka's majority decision in *Rodriguez v. British Columbia (Attorney General)*[2] and develop the reasoning and embrace the result in the dissenting opinions of former Chief Justice Lamer and Justice McLachlin (as she then was) in *Rodriguez*.[3] I must argue that Justice Sopinka was incorrect in concluding that there was no breach of section 7 and that, even if there was a breach of section 15, such a breach would be saved by section 1. I do this in this final chapter as some of the arguments to be made against Justice Sopinka's decision to uphold the current prohibition on assisted suicide rely on arguments presented earlier in the book.

SECTION 7

In his decision in *Rodriguez*, Justice Sopinka, for the majority, accepts the claim made by Sue Rodriguez that the *Criminal Code* provision prohibiting assisted suicide (s. 241(b)) infringes section 7 insofar as it infringes the right to security of the person. However, he claims that it does so in a way that is not contrary to the principles of fundamental justice and, therefore, does not breach section 7.[4] Justice Sopinka argues that section 241(b) breaches section 7 only if 'the blanket prohibition on assisted suicide is arbitrary or unfair in that it is unrelated to the state's interest in protecting the vulnerable, and that it lacks a foundation in the legal tradition and societal beliefs which are said to be represented by the prohibition.'[5] He then finds the prohibition to be related to the state's interest and finds that it has a foundation in the legal tradition and societal beliefs with respect to sanctity of life.

At least two counter-arguments can be made to this argument. First, it can be argued that Justice Sopinka wrongly imports the consideration of societal interests into the section 7 analysis instead of leaving it for the section 1 analysis. Second, it can be argued that Justice Sopinka wrongly concludes that the blanket prohibition has a foundation in the legal tradition and societal beliefs which are said to be represented by the prohibition.

Justice McLachlin primarily engages with the first of these counter-arguments. I will engage with the latter. I do so for two reasons. First, I subscribe to Justice McLachlin's analysis of the proper analytical place for the balancing of societal interests and cannot add to her analysis.[6] Second, if the foundation claimed by Justice Sopinka can be pulled out from under the prohibition, then his argument fails regardless of where the balancing of societal interests belongs.

Justice Sopinka postulates a sanctity of life principle as the relevant principle of fundamental justice: 'Section 241(b) has as its purpose the protection of the vulnerable who might be induced in moments of weakness to commit suicide. This purpose is grounded in the state interest in protecting life and reflects the policy of the state that human life should not be depreciated by allowing life to be taken. This policy finds expression not only in the provisions of our Criminal Code which prohibit murder and other violent acts against others notwithstanding the consent of the victim, but also in the policy against capital punishment and, until its repeal, attempted suicide. This is not only a policy of the state, however, but is part of our fundamental conception of the sanctity of human life.'[7]

He acknowledges that the sanctity of life principle has 'certain limitations and qualifications reflective of personal autonomy and dignity.'[8] For his argument to succeed, he must defend the claim that these limitations and qualifications do not apply to assisted suicide. Justice Sopinka fails to do this. He fails to distinguish suicide and the withholding and withdrawal of potentially life-sustaining treatment (to which the qualifications of the principle apply) from assisted suicide (to which he wants to conclude the qualifications do not apply).

Suicide

Justice Sopinka acknowledges that the principle of sanctity of life does not provide a foundation for a prohibition on suicide. Indeed, he recognizes the fact that attempted suicide was removed from the *Criminal Code* in 1972. But he claims: 'The fact of this decriminalization does not aid us particularly in this analysis, however. Unlike the partial decriminalization of abortion, the decriminalization of attempted suicide cannot be said to represent a consensus by Parliament or by Canadians in general that the autonomy interest of those wishing to kill themselves is paramount to the state interest in protecting the life of its citizens. Rather, the matter of suicide was seen to have its roots and its solutions in sciences outside the law, and for that reason not to mandate a legal remedy. Since that time, there have been some attempts to decriminalize assistance to suicide through private members bills, but none has been successful.'[9]

Justice McLachlin observes: 'My colleague Sopinka J has noted that the decriminalization of suicide reflects Parliament's decision that the matter is best left to sciences outside the law. He suggests that it does not reveal any consensus that the autonomy interest of those who wish to end their lives is paramount to a state interest in protecting life. I agree. But this conclusion begs the question. What is the difference between suicide and assisted suicide that justifies making the one lawful and the other a crime, that justifies allowing some this choice, while denying it to others?'[10]

Justice Sopinka's argument can be unpacked as follows:

Premise 1: Suicide was decriminalized because it was seen to have its roots and its solutions in sciences outside the law, and for that reason not to mandate a legal remedy.

Premise 2: Suicide was not decriminalized as a result of consensus that the autonomy interest of those wishing to kill themselves is paramount to the state interest in protecting the life of its citizens.

Premise 3 (implied): The only argument for decriminalizing assisted suicide is the argument that the autonomy interest of those wishing to kill themselves is paramount to the state interest in protecting the lives of its citizens.

Premise 4: No attempts to decriminalize assisted suicide have been successful.

Conclusion: The decriminalization of suicide does not logically imply anything about the appropriate legal response to assisted suicide.

At least four responses that can be made to this argument. First, following Chief Justice Lamer, one can deny the truth of Premise 2 and link the decriminalization of attempted suicide to Parliament's views on autonomy: 'I also take the repeal of the offence of attempted suicide to indicate Parliament's unwillingness to enforce the protection of a group containing many vulnerable people (i.e., those contemplating suicide) over and against the freely determined will of an individual set on terminating his or her life. Self-determination was now considered the paramount factor in the state regulation of suicide. If no external interference or intervention could be demonstrated, the act of attempting suicide could no longer give rise to criminal liability. Where such interference and intervention was present, and therefore the evidence of self-determination less reliable, the offence of assisted suicide could then be triggered.'[11]

Second, one can deny the truth of the implied Premise 3. An argument for decriminalizing assisted suicide could well be grounded in the premise that assisted suicide, like suicide, has its roots and solutions in sciences outside the law and, for that reason, does not mandate a legal remedy. Therefore, it might be concluded, assisted suicide, like suicide, should be decriminalized and dealt with outside the criminal law. Third, one can note that Premise 4 takes the argument in the direction of begging the question; the question is whether assisted suicide should be decriminalized. The very concept of decriminalization implies that the act is currently criminal. Fourth, one can note, once the argument is unpacked, that the conclusion simply does not follow from the premises. Thus, one can conclude that Justice Sopinka fails to prove that there is a basis for distinguishing between assisted suicide and attempted suicide. Yet this is exactly what he must prove to maintain that the sanctity of life principle operates as a principle of fundamental justice in the context of assisted suicide but not attempted suicide.

Withholding and Withdrawal of
Potentially Life-Sustaining Treatment

Justice Sopinka also acknowledges that the principle of sanctity of life does not provide a foundation for a prohibition on the withholding and withdrawal of potentially life-sustaining treatment. He notes that:

'Canadian courts have recognized a common law right of patients to refuse consent to medical treatment, or to demand that treatment, once commenced, be withdrawn or discontinued (*Ciarlariello* v. *Schacter*, [1993] 2 S.C.R. 119). This right has been specifically recognized to exist even if the withdrawal from or refusal of treatment may result in death (*Nancy B.* v. *Hotel-Dieu de Quebec* (1992), 86 D.L.R. (4th) 385 (Que.S.C.); and *Malette* v. *Shulman* (1990), 72 O.R. (2d) 417 (C.A.)).'[12]

Then he attempts to distinguish assisted suicide from the withholding and withdrawal of potentially life-sustaining treatment. He refers to at least two bases on which commentators and other jurisdictions have grounded the distinction: active/passive and natural/unnatural.[13] He then makes the following argument: 'Whether or not one agrees that the active vs passive distinction is maintainable, however, the fact remains that under our common law, the physician has no choice but to accept the patient's instructions to discontinue treatment. To continue to treat the patient when the patient has withdrawn consent to that treatment constitutes battery (*Ciarlariello* and *Nancy B.*, supra). The doctor is therefore not required to make a choice which will result in the patient's death as he would be if he chose to assist a suicide or to perform active euthanasia.'[14]

The commentators' versions of the active/passive and natural/ unnatural distinctions have been discussed and rejected already in this book. Justice Sopinka's argument, however, requires more detailed consideration. His argument can be unpacked as follows:

Premise 1: Under the common law, the physician has no choice but to accept the patient's instructions to discontinue treatment.

Conclusion 1: Therefore, under the common law, when withholding or withdrawing life-sustaining treatment, the doctor is not required to make a choice which will result in the patient's death.

Premise 2: With assisted suicide, the physician is required to make a choice which will result in the patient's death.

Conclusion 2: Therefore, the discontinuation of treatment is different from assisted suicide.

Premise 3: If a distinction can be drawn between the discontinuation of treatment and assisted suicide, then the qualifications on the principle of sanctity of life that apply to the discontinuation of treatment do not necessarily apply to assisted suicide.

Conclusion 3: Therefore, the qualifications on the principle of sanctity of life that apply to the discontinuation of treatment do not necessarily apply to assisted suicide.

The problem with this argument lies in the use of the expression 'required to make a choice which will result in the patient's death.' What does Justice Sopinka mean by this expression? From the sentences found around this expression, it appears that he means 'must perform an act, not legally required, that will result in the patient's death.' This then generates three possible bases for his distinction between assisted suicide and euthanasia, on the one hand, and the withholding and withdrawal of treatment, on the other: (1) assisted suicide and euthanasia are acts, while withholding and withdrawal of treatment are not; and/or (2) assisted suicide and euthanasia cause the patient's death, while withholding and withdrawal do not; and/or (3) the law requires that physicians withhold and withdraw treatment but that they not perform assisted suicide or euthanasia. However, these distinctions are not sustainable.

Assisted suicide and euthanasia are acts; withholding and withdrawal are not. Earlier in this book, I considered and rejected reliance on a distinction between acts and omissions in the context of establishing the appropriate legal status for various forms of assisted death.[15]

Assisted suicide and euthanasia cause the patient's death; withholding and withdrawal do not. Earlier in this book, I considered and rejected reliance on the causation distinction in the context of establishing the appropriate legal status for various forms of assisted death.[16]

The law requires that physicians withhold and withdraw treatment but do not provide assisted suicide and euthanasia. This distinction begs the question of legality of assisted suicide and euthanasia. This argument is grounded in the assumption that assisted suicide is illegal, but that is precisely what is at issue. Furthermore, not so many years ago, it was not recognized that individuals had the right to refuse treatment and that physicians had an obligation to respect refusals of treatment. The common practice with respect to refusals was challenged and the common law evolved. The challenge is now being launched against the law with respect to assisted suicide. The fact that refusals of treatment are now legal and assisted suicide is not cannot ground a conclusion that they are different and therefore they can be treated differently.

One might also think that there is a distinction grounded in the notion of choice embedded in Justice Sopinka's argument. However, the idea of choosing – meaning choosing between options – will not do any work for Justice Sopinka. Within the law, there is no choice with respect to the withholding and withdrawal of treatment or assisted suicide and euthanasia. Outside of the law, whether the case involves the withholding or withdrawal of potentially life-sustaining treatment, assisted suicide, or euthanasia, a physician faces a choice between an option that results in the patient's death and an option that does not. Therefore, it is false that in one case one is required to make a choice, while in the other one is not.

Justice Sopinka concludes: 'Regardless of one's personal views as to whether the distinctions drawn between withdrawal of treatment and palliative care, on the one hand, and assisted suicide on the other are practically compelling, the fact remains that these distinctions are maintained and can be persuasively defended.'[17] However, he fails to provide a persuasive defence. He therefore fails to provide a basis for distinguishing between assisted suicide and the withholding and withdrawal of potentially life-sustaining treatment.

As Justice Cory writes in dissent in *Rodriguez*: 'I can see no difference between permitting a patient of sound mind to choose death with dignity by refusing treatment and permitting a patient of sound mind who is terminally ill to choose death with dignity by terminating life preserving treatment, even if, because of incapacity, that step has to be physically taken by another on her instructions. Nor can I see any reason for failing to extend that same permission so that a terminally ill patient facing death may put an end to her life through the intermediary of another.'[18]

Life-Shortening Palliative Treatment

Finally, Justice Sopinka acknowledges that the principle of sanctity of life does not provide a foundation for a prohibition on the provision of potentially life-shortening palliative treatment. He notes that 'doctors may deliver palliative care to terminally ill patients without fear of sanction.'[19] However, he quickly attempts to distinguish assisted suicide from the provision of potentially life-shortening palliative treatment:

> The administration of drugs designed for pain control in dosages which the physician knows will hasten death constitutes active contribution to death by any standard. However, the distinction drawn here is one based upon intention – in the case of palliative care the intention is to ease pain,

which has the effect of hastening death, while in the case of assisted suicide, the intention is undeniably to cause death. The Law Reform Commission, although it recommended the continued criminal prohibition of
both euthanasia and assisted suicide, stated, at p. 70 of the Working
Paper, that a doctor should never refuse palliative care to a terminally ill
person only because it may hasten death. In my view, distinctions based
upon intent are important, and in fact form the basis of our criminal law.
While factually the distinction may, at times, be difficult to draw, legally it
is clear. The fact that in some cases, the third party will, under the guise of
palliative care, commit euthanasia or assist in suicide and go unsanc-
tioned due to the difficulty of proof cannot be said to render the existence
of the prohibition fundamentally unjust.[20]

This argument is vulnerable to the counter-arguments made to the
argument from intention considered and rejected earlier. 'Intent' can
mean either subjective foresight or motive or goal. Insofar as intent is
subjective foresight, it fails to serve the purpose of distinguishing
between the provision of potentially life-shortening palliative treatment and assisted suicide as, in both cases, there is subjective foresight
of death. Insofar as intent is motive or goal, it also fails to serve the
purpose as, in both cases, the motive is to alleviate suffering. Therefore, Justice Sopinka fails to sustain the distinction between life-
shortening palliative treatment and assisted suicide.

Given Justice Sopinka's failure to sustain a distinction between
assisted suicide, on the one hand, and attempted suicide, the withholding and withdrawal of potentially life-sustaining treatment and the
provision of potentially life-shortening palliative treatment, on the
other, he cannot legitimately claim a foundation for the prohibition on
assisted suicide in the legal tradition and societal beliefs which are said
to be represented by the prohibition.

Additional Arguments

Justice Sopinka makes three additional arguments in support of his
claim that the prohibition on assisted suicide is not contrary to the
principles of fundamental justice. First he argues:

To the extent that there is a consensus, it is that human life must be
respected and we must be careful not to undermine the institutions that
protect it.

This consensus finds legal expression in our legal system which prohibits capital punishment. This prohibition is supported, in part, on the basis that allowing the state to kill will cheapen the value of human life and thus the state will serve in a sense as a role model for individuals in society. The prohibition against assisted suicide serves a similar purpose. In upholding the respect for life, it may discourage those who consider that life is unbearable at a particular moment, or who perceive themselves to be a burden upon others, from committing suicide. To permit a physician to lawfully participate in taking life would send a signal that there are circumstances in which the state approves of suicide.[21]

There are at least two problems with this argument. First, the consensus that 'human life must be protected and we must be careful not to undermine the institutions that protect it' is limited. As noted earlier, life is only a limited value. Second, Justice Sopinka claims that 'permitting a physician to lawfully participate in taking life would send a signal that there are circumstances in which the state approves of suicide.' However, there is a contestable implied premise in his argument. To get from this first premise to his conclusion that assisted suicide should remain illegal, Justice Sopinka must add the premise 'it is wrong for the state to send a signal that there are circumstances in which the state approves of suicide.' But, by decriminalizing suicide, on Justice Sopinka's logic the state has already sent this very signal. Furthermore, it is not so clear that it would be wrong to send this signal. Finally, not prohibiting activity A is different from approving of activity A. I may well argue that smoking should not be prohibited by the state but my argument does not logically entail that I approve of smoking.

Justice Sopinka's second additional argument is: 'I also place some significance in the fact that the official position of various medical associations is against decriminalizing assisted suicide (Canadian Medical Association, British Medical Association, Council of Ethical and Judicial Affairs of the American Medical Association, World Medical Association and the American Nurses Association).'[22] However, the jurisprudential relevance of these official positions is assumed but not defended. Furthermore, while Justice Sopinka cites the official positions of these various health care professional associations, he fails to note that these official positions do not reflect consensus within the professions. Health care providers are clearly split on the issue of the decriminalization of assisted suicide, and there is no survey that shows that even a bare majority of Canadian physicians or nurses oppose decriminalization of assisted suicide.[23] The professional consensus upon which Justice Sopinka seeks to ground a claim of a principle of fundamental justice is shaky indeed. Furthermore, it is not clear why the opinions of health care providers should matter more than the opinions of the general public (if, indeed, either should matter for the determination of the principles of fundamental justice). The public consensus runs counter to what Justice Sopinka presents as the professional consensus.[24]

Justice Sopinka's third additional argument is: 'Given concerns about abuse that have been expressed and the great difficulty in creating appropriate safeguards to prevent these, it can not be said that the blanket prohibition on assisted suicide is arbitrary or unfair, or that it is not reflective of fundamental values at play in our society.'[25] As I argued earlier in the chapter on freedom, competence, and inequality, the concerns about abuse and threats to the well-being of the vulnerable are as serious for the withholding and withdrawal of life-sustaining treatment as they are for assisted suicide and euthanasia. Therefore, if protection of the vulnerable is a principle of fundamental justice, then it grounds prohibiting all forms of voluntary assisted death equally. Given that Justice Sopinka supports a permissive regime for the withholding and withdrawal of potentially life-sustaining treatment, he cannot use the concerns he refers to here as the foundation for finding that a prohibitive regime with respect to assisted suicide and euthanasia is not in breach of section 7 of the *Charter*.

Following this close consideration of Justice Sopinka's reasons, it can be concluded, contrary to his conclusion, that the prohibition on assisted suicide does constitute a breach of section 7 of the *Charter*. The question of whether it can be justified under section 1 must therefore now be considered.

SECTION 1

Justice Sopinka assumes without deciding a breach of section 15 of the *Charter* and so, despite finding no section 7 breach, he considers section 1. Section 1 of the *Charter* states: 'The Canadian Charter of Rights and Freedoms guarantees the rights and freedoms set out in it subject only to such reasonable limits prescribed by law as can be demonstrably justified in a free and democratic society.' According to the Supreme Court of Canada, for a breach of a *Charter* right or freedom to be demonstrably justified there must be a pressing and substantial objective and there must be proportionality between the means and the ends of the legislation. For there to be proportionality, there must be a rational connection between the means taken and the end sought, there must be minimal impairment of the protected right or freedom, and there must be proportionality between the objective and the deleterious effects of the legislation as well as between the deleterious and salutary effects.[26] Justice Sopinka argues that section 241(b) passes all aspects of the section 1 analysis.

First, Justice Sopinka claims that the pressing and substantial objective of the legislation is grounded in 'the respect for and the desire to protect human life.' He then refers back to his discussion of section 7 for the purpose of the legislation. Drawing on his earlier discussion, it can be concluded that Justice Sopinka believes that the objective of the legislation is 'the protection of the vulnerable who might be induced in moments of weakness to commit suicide.'[27]

With respect to proportionality, Justice Sopinka asserts a rational connection between the means and ends of the legislation. He then argues that the legislation minimally impairs the rights and that the deleterious effects of the legislation are proportionate to the objectives. Justice Sopinka argues as follows:

> Section 241(b) protects all individuals against the control of others over their lives. To introduce an exception to this blanket protection for certain groups would create an inequality. As I have sought to demonstrate in my discussion of section 7, this protection is grounded on a substantial consensus among western countries, medical organizations and our own Law Reform Commission that in order to effectively protect life and those who are vulnerable in society, a prohibition without exception on the giving of assistance to commit suicide is the best approach. Attempts to fine tune this approach by creating exceptions have been unsatisfactory and have tended to support the theory of the 'slippery slope.' The formulation of safeguards to prevent excesses has been unsatisfactory and has failed to allay fears that a relaxation of the clear standard set by the law will undermine the protection of life and will lead to abuses of the exception.[28]

Later, he says: 'There is no halfway measure that could be relied upon with assurance to fully achieve the legislation's purpose; first because the purpose extends to the protection of the life of the terminally ill. Part of this purpose, as I have explained above, is to discourage the terminally ill from choosing death over life. Secondly, even if the latter consideration can be stripped from the legislative purpose, we have no assurance that the exception can be made to limit the taking of life to those who are terminally ill and genuinely desire death.'[29]

Justice Sopinka's argument fails for its reliance on concerns about voluntariness and the possibility of abuse as well as the slippery slope argument – concerns and an argument that have already been considered and rejected earlier. In addition, it can be argued with as much authority as is available for Justice Sopinka's claim to the contrary that it *is* possible to erect barriers on the slippery slope that would take us from permitting assisted suicide freely chosen by the competent to assisted suicide forced upon the vulnerable. As noted by Chief Justice Lamer and Justice McLachlin (both in dissent), safeguards can be designed to ensure that decisions to commit assisted suicide are free and informed.[30] By putting in place such safeguards, the legislative regime would no longer capture everyone who might wish to commit an assisted suicide but rather would capture only those who are vulnerable and in need of protection. It would, thereby, minimally impair *Charter* rights.

Finally, as noted by Benjamin Freedman, in 'The Rodriguez Case: Sticky Questions and Slippery Answers,' slippery slope arguments cannot be used in the context of section 1 justifications for breaches of *Charter* rights: 'First, courts are unequipped to gather, assess and weigh the complicated empirical evidence that needs to be brought to bear in such a discussion, as was evident in both Justice Sopinka's opinion and in the dissenting judgments. But there is a deeper, far more fundamental reason. Properly understood, slippery slope arguments cannot satisfy this requirement. They are cautionary in nature, providing reasons to pause, to reconsider, to temporize and to carefully weigh, but by their nature, they are not knock-down, conclusory points. A slippery slope consideration is, by definition, speculative, and so it cannot play the role of satisfying the burden of proof required [i.e., being "demonstrably justified"].'[31]

CONCLUSION

It can therefore be concluded that section 241(b) of the *Criminal Code* breaches sections 7 and 15 of the *Charter* and cannot be saved under section 1. The current regime which requires respect for free and informed refusals of potentially life-sustaining treatment made by competent adults and yet prohibits assisted suicide is unconstitutional.

Active Euthanasia and Assisted Suicide Crown Counsel Policy Manual, Province of British Columbia

[Note: The enactment of the Criminal Code is a federal jurisdiction, however, the administration of justice is a provincial responsibility. Therefore, the Attorney-General of each province has discretion as to whether charges are laid. In accordance with these responsibilities, British Columbia, alone among Canada's provinces and territories, has developed the following guidelines to deal with 'compassionate deaths.']

A. *Active Euthanasia and Assisted Suicide Crown Counsel Policy Manual,* **Province of BC Ministry of Attorney General Criminal Justice Branch (Policy 11-3-93, File no. 56880-01, Eut 1)**

These guidelines apply in cases where a police report to Crown Counsel reveals a person, motivated by compassion for the deceased, participated in causing a death.

In considering these cases, Crown Counsel will apply the general Charge Approval Policy and will only approve a prosecution where there is a substantial likelihood of conviction and the public interest requires a prosecution.

Given the complex nature of the legal issues and the evolution of palliative care, charging decisions will be made on a case-by-case basis following an examination of the facts and circumstances of each case and taking into consideration the following additional factors in applying the general Charge Approval Policy. The charging decision will be made by Regional

Crown Counsel in consultation with the Director of Policy and Legal Services.

Substantial Likelihood of Conviction

In considering whether there is a substantial likelihood of conviction, Crown Counsel must characterize the conduct of the person involved in a death. For the purpose of this policy, this conduct, and the resulting legal consequences are divided into four categories.

'Active-euthanasia' means intentionally terminating early, for compassionate reasons, the life of a person who is terminally ill or whose suffering is unbearable. This conduct is culpable homicide under section 222 of the Criminal Code and may constitute the offences of murder or manslaughter or criminal negligence causing death.

'Assisted suicide' means advising, encouraging or assisting another person to perform an act that intentionally brings about his or her own death. This conduct is an offense of either counseling or aiding suicide under section 241 of the Criminal Code.

'Palliative care' means a qualified medical practitioner, or a person acting under the general supervision of a qualified medical practitioner administering medication or other treatment to a terminally ill patient with the intention of relieving pain or suffering even though this may hasten death. This conduct, when provided or administered according to accepted ethical medical standards, is not subject to criminal prosecution.

'Withholding or withdrawing treatment' means a qualified medical practitioner, with consent by or on behalf of the patient, discontinuing or not intervening with medical procedures to prolong life beyond its natural length. This conduct, when provided or administered according to accepted ethical medical standards, is not subject to criminal prosecution.

The factors to be considered by Crown Counsel in characterizing the conduct of the person involved in a death include:

1 The provable intention of the person who caused, accelerated, counselled or assisted the death, recognizing the criminal intents necessary for murder and counselling or aiding suicide.

2 Where the conduct involves a physician and a patient, the position of the Canadian Medical Association and expert medical opinions as to generally recognized and accepted ethical medical practices:

... there are conditions of ill health and impending inevitable death where an order ... by the attending doctor of 'no resuscitation' is appropriate and ethically acceptable.*

... an ethical physician 'will allow death to occur with dignity and comfort when death of the body appears to be inevitable [and] may support the body when clinical death of the brain has occurred, but need not prolong life by unusual or heroic means.'**

The withholding or withdrawal of inappropriate, futile or unwanted medical treatment and the provision of compassionate palliative care, even when that shortens life, is considered good and ethical medical practice.†

3 Whether, with reference to the following considerations, the acts of a qualified medical practitioner, or a person acting under the general supervision of a qualified medical practitioner, constitute 'palliative care':

a) As stated by Mr Justice Sopinka, in *Rodriguez v. Attorney General of Canada et al*, Supreme Court of Canada, September 30, 1993:

> The administration of drugs designed for pain control in dosages which the physician knows will hasten death constitute active contribution to death by any standard. However, the distinction drawn here is one based upon intention - in the case of palliative care the intention is to ease pain, which has the effect of hastening death, while in the case of assisted suicide, the intention is undeniably to cause death. The Law Reform Commission, although it recommended the continued criminal prohibition of both euthanasia and assisted suicide, stated, at p. 70 of the Working Paper, that a doctor should never refuse palliative care to a terminally ill person because it may hasten death. In my view, distinctions based upon intent are important, and in fact form the basis of our criminal law. While factually the distinction may, at times, be difficult to draw, legally it is clear ... (at page 34)

---

*Canadian Medical Association, *Canadian Physicians and Euthanasia*, 1993, 5.
**Ibid. 19, quoting from the Canadian Medical Association, *Code of Ethics*, CMA, Ottawa, 1990: items 18 and 19.
† Ibid. 20.

b) whether the patient was terminally ill and near death with no
   hope of recovery
c) whether the patient's condition was associated with severe and
   unrelenting suffering
d) whether accepted ethical medical practices were followed: and
e) whether the patient was participating in a palliative care program
   or palliative care treatment plan.

4 Whether, with reference to the following considerations, the acts of a
  qualified medical practitioner constitute 'withholding or withdrawing treatment':

a) Under the common law, a physician must accept the patient's
   instructions to refuse or discontinue medical treatment although
   such treatment may well prolong life. Canadian Courts have recognized this right, see *Malette* v. *Shulman* (1990) 72 O.R.(2d) 417
   (Ont. C.A.). As stated by Sopinka, J. in *Rodriguez*, supra: 'To continue to treat the patient when the patient has withdrawn consent
   to that treatment constitutes battery (*Ciarlariello* and *Nancy B.*,
   supra.) The doctor is therefore not required to make a choice
   which will result in the patient's death as he would be if he chose
   to assist a suicide or to perform active euthanasia' (at page 34).
b) where the deceased refused treatment or revoked consent to the
   treatment, whether such refusal or revocation was fully informed
   and freely done. This will include consideration of whether:

   i)   the patient clearly understood his or her medical condition
        and that it may result in death if treatment was discontinued
        or not engaged
   ii) the patient was mentally incompetent, depressed, or other-
        wise vulnerable
   iii) the patient's refusal of treatment or revocation of consent and
        the act of withholding or withdrawing treatment occurred
        contemporaneously
   iv) the patient was informed and understood his or her ongoing
        right to reconsider the refusal or revocation of consent
   v)   there is any evidence the patient reconsidered his or her
        initial refusal or revocation of, consent
   vi) anyone pressured the patient to refuse treatment or revoke
        consent to the treatment and

vii) accepted ethical medical practices were followed.

c) where the deceased was unable to refuse treatment or revoke consent to treatment, consideration of whether:

    i)   there were instructions given to the qualified medical practitioner by another person or entity authorized to refuse treatment or revoke consent to treatment on behalf of the patient, for example, the existence of a court order or power of attorney for health care

    ii) here was evidence that withholding or withdrawal of treatment was what the patient would have requested had he or she been able to refuse treatment or revoke consent to treatment: and

    iii) accepted ethical medical practices were followed.

Public Interest

If Crown Counsel has determined there is a substantial likelihood of conviction, he or she must also be satisfied the public interest requires a prosecution. In determining the public interest, the specific factors to be considered include, but are not restricted to, the public interest factors outlined in the general Charge Approval Policy and the following:

1 The importance of supporting proper professional and ethical standards within the health care professions
2 Society's interest in the protection of vulnerable persons and
3 Society's interest in protecting the sanctity of human life, recognizing this does not require life to be preserved at all cost.

B. Quality Control – Charge Approval Policy Crown Counsel Policy Manual, Province of British Columbia, Ministry of Attorney General, Criminal Justice Branch (Policy 2-26-91, File no. 55100-00)

Section 504 of the *Criminal Code* allows anyone to lay, and directs a justice to receive, an Information alleging a criminal offense. In British Columbia, it has long been the policy of this Ministry of Attorney General that Crown Counsel review all allegations of criminal conduct and apply a single, consistent charging standard before charges are approved and an Information laid. This system of charge approval has received the endorsement of the Justice Reform Commission and the Discretion to Prosecute Inquiry.

The charging standard and procedure to be followed are set out below. Any Informations that are laid without the prior approval of Crown Counsel should be dealt with under the private prosecutions policy, see PRI 1.

Charge Standard

Allegations must be examined to determine whether there is a substantial likelihood of conviction and if so, whether the public interest requires a prosecution of the accused.

Substantial Likelihood of Conviction

In determining whether a charge should be laid, Counsel must first conclude that it is likely there will be a conviction after considering all relevant matters including the available evidence, the anticipated defense and the applicable law. A substantial likelihood of conviction is significantly more a *prima facie* case, but considerably less than a virtual certainty of conviction.

During the charge approval process, Crown Counsel does not have the benefit of hearing the testimony of Crown witnesses, either in direct or cross-examination. Nor does Crown Counsel have the benefit of hearing the defence evidence, if any. During the course of a trial, the Crown's case may be materially stronger or weaker than counsel's initial assessment at the early charge approval stage. For this reason, Crown Counsel must be flexible in applying the substantial likelihood of conviction standard recognizing that the more serious the allegation, the greater the interests of justice in ensuring that provable charges are prosecuted.

Public Interest

Counsel must next determine whether the public interest dictates a prosecution. There are a number of factors counsel should consider in assessing the public interest in a prosecution:

(a) The nature and seriousness of the allegations
(b) the harm caused to the victim, if any

(c) the personal circumstances of the accused, including his or her criminal record

(d) the likelihood of achieving the desired result without a court proceeding, including an assessment of the available alternatives to prosecution and

(e) the cost of a prosecution compared to the social benefit to be gained by it. This will include considerations such as the degree to which this offense (as opposed to this offender) represents a community problem which cannot be effectively dealt with otherwise.

In considering the public interest hard and fast rules cannot be imposed and flexibility in decision making at the local level is essential if the Ministry is to respond to the legitimate concerns of each community.

Applying the Charge Standard

If Counsel is to accurately apply the charge standard, the Report to Crown Counsel (RTCC) must provide an accurate and detailed statement of the evidence available. The following are the basic requirements for every RTCC:

(a) A comprehensive description of the evidence supporting each element of the suggested charge(s)

(b) where the evidence of a civilian witness is necessary to prove an essential element of the charge (except for minor offenses), a copy of that person's written statement

(c) necessary evidence check sheets

(d) copies of all documents required to prove the chargers)

(e) a detailed summary or written copy of the accused's statements) and

(f) accused's criminal record (if any).

There may be cases where the RTCC will not comply with the quality control standards. The RTCC should then be returned to the investigator with a request for additional information before a charge is approved. If the accused is in custody, Crown should not seek to detain the accused in custody without sufficient written material from the police to justify both the charge and the detention.

If the offense is serious and there is sufficient evidence to charge the detained accused but insufficient information to determine Crown's position on release, resort may be had to s.516 to adjourn the show cause. This should be used only where it appears necessary to protect the public.

In applying the charge standard Crown Counsel s important obligations are to:

(i)   make the decision in a timely manner
(ii) record the reasons for the decision and
(iii) where appropriate, communicate with those affected, including the police, so that they understand the reasons for the decision.

Notes

Introduction

1 I will demonstrate this absence in Chapter 1.
2 M.B. Kapp, 'Treating Medical Charts Near the End of Life: How Legal Anxieties Inhibit Good Patient Deaths' (1997) 28(3) Univ. Toledo L. Rev. 521; T. R. Fried et al., 'Limits of Patient Autonomy: Physician Attitudes and Practices Regarding Life-Sustaining Treatments and Euthanasia' (1993) 153(6) Arch. Intern. Med. 722; M.Z. Solomon et al., 'Decisions Near the End of Life: Professional Views on Life-Sustaining Treatments' (1993) 83(1) Am. J. Public Health 14.
3 Fried et al., 'Limits of Patient Autonomy,' supra, n2; K.A. Puntillo et al., 'End-of-Life Issues in Intensive Care Units: A National Random Survey of Nurses' Knowledge and Beliefs' (2001) 10(4) Am. J. Crit. Care 216; C.S. Hill Jr., 'The Barriers to Adequate Pain Management with Opioid Analgesics' (1993) 20(2 Suppl. 1) Semin. Oncol. 1; J. Alaeddini et al., 'Physician Attitudes toward Palliative Care at Community Teaching Hospitals' (2000) 15(2) Hosp. J. 67; A.C. Carver et al., 'End-of-Life Care: A Survey of U.S. Neurologists' Attitudes, Behavior and Knowledge' (1999) 53(2) Neurology 284; and Kapp, 'Treating Medical Charts Near the End of Life,' supra, n2. See testimony before the Special Senate Committee on Euthanasia and Assisted Suicide of Carol Rees from Action Life, Monique Coupal from the Fédération québécoise des centres d'hébèrgement et de soins de longue durée, and Patricia Rodney. Senate of Canada, *Proceedings of the Senate Special Committee on Euthanasia and Assisted Suicide* [hereinafter cited as *Senate Special Cte.*], No. 8 (1 June 1994) at 11, No. 32 (17 Oct. 1994) at 39, and No. 15 (27 Sept. 1994) at 129, respectively.
4 *Nancy B. v. Hôtel-Dieu de Québec* (1992), 86 D.L.R. (4th) 385 (Que. Sup. Ct.).

5 Ibid.
6 This argument is found in many decisions. See, e.g., Justice Beard's reasons in *Sawatzky* v. *Riverview Health Centre Inc.*, [1998] M.J. No. 506 (Q.B.) at para. 5, online: QL (MJ) [hereinafter *Sawatzky*]: 'Those questions raise serious legal, moral, ethical, medical and practical issues on which there is unlikely to ever be complete agreement ... While the courts may be an appropriate place to start the discussion of these issues in that the courts can clarify the existing state of the law in light of the Charter of Rights and Freedoms, it may be for the government to resolve any moral or ethical questions that remain at the end of the day. The government can ensure a much wider debate including all interested sectors of society, while a court proceeding is, by necessity, relatively narrow and limited even if some interventions are allowed.'
7 *Senate Special Cte.*, No. 20 (17 Oct. 1994) at 8.
8 A review of the treatment of euthanasia cases across the country is found in Chapter 1.
9 See, e.g., testimony of Thomas Sigurdson. *Senate Special Cte.*, No. 15 (27 Sept. 1994) at 119–23. See also supra, n3.
10 See, e.g., the testimony of Russell Ogden and Louise Normandin Miller, *Senate Special Cte.*, No. 14 (26 Sept. 1994) and No. 5 (11 May 1994), respectively.
11 For example, Scott Mataya, Robert Latimer, Jean Brush, and Nancy Morrison. Their cases are all summarized and referenced fully in Chapter 1.
12 For example, Canadian Austin Bastable died with the assistance of Jack Kevorkian on 6 May 1996. 'Austin Bastable dies with the aid of Dr Jack Kevorkian,' Canadian News Bulletins [hereinafter CNB] (1 April to 31 May 1996), online: Deathnet < http://www.rights.org/deathnet/open.html>
13 These definitions are similar to, but in most cases modifications of, the definitions adopted by the Special Senate Committee on Euthanasia and Assisted Suicide in *Of Life and Death: Report of the Special Senate Committee on Euthanasia and Assisted Suicide* [hereinafter *Of Life and Death*] (June 1995) at 13–15.
14 James Bernat, 'Ethical and Legal Issues in Palliative Care' (2001) 19(4) Neurology.
15 Indeed, I have argued elsewhere for legally requiring respect for advance directives. See J. Downie, '"Where There Is a Will, There May Be a Better Way": Legislating Advance Directives' (1992) 12(3) Health L. Can. 73.
16 See, e.g., Yale Kamisar, 'Against Assisted Suicide – Even a Very Limited Form' (1995) 72 U. Det. Mercy L. Rev. 735; and Daniel Callahan, 'Self-

Extinction: The Morality of the Helping Hand,' in Robert Weir ed., *Physician-Assisted Suicide* (Bloomington: Indiana University Press, 1997) (re: active/passive and intention); and the President's Commission for the Study of Ethical Problems in Medicine and Biomedical and Behavioral Research, *Deciding to Forego Life-Sustaining Treatment: A Report of the Ethical, Medical, and Legal Issues in Treatment Decisions* (Washington, DC: Government Printing Office, 1983) (re: causation).

17 For example, the majority of the Special Senate Committee on Euthanasia and Assisted Suicide, supra, n13, and the majority of the Supreme Court of Canada in *Rodriguez v. British Columbia (Attorney General)*, [1993] 3 S.C.R. 519.

18 *Canadian Charter of Rights and Freedoms*, Part I of the *Constitution Act*, being Schedule – to the *Canada Act 1982* (U.K.).

1 Withholding and Withdrawal of Potentially Life-Sustaining Treatment from Competent Persons

1 *Criminal Code*, R.S.C. 1985, c. C-46.

2 *R. v. Brooks* (1902), 5 C.C.C. 372 (B.C.S.C.)

3 *Hôpital Notre-Dame v. Patry* (1972), C.A. 579 (Que. C.A.).

4 Other cases have, of course, considered the legal status of the withholding and withdrawal of potentially life-sustaining treatment. However, as these did not refer to the *Criminal Code* or other pieces of legislation, they will be discussed in the subsequent section on the common law. Furthermore, although *Procureur Général du Canada c. Hôpital Notre-Dame et Niemiec*, [1984] C.S. 426 (Que.S.C.) [hereinafter *Niemiec*] did refer to the *Criminal Code* and, in the result, went in the opposite direction to *British Columbia (Attorney General) v. Astaforoff*, [1983] 6 W.W.R. 322 at 326 (B.C.S.C.); aff'd. [1984] 4 W.W.R. 385 (B.C.C.A.) [hereinafter *Astaforoff*], I will not discuss it here; the analysis of the *Criminal Code* refers to suicide, not negligence (the part of the *Criminal Code* at issue here).

5 *Nancy B. v. Hôtel-Dieu de Québec* (1992), 86 D.L.R. (4th) 385 (Que.S.C.) [hereinafter *Nancy B.*].

6 Ibid. at 393.

7 He quoted approvingly (*Nancy B.*, supra, n5 at 392–3) from the Law Reform Commission of Canada, Working Paper 28: 'Section 199 [now s. 217] of the *Criminal Code*, read in isolation, seems to imply that a physician who has undertaken treatment is not permitted to terminate it if this involves a risk to the life of the patient. If this were the case, the law would require the use of aggressive and useless therapy. It would also have the effect, in many cases,

of causing doctors to hesitate seriously before undertaking treatment, for fear of not being permitted to terminate it later, when it no longer appears to be useful. If this were the actual implication of the rule, then the rule would be absurd and would have disastrous effects on medical practice.'

8 *Nancy B.*, supra, n5 at 394.

9 *Astaforoff*, supra, n4 at 326.

10 *Health Care Consent Act, 1996*, S.O. 1996, c. 2.; *Health Care (Consent) and Care Facility (Admission) Act*, S.B.C. 1996, C.181; and *Consent to Treatment and Health Care Directives Act*, S.P.E.I. 1996, C-17.2.

11 Section 4 *Health Care (Consent) and Care Facility (Admission) Act*, ibid.; and s. 4 *Consent to Treatment and Health Care Directives Act*, ibid.

12 *Hospitals Act*, R.S.N.S. 1989, c. 208, s. 4.

13 Ibid. at s. 12.

14 Ibid. at s. 36.

15 *Rodriguez v. British Columbia (Attorney General)*, [1993] 3 S.C.R. 519 at 588 [hereinafter *Rodriguez*].

16 Ibid. at 598.

17 Ibid. at 606.

18 For example, *Niemiec*, supra, n4 and *Astaforoff*, supra n4. In *Astaforoff*, a B.C. court held that the corrections authorities did not have a duty to forcibly feed a Doukhobor prisoner on a hunger strike even though she was likely to die without force-feeding. In *Niemiec*, a Quebec court held that a prisoner did not have the right to have his refusal of treatment and force-feeding respected (Niemiec, a prisoner awaiting deportation from Canada, had put a metal wire into his throat). The court held that to respect his refusal would be to assist in his suicide which would be illegal. It is interesting to note that given *obiter dicta* about the American case of Elizabeth Bouvia (*Bouvia v. Superior Court*, 225 Cal. Rptr. 297 (Cal. C.A. 1986)), it seems likely that the *Niemiec* court would not permit the withholding of nutrition and hydration from a non-terminally ill quadriplegic patient.

19 It is interesting to note that the cases Justice Sopinka relied upon in *Rodriguez*, supra, n15, do not in fact provide the solid common law foundation he seeks. In *Ciarlariello v. Schacter*, [1993] 2 S.C.R. 119 [hereinafter *Ciarlariello*], frequently thought to stand for the proposition that there is a common law right to refuse potentially life-sustaining treatment, Justice Cory wrote for the Court at 135: 'It should not be forgotten that every patient has a right to bodily integrity. This encompasses the right to determine what medical procedures will be accepted and the extent to which they will be accepted. Everyone has the right to decide what is to be done to one's own body. This includes the right to be free from medical treatment to which the

individual does not consent. This concept of individual autonomy is fundamental to the common law and is the basis for the requirement that disclosure be made to a patient. If, during the course of a medical procedure a patient withdraws the consent to that procedure, then the doctors must halt the process. This duty to stop does no more than recognize every individual's basic right to make decisions concerning his or her own body.'

This is indeed a strong statement and would appear to support the proposition stated above. However, it must be noted that later, in a portion of the judgment seemingly ignored by those who would cite *Ciarlariello* as standing for the proposition that refusals of potentially life-sustaining treatment must be respected, Justice Cory also stated at 136 that '[i]n any event, the patient's right to bodily integrity provides the basis for the withdrawal of a consent to a medical procedure even while it is underway. Thus, if it is found that the consent is effectively withdrawn during the course of the proceeding, then it must be terminated. *This must be the result except in those circumstances where the medical evidence suggests that to terminate the process would be either life-threatening or pose immediate and serious problems to the health of the patient*' (emphasis added). *Ciarlariello* therefore stands only for the proposition that there is a common law right to refuse treatment as long as the withdrawal of the treatment would *not* be life-threatening.

Malette v. *Shulman* (1990), 72 O.R. (2d) 417 (C.A.) [hereinafter *Malette*] also limits the right to refuse potentially life-shortening treatment. At first glance, the case seems to set a significant precedent for respecting advance directives. However, at 428, the Court of Appeal explicitly rejected the extension of the reasoning in this case to cases involving patients who have been diagnosed as terminally or incurably ill or patients in a persistent vegetative state: 'I should emphasize that in deciding this case the court is not called upon to consider the law that may be applicable to the many situations in which objection may be taken to the use or continued use of medical treatment to save or prolong a patient's life. The court's role, especially in a matter as sensitive as this, is limited to resolving the issues raised by the facts presented in this particular case. On these facts, we are not concerned with a patient who has been diagnosed as terminally ill or incurably ill who seeks by way of advance directive or 'living will' to reject medical treatment so that she may die with dignity; neither are we concerned with a patient in an irreversibly vegetative state whose family seeks to withdraw medical treatment in order to end her life; nor is this a case in which an otherwise healthy patient wishes for some reason or other to terminate her life. There is no element of suicide or euthanasia in this case.' Therefore, while this case does require respect for some advance directives, it does not require respect for them in the context of traditional assisted death scenarios (e.g., a terminally ill patient refusing life-sustaining treatment or the family of a patient in a persistent vegetative state seeking the withdrawal of treatment).

In *Nancy B.*, supra, n5, a woman was found to be entitled to have her refusal of potentially life-sustaining treatment respected. However, the court did *not* ground this entitlement in a common law right. The decision was grounded in the Quebec *Civil Code*, Section 19.1: 'No person may be made to undergo care of any nature, whether for examination, specimen taking, removal of tissue, treatment or any other act, except with his consent.' However, despite the fact that the *Rodriguez* comments stand on shakier ground than indicated by Justice Sopinka, the comments nonetheless in themselves establish a common law right to refuse potentially life-sustaining treatment.

20 A useful discussion of the law in relation to mature minors is found in Joan Gilmour, 'Children, Adolescents, and Health Care,' in J. Downie, T. Caulfield, and C. Flood, eds., *Canadian Health Law and Policy*, 2nd ed. (Toronto: Butterworths, 2002) 205–49.

21 Several regulations that govern hospital management specifically address mature minors' consent to treatment. These include: Section 55(1) of the *Hospital Standards Regulations, 1980*, Sask. Reg. 331/79, s. 55, made pursuant to *The Hospital Standards Act*, R.S.S. 1978, c. H-10; section 48 of the *Hospital Management Regulations*, EC574/76 as am., made pursuant to the *Hospitals Act*, R.S.P.E.I. 1988, c. H-10; section 26(1) and (2) of the *Hospital Management Regulation*, R.R.O. 1990, Reg. 965, made pursuant to the *Public Hospitals Act*, R.S.O. 1990, c. P-40; and section 87 of the *Hospital Standards Regulations*, R.R.N.W.T. 1990, c. T-6, s. 87 made pursuant to the *Territorial Hospital Insurance Services Act*, R.S.N.W.T. 1988, c. T-3. However, the first three concern consent to non-emergency surgery (they make both the minor's consent and parental consent necessary but not sufficient) and thus would have limited bearing on refusals of potentially life-sustaining treatment. They would affect the ability to get treatment without parental consent but, if a mature minor refuses treatment, parental wishes are irrelevant. In addition, the Ontario regulations are inconsistent with the recent Ontario consent legislation discussed *infra* and would likely be held to be of no legal effect in the face of a contested mature minor consent case.

The fourth concerns discharge from hospital. If a patient is a minor, the parent or guardian must sign a statement releasing the hospital and the attending medical practitioner from responsibility for the discharge. However, this has *no limiting effect* on the mature minor's right to refuse treatment. I will therefore not consider these regulations further.

22 'Sec. 4. Capacity. – (1) A person is capable with respect to a treatment, admission to a care facility or a personal assistance service if the person is able to understand the information that is relevant to making a decision about the treatment, admission or personal assistance service, as the case may be, and able to appreciate the reasonably foreseeable consequences of a decision or lack of decision. *Health Care Consent Act*, supra, n10.

23 The law respecting consent to medical treatment of persons who have attained the age of majority applies, in all respects, to minors who have attained the age of 16 years in the same manner as if they had attained the age of majority. *Medical Consent of Minors Act*, R.S.N.B. 1973, c. M-6.1, s. 2.

24 'S.17.(2) Subject to subsection (3), an infant may consent to health care whether or not that health care would, in the absence of consent, constitute a trespass to the infant's person, and if an infant provides that consent, the consent is effective and it is not necessary to obtain a consent to the health care from the infant's parent or guardian. (3) A request for or consent, agreement or acquiescence to health care by an infant does not constitute consent to the health care for the purposes of subsection (2) unless the health care provider providing the health care (a) has explained to the infant and has been satisfied that the infant understands the nature and consequences and the reasonably foreseeable benefits and risks of the health care.' *Infants Act*, R.S.B.C. 1996, c. 223.

This legislation (then s.16) withstood a constitutional challenge in *Ney* v. *Canada (Attorney General)*, [1993] B.C.J. No. 993 May 3, 1993. B.C.S.C.) [hereinafter *Ney*] at 59: 'Because I am of the view that section 16, when read properly, does no more than codify the common law rules and provide certainty with regard to those to whom they apply, and because no complaint is made about the common law, I cannot hold the section to be unconstitutional.'

25 Sec.3. (1) The consent to medical treatment of a minor who has not attained the age of sixteen years is as effective as it would be if he had attained the age of majority where, in the opinion of a legally qualified medical practitioner or legally qualified dentist attending the minor, supported by the written opinion of one other legally qualified medical practitioner or legally qualified dentist, as the case may be, (a) the minor is capable of understanding the nature and consequences of a medical treatment, *and (b) the medical treatment and the procedure to be used is in the best interests of the minor and his continuing health and well-being.' Medical Consent of Minors Act,* supra, n23. Emphasis added.

26 Sec. 17.(2) Subject to subsection (3), an infant may consent to health care
   whether or not that health care would, in the absence of consent, constitute
   a trespass to the infant's person, and if an infant provides that consent, the
   consent is effective and it is not necessary to obtain a consent to the health
   care from the infant's parent or guardian. (3) A request for or consent,
   agreement or acquiescence to health care by an infant does not constitute
   consent to the health care for the purposes of subsection (2) unless the
   health care provider providing the health care (a) has explained to the
   infant and has been satisfied that the infant understands the nature and
   consequences and the reasonably foreseeable benefits and risks of the
   health care, and (b) *has made reasonable efforts to determine and has concluded
   that the health care is in the infant's best interests.' Infants Act*, supra, n24.
   Emphasis added.
27 *Child and Family Services Amendment Act*, S.M. 1995, c. 23, s. 25(2).
28 Ibid. at s. 25(9).
29 *Civil Code of Quebec*, art. 14 para. 2.
30 Ibid., art. 16 para. 2 and art. 23. See R. Kouri and S. Philips-Nootens, 'Civil
   Liability of Physicians Under Quebec Law' in J. Downie, T. Caulfield, C.
   Flood, eds., *Canadian Health Law and Policy*, 2nd ed. (Toronto: Butterworths,
   2002) 533–85.
31 *B.H. (Next Friend of)* v. *Alberta (Director of Child Welfare)* 2002 ABQB 371,
   [2002] A.J. No. 518 Alta. C.Q.B., 10 April 2002 at para. 44.
32 *Child Welfare Act* S.A. 1984 C-8.1 s. 1(2) and 2. Affirmed on appeal but not
   on this point as the court said that this point was 'academic' given the facts.
   2002 ABCA 109, [2002] A.J. No. 568 A.C.A., 1 May 2002.
33 *C.A.S. Metro Toronto* v. *K.* (1985), 48 R.F.L. (2d) 164 (Ont. Fam. Ct.) [hereinaf-
   ter *L.D.K.*]; *Re Y.(A.)* (1993), 111 Nfld. & P.E.I.R. 91 [hereinafter *A.Y.*]; *Walker
   (Litigation Guardian of)* v. *Region 2 Hospital Corp.* (1994) 116 D.L.R. (4th) 477
   (N.B.C.A.) [hereinafter *Walker*].
34 For example, American courts in *In re Quinlan*, 355 A. 2d 647 (N.J.S.C. 1976),
   rev'g 348 A.2d 801 (1975), *cert.* denied 429 U.S. 922 (1976) [hereinafter *Quinlan*] and *Cruzan* v. *Director, Missouri Dep't of Health* 110 S.Ct. 2841 (1990)
   [hereinafter *Cruzan*].
35 The Special Senate Committee on Euthanasia and Assisted Suicide, which
   heard 138 presentations and received thousands of written submissions,
   received only one submission against the withdrawal of potentially life-sustaining treatment. According to their written brief (on file with the Library of
   Parliament and the author) at p. 13, the Lubavitch–B.C. Jewish community
   opposes all withdrawal of life-sustaining treatment: 'The discontinuation of
   any medical treatment such as respirator, oxygen, intravenous, nasal-gastric

feeding or pharmacological treatment cannot be endorsed. It would only be possible to take these actions if the physician knew with absolute certainty that his conduct was not interrupting life. Such a determination is impossible for anyone to make with absolute and total certainty. Therefore, once initiated, instrumental support of vital life processes should not be interrupted unless and until death has been determined.'

36 *Johnston* v. *Wellesley Hospital* (1971), 17 D.L.R. (3d) 139 (Ont. H.C.).

37 Ibid. at 145. Justice Addy quoted approvingly at 145 from Lord Nathan in *Medical Negligence* (1957) at 176: 'It is suggested that the most satisfactory solution of the problem is to rule that an infant who is capable of appreciating fully the nature and consequences of a particular operation or of particular treatment can give an effective consent thereto, and in such cases the consent of the guardian is unnecessary; but that where the infant is without that capacity, any apparent consent by him or her will be a nullity, the sole right to consent being vested in the guardian.'

38 *J.S.C.* v. *Wren*, [1987] 2 W.W.R. 669 (Alta. C.A.).

39 Justice Kerans, for the Alberta Court of Appeal, quoted approvingly at 672 from the decision of Lord Scarman in *Gillick* v. *West Norfolk & Wisbech Area Health Authority*, [1985] 3 W.L.R. 830, [1985] 3 All E.R. 402 (H.L.) at 423: 'In the light of the foregoing I would hold that as a matter of law the parental right to determine whether or not their minor child below the age of 16 will have medical treatment terminates if and when the child achieves a sufficient understanding and intelligence to enable him or her to understand fully what is proposed.'

40 I will not consider *Children's Aid Society of Metropolitan Toronto* v. *S.H.*, [1996] O.J. No. 2578, 15 July 1996, Justice Wilson Ontario Court of Justice (General Division), the case of an anorexic adolescent taken to a Consent and Capacity Review Board in Ontario (described in R. Geist, D. Katzman, and J. Colangelo. 'The *Consent to Treatment Act* and an Adolescent with Anorexia Nervosa' (1996) 16 Health L. Can. 110) or *Re Dueck* (1999), 171 D.L.R. (4th) 761. These recent cases involve refusals of treatment by minors but will not be considered herein because in each of these cases, the minor was found not to be a mature minor. Nothing in the reasons contribute to the analysis of the status and scope of the mature minor rule at common law.

41 'She has wisdom and maturity beyond her years and I think it would be safe to say that she has all of the positive attributes that any parent would want in a child. She has a well thought out, firm and clear religious belief. In my view, no amount of counselling from whatever source or pressure from her parents or anyone else, including an order of this court, would shake or alter her religious beliefs.' *L.D.K.*, supra, n33 at 171.

42 Ibid.

43 *A.Y.*, supra, n33 at 96.

44 Ibid. at 93.

45 *Walker*, supra, n33 at 487.

46 See, e.g., E.I. Picard and G.B. Robertson, *Legal Liability of Doctors and Hospitals in Canada*, 3rd ed. (Toronto: Carswell, 1996) at 72; G.B. Robertson, *Mental Disability and the Law in Canada*, 2nd ed. (Toronto: Carswell, 1994) at 157–8; and G. Sharpe, *The Law and Medicine in Canada*, 2nd ed. (Toronto: Carswell, 1987) at 69.

47 *L.D.K.*, supra, n33 at 170.

48 *Child Welfare Act*, R.S.O. 1980, c. 66.

49 'I am not satisfied on the medical evidence which I have heard that in this particular case – and every case is different – I am not satisfied that in this particular case the use of blood products as a follow-up to chemotherapy is considered essential by the qualified medical practitioner from whom I have heard and in whom I have considerable confidence.' *A.Y.*, supra, n33 at 95. '[A]s always with matters involving children or young persons who are below the age at which the law allows them to deal with matters independently of officials and courts, what the court must take into consideration and be guided by is, in all respects, the *best interests* of the child.' Ibid. at 96. Emphasis added.

50 '[T]he evidence here is overwhelming that Joshua is sufficiently mature and that, in the circumstances, *the proposed treatment is in his best interests and his continuing well-being.*' *Walker*, supra, n33 at 489. Emphasis added.

51 *Ney*, supra, n24 at 51 and 53; C.J.B.C. McEachern in *R.* v. *D.D.W.*, [1997] B.C.J. No. 744, 27 March 1997 B.C.C.A. (for himself with Hall filing concurring reasons) at para. 29–30; and *Kennett Estate* v. *Manitoba (Attorney-General)*, [1998] M.J. No. 131, 18 March 1998, Jewers J. Manitoba Court of Queen's Bench at para. 13.

52 *Ney*, supra n24 at 58. Emphasis added.

53 *R.* v. *D.D.W.*, supra n51 at para. 29–30.

54 *Kennett Estate* v. *Manitoba (Attorney-General)*, supra, n51 at para. 13.

55 *Van Mol (Guardian ad litem of)* v. *Ashmore*, [1999] B.C.J. No. 31 (B.C.C.A.), online: QL (CJ).

56 Ibid. at para. 143.

57 This conclusion applies everywhere in Canada except in those provinces with legislation on the issue (as previously discussed).

58 *Child and Family Services of Manitoba* v. *R.L.*, [1997] M.J. No. 568, online: QL (MJ).

59 Ibid. at para 17.

60 *Sawatzky* v. *Riverview Health Centre Inc.*, [1998] M.J. No. 506 (Q.B.), online: QL (MJ) [hereinafter *Sawatzky*].
61 Ibid. at para. 26.
62 Ibid. at para. 5.
63 Ibid. at para. 26.

2 The Provision of Potentially Life-Shortening Palliative Treatment

1 Anne Mullens, 'Society must lead in determining Canadian position on euthanasia, doctors say' (15 April 1993) 148 Can. Med. Assoc. J. 1363 at 1367.
2 Ibid. At 1367, Mullens reports that the Royal Canadian Mounted Police decided not to lay charges 'primarily because both families refused to press charges and praised Graff for his compassionate care.'
3 Verdicts of the Coroner's Jury, appended to the brief of the Office of the Chief Coroner of Ontario submitted to the Special Senate Committee on Euthanasia and Assisted Suicide, on file with the Library of Parliament and the author.
4 See Dr Young's testimony before the Special Senate Committee on Euthanasia and Assisted Suicide. Senate of Canada, *Senate Special Cte.*, No. 20 (17 Oct. 1994) at 18.
5 *Rodriguez* v. *British Columbia (Attorney General)*, [1993] 3 S.C.R. 519 at 607.

3 Assisted Suicide

1 A fourth case could have been significant. Early in 1998, an elderly man in Manitoba, Bert Doerksen, was charged under s. 241(b) in the death of his chronically ill wife (she was found dead by carbon monoxide poisoning in the garage of their home). This case had the potential to undercut the legal prohibition against assisted suicide (i.e., if the evidence had been convincing and yet a jury had refused to convict). However, the Crown ultimately decided not to proceed on the charge as Mr Doerksen was too ill to stand trial.
2 *Rodriguez* v. *British Columbia (Attorney General)*, [1993] 3 S.C.R. 519 [hereinafter *Rodriguez*].
3 She took an overdose of morphine and secobarbital. 'Special Prosecutor to Decide Whether to Charge Member of Parliament' Canadian News Bulletins [hereinafter CNB] (1 Jan. to 31 Jan. 1995), online: Deathnet <http://www.rights.org/deathnet/open.html>.
4 Robert T.C. Johnston, 'Letter from Robert Johnson to H.N. Yacowar (Acting

Assistant Attorney General of Vancouver) Re: Investigation into the death of Susan Jane Rodriguez,' 21 June 1995, on file with the author.

5 'Senator Carstairs contends that Mary Jane Fogarty case will be used as a precedent' CNB (1 Nov. to 31 Dec. 1995), online: Deathnet <http://www.rights.org/deathnet/open.html>.

6 In 1962, three Inuit men were charged and convicted with assisting the suicide of Chief Aleak Kolitalik. There are no official records of this case. However, through interviews with the arresting officer and the Crown counsel at trial, it has been reconstructed and is described in Anne Mullens, *Timely Death: What We Can Expect and What We Need to Know* (Toronto: Vintage Canada, 1996): 52–7.

7 'Canada's first assisted suicide charge in 32 years' CNB (1 Jan. to 31 Jan. 1995), online: Deathnet <http://www.rights.org/deathnet/open.html>.

8 'Canadian doctor charged with assisting a suicide' CNB (1 April to 31 May), online: Deathnet <http://www.rights.org/deathnet/open.html>.

9 'Aids doctor faces additional charges' CNB (1 May to 31 May 1997), online: Deathnet <http://www.rights.org/deathnet/open.html>; 'Aids doctor convicted of assisting suicides' CNB (1 Dec. to 31 Dec. 1997), online: Deathnet <http://www.rights/org/deathnet/open.html>.

10 Russel Ogden, *Euthanasia, Assisted Suicide and AIDS* (Pitt Meadows, BC: Perreault Goedman Publishing, 1994), and Neil Searles, 'Silence Doesn't Obliterate the Truth: A Manitoba Survey on Physician Assisted Suicide and Euthanasia' 4(3) Health L.Rev. (1995) 9–16. That we do not know exactly *how often* it is happening is not surprising given its illegality.

11 There have already been six significant changes in the constitution of the Court. First, Justices La Forest and Gonthier, one of the judges in the majority in *Rodriguez*, supra, n2, retired and, second, Justice Sopinka, the author of the majority decision, died suddenly on 24 Nov. 1997. Since then, Justices Cory and L'Heureux-Dubé and Chief Justice Lamer have retired (all of these judges were in dissent in *Rodriguez*). There is no indication how the six new judges might affect a decision in a subsequent assisted suicide case.

12 Note that the Supreme Court can and does reverse itself (albeit rarely). See, e.g., *Brooks* v. *Canada Safeway Ltd.*, [1989] 1 S.C.R. 1219 overruling *Bliss* v. *Attorney General of Canada*, [1979] 1 S.C.R. 183. In *Bliss*, the Supreme Court of Canada held that discrimination on the basis of pregnancy is not discrimination on the basis of sex. In *Brooks*, the Court explicitly overruled this holding.

4 Euthanasia

1 *R.* v. *Lewis*, [1979] 2 S.C.R. 821 at 831.

2 Ibid. at 833.

3 See Eric Colvin, *Principles of Criminal Law*, 2nd ed. (Scarborough: Thomson Professional Publishing, 1991) at 212–17 for a discussion of these exceptions.

4 Motive can go to sentencing for manslaughter since it does not have a mandatory minimum sentence and so the judge looks to sentencing guidelines.

5 '8.(3) Every rule and principle of the common law that renders any circumstance a justification or excuse for an act or a defence to a charge continues in force and applies in respect of proceedings for an offence under this Act or any other Act of Parliament except in so far as they are altered by or are inconsistent with this Act or any other Act of Parliament.'

6 *R.* v. *Latimer*, [2001] 1 S.C.R. 3, 193 D.L.R. (4th) 577 (S.C.C.) [hereinafter *Latimer 1*]. Other cases involving euthanasia might provide more compelling factual bases for arguing a defence of necessity. Consider, e.g., the situation described in *R.* v. *Morrison*. However, the Supreme Court of Canada has given the defence of necessity very limited scope: *Perka* v. *The Queen* (1984), 14 C.C.C. 93d 385 (S.C.C.).

7 I mention the province in describing each case because prosecutorial discretion is exercised at a provincial level, and it is important to see where and how prosecutorial discretion is being exercised across the country.

8 Edward Keyserlingk, 'Nontreatment in the Best Interests of the Child' (1989) 32 McGill L.J. at 416–17.

9 This case was described by Dr James Cairns, Deputy Chief Coroner, Province of Ontario, in his testimony to the Senate Committee on Euthanasia and Assisted Suicide, Senate of Canada, *Proceedings of the Senate Special Committee on Euthanasia and Assisted Suicide*, [hereinafter *Special Senate Cte.*] No. 20 (17 Oct. 1994) at 7 and 13.

10 *R* v. *Mataya* (unreported Ontario Court of Justice (General Division), 24 Aug. 1992 Wren J. without a jury) [hereinafter *Mataya*].

11 '245. Every one who administers or causes to be administered to any person or causes any person to take poison or any other destructive or noxious thing is guilty of an indictable offence and liable (a) to imprisonment for a term not exceeding fourteen years, if he intends thereby to endanger the life of or to cause bodily harm to that person; or (b) to imprisonment for a term not exceeding two years, if he intends thereby to aggrieve or annoy that person.'

12 *Mataya*, supra, n10 at 254.

13 The CPMQ placed the physician on 'three months probation, he was ordered to consult with another doctor within 72 hours of taking on a new patient, and to consult with a colleague before administering large daily doses of morphine.' Special Senate Committee on Euthanasia and Assisted Suicide, *Of Life and Death: Report of the Special Senate Committee on Euthanasia and Assisted Suicide* [hereinafter *Of Life and Death*] (June 1995) at A-29.

14 Joan Gilmour, 'Dying Legally: The Legal Implications of Withholding and Withdrawing Life Support in Canada' (J.S.D. thesis, Stanford University, 1993) 216. Gilmour rightly notes the possibility that the CPMQ decision was affected by the unsuccessful prosecutions launched against Dr Henry Morgentaler in Quebec. Juries repeatedly refused to convict Dr Morgentaler despite the fact that abortion was illegal under the *Criminal Code* and the prosecution had proven that he had provided abortions. For more on this, see *Morgentaler* v. *The Queen*, [1976] 1 S.C.R. 616.

15 *R.* v. *de la Rocha* (2 April 1993), Timmins (Ont. Ct. (Gen. Div.)).

16 The Ontario College of Physicians and Surgeons reviewed the case and gave Dr. de la Rocha the *option* of developing a protocol on the withdrawal of life-support from terminally ill patients or a 90-day suspension of his licence to practice medicine. B. Sneiderman, J. Irvine, and P. Osborne, *Canadian Medical Law: An Introduction for Physicians, Nurses, and Other Health Care Professionals*, 2nd ed. (Toronto: Carswell, 1995) at 548.

17 Mr David Thomas, Crown Attorney's Office, Timmins, Ontario, testimony before the Special Senate Committee on Euthanasia and Assisted Suicide. *Senate Special Cte.*, No. 29 (12 Dec. 1994) at 42–3.

18 *R.* v. *Latimer* (1995), 126 D.L.R. (4th) 203 (Sask. C.A.) [hereinafter *Latimer 2*].

19 *R.* v. *Latimer*, [1997] 1 S.C.R. 217 [hereinafter *Latimer 3*].

20 *R.* v. *Latimer*, [1997] S.J. No. 701 (Sask.Q.B.), online: QL (SJ) [hereinafter *Latimer 4*].

21 *R.* v. *Latimer*, [1998] S.J. No. 731 [Sask. C.A.][hereinafter *Latimer 5*].

22 *Latimer 1*, supra, n6.

23 *R.* v. *Myers* (23 Dec. 1994), Halifax, (N.S.S.C.). The agreed statement of facts is reproduced, in part, in Chief Justice Bayda's decision in *Latimer 2*, supra, n18 at 256–7.

24 Justice Cacchione's oral judgment is reproduced in part in Chief Justice Bayda's reasons in *Latimer 2*, supra, n18 at 258.

25 *R.* v. *Brush* (2 March 1995) Toronto (Ont. Ct. J. (Prov. Div.)).

26 Sneiderman et al., supra, n16 at 542.

27 It is not clear why he was charged with attempted murder instead of assisted suicide given that his mother put the pills to her mouth and swallowed them.

28 'Edmonton man given "suspended sentence" for assisting his mother's death' *Canadian News Bulletins* (1 April to 30 April 1995), online: Deathnet <http://www.rights.org/deathnet/open.html>.

29 Judge Randall believed that it was possible that the intravenous tip had become dislodged from the femoral vein prior to the injection of the potassium chloride. Therefore, although it was possible that Paul Mills's death was caused by a lethal injection of potassium chloride, it was also possible that the potassium chloride did not reach his blood stream and his death was caused by the irreversible infection that set in after his final surgery. *R. v. Morrison*, [1998] N.S.J. No. 75, online: QL (NSJ).

30 *R. v. Morrison*, [1998] N.S.J. No. 441, online: QL (NSJ).

31 Letter dated 25 March 1999 to Dr Nancy Morrison from Dr Patricia Pearce, Chair, Investigation Committee 'A', Re: Complaint of Dr Cameron Little, available from the College of Physicians and Surgeons of Nova Scotia.

5 The Values

1 *Rodriguez v. British Columbia (Attorney General)*, [1993] 3 S.C.R. 519 [hereinafter *Rodriguez*] at para. 186.

2 For a discussion of equality and assisted suicide see, e.g., the reasons of Chief Justice Lamer in *Rodriguez*, ibid.

3 *Schloendorff v. Society of New York Hospital*, 105 N.E. 92 at 93 (N.Y.Ct. App. 1914).

4 *Hopp v. Lepp* (1980), 112 D.L.R. (3d) 67 (S.C.C.).

5 *Reibl v. Hughes* (1980), 114 D.L.R. (3d) 1 (S.C.C.).

6 *Ciarlariello v. Schacter*, [1993] 2 S.C.R. 119 at 135.

7 *R. v. Ewanchuk*, [1999] 1 S.C.R. 330 at para. 28.

8 *R. v. Jones*, [1994] 2 S.C.R. 229.

9 *R. v. White*, [1999] S.C.J. No. 28 at para. 43–4, online: QL (SCJ) [hereinafter *White*].

10 Wilson J. in *Thomson Newspapers Ltd. v. Canada (Director of Investigation and Research)*, [1990] 1 S.C.R. 425 at 480 [hereinafter *Thomson*].

11 Chief Justice Dickson for the majority in *R. v. Morgentaler*, [1988] 1 S.C.R. 30 at 53 [hereinafter *Morgentaler*].

12 See, e.g., Chief Justice Dickson in *R. v. Big M. Drug Mart Ltd.*, [1985] 1 S.C.R. 295 [hereinafter *Big M.*].

13 Ibid. at 337.

14 *Morgentaler*, supra, n11 at 164.

15 Ibid. at 56. He did not disavow a broader view of security of the person. Rather, he left it for another case at another time: 'It is not necessary in this

case to determine whether the right extends further, to protect either interests central to personal autonomy, such as a right to privacy, or interests
unrelated to criminal justice.'

16 Ibid. at 171.

17 Ibid. at 173.

18 *Rodriguez*, supra, n1 at 588.

19 Obviously, much has been written on liberty under s. 7 of the *Charter*. For
example, the reader is also referred to *R.B.* v. *Children's Aid Society of Metropolitan Toronto*, [1995] 1 S.C.R. 315 [hereinafter *Sheena B.*], and *Godbout* v.
Longueil (City), [1997] 3 S.C.R. 844 for further examples of cases in which the
Court has found that autonomy lies at the heart of the s. 7 rights. However,
the discussion in this chapter is limited by the needs of the book. For the
purposes of exploring what the law should be with respect to voluntary
assisted death, it is sufficient to demonstrate that the Supreme Court of
Canada has strongly endorsed a view that s. 7 protects personal autonomy
(especially including choices concerning one's own body).

20 *R.* v. *Dyment*, [1988] 2 S.C.R. 417 at 427 [hereinafter *Dyment*].

21 *R.* v. *Plant*, [1993] 3 S.C.R. 281 at 292.

22 See, e.g., *R.* v. *Godoy*, [1988] S.C.J. No. 85 at para. 19, online: QL (SCJ).

23 'Section 2. Everyone has the following fundamental freedoms: (a) freedom
of conscience and religion; (b) freedom of thought, belief, opinion and
expression, including freedom of the press and other media of communication; (c) freedom of peaceful assembly; and (d) freedom of association.'

24 *Big M*, supra, n12 at 346–7.

25 *C.B.C.* v. *New Brunswick*, [1996] 3 S.C.R. 480 at para. 63, quoting from Justice
La Forest in dissent in *RJR MacDonald Inc.* v. *Canada (Attorney General)*,
[1995] 3 S.C.R. 199 at para. 72–4. Emphasis added.

26 *Lavigne* v. *Ontario Public Service Employees Union (OPSEU)*, [1991] 2 S.C.R.
211 at para. 58. Emphasis added. While Justice La Forest was writing for
only three of the justices, Justice McLachlin's concurring reasons are consistent with this quote on this issue. Thus, at least a majority of the Court (only
seven judges sat) embraced this conception of the values behind the freedom of association protected by s. 2.

27 *Health Care Consent Act, 1996*, S.O. 1996, c. 2; *Health Care (Consent) and Care
Facility (Admission) Act*, S.B.C. 1996, C.181; *Hospitals Act*, R.S.N.S. 1989,
c. 208; *Health Act*, S.Y.T. 1989–90, c. 36; *Dependent Adults Act*, S.S. 1989–90,
c. D-25.1; *Civil Code of Quebec*, Art. 11, C.C.Q.; *Health Care Directives Act*,
S.M. 1992, c. 33. Note that I am not making a positivist appeal to the status
of the withholding and withdrawal of potentially life-sustaining treatment;
I am appealing to the status of consent to treatment in general.

28 '*Sec. 10 No treatment without consent.* – (1) a health practitioner who proposes a treatment for a person shall not administer the treatment, and shall take reasonable steps to ensure that it is not administered unless, (a) he or she is of the opinion that the person is capable with respect to the treatment, and the person has given consent; or (b) he or she is of the opinion that the person is incapable with respect to the treatment, and the person's substitute decision-maker has given consent on the person's behalf in accordance with this Act.'

'*Sec. 21 Principles for giving or refusing consent.* – (1) A person who gives or refuses consent to a treatment on an incapable person's behalf shall do so in accordance with the following principles: (1) If the person knows of a wish applicable to the circumstances that the incapable person expressed while capable and after attaining 16 years of age, the person shall give or refuse consent in accordance with the wish. (2) If the person does not know of a wish applicable to the circumstances that the incapable person expressed while capable and after attaining 16 years of age, or if it is impossible to comply with the wish, the person shall act in the incapable person's best interests.

29 '*Sec. 1 Purposes.* – The purposes of this Act are, (c) to enhance the autonomy of persons for whom treatment is proposed, persons for whom admission to a care facility is proposed and persons who are to receive personal assistance services by ... (iii) requiring that wishes with respect to treatment, admission to a care facility or personal assistance services, expressed by persons while capable and after attaining 16 years of age, be adhered to.'

30 *R.* v. *Cuerrier*, [1998] 2 S.C.R. 371 at para. 12. Emphasis added.

31 Supra, n7 at para. 28. Emphasis added.

32 See, e.g., the quotations referenced in nn 7, 10, 18, 21, and 24.

33 For example, in discussions of dignity under s. 15 of the *Charter*.

34 Justice Sopinka for the majority in *Rodriguez*, supra, n1 at para. 26.

35 *R.* v. *Stillman*, [1997] 1 S.C.R. 607 at para. 88 [hereinafter *Stillman*].

36 Other areas of the common law could also be referred to. For example, loss of dignity is a compensable damage in personal injury litigation (see, e.g., *Norberg* v. *Wynrib*, [1992] 2 S.C.R. 226). However, the three examples discussed should suffice to support the claim that dignity is a foundational value in the common law.

37 Supra, n20 at 431–2.

38 *Hill* v. *Church of Scientology of Toronto*, [1995] 2 S.C.R. 1130 at para. 117 [hereinafter *Hill*].

39 Supra, n9 at para. 43.

40 Supra, n38 at para. 120. Similarly, although all writing in dissent (but not

specifically on this issue): Justice L'Heureux-Dubé in *R.* v. *O'Connor*, [1995] 4 S.C.R. 411 at para. 63 wrote: 'This Court has repeatedly recognized that human dignity is at the heart of the *Charter*'; Justice L'Heureux-Dubé wrote in *Egan* v. *Canada*, [1995] 2 S.C.R. 513 at para. 36, 'this Court has recognized that inherent human dignity is at the heart of individual rights in a free and democratic society'; Justices Cory and Iacobucci in *R.* v. *Zundel*, [1992] 2 S.C.R. 731 at para. 136 [hereinafter *Zundel*], 'as a fundamental document setting out essential features of our vision of democracy, the *Charter* provides us with indications as to which values go to the very core of our political structure. A democratic society capable of giving effect to the *Charter's* guarantees is one which strives toward creating a community committed to equality, liberty and human dignity.'

41 It might also be argued that dignity lies at the heart of s. 27: 'This *Charter* shall be interpreted in a manner consistent with the preservation and enhancement of the multicultural heritage of Canadians.' Indeed, Justices Cory and Iacobucci wrote in *Zundel*, supra n40 at para. 156: 'It [s. 27] supports the protection of the collective rights, the cultural integrity and dignity of Canada's ethnic groups. In doing so it enhances the dignity and sense of self worth of every individual member of those groups and thereby enhances society as a whole.' However, Justices Cory and Iacobucci were in dissent in *Zundel*, and the relationship between dignity and s. 27 has not been articulated elsewhere in the Supreme Court jurisprudence.

42 *R.* v. *Amway Corp.*, [1989] 1 S.C.R. 21 at 36.

43 *R.* v. *Smith*, [1987] 1 S.C.R. 1045 per Justice Lamer (for himself and Chief Justice Dickson and with Justice La Forest on this point) and Justice McIntyre in dissent (Justice Le Dain agreed with him on the test for cruel and unusual punishment under s. 12).

44 Justice Cory was writing in dissent in *Kindler* v. *Canada (Minister of Justice)*, [1991] 2 S.C.R. 779 [hereinafter *Kindler*]. However, his reasons re: dignity appear to have been endorsed by the majority in *Rodriguez* at para. 25: 'The importance of the concept of human dignity in our society was enunciated by Cory J. (dissenting, Lamer C.J.C. concurring) in *Kindler* v. *Canada (Minister of Justice)*, [1991] 2 S.C.R. 779 at 813. Respect for dignity underlies many of the rights and freedoms in the *Charter*.'

45 *Law* v. *Canada (Minister of Employment and Immigration)*, [1999] 1 S.C.R. 497 [hereinafter *Law*].

46 Section 15 provides that '[e]very individual is equal before and under the law and has the right to the equal protection and equal benefit of the law without discrimination and, in particular, without discrimination based on

race, national or ethnic origin, colour, religion, sex, age or mental or physical disability.'

47 Supra, n45 at para. 51.

48 Ibid. at para. 53.

49 Other examples, are again, available. For example, the working rule to assess compliance with the definition of 'convention refugee' in s. 2(1) of the *Immigration Act* invokes the concept of dignity (see Justice La Forest for the Court in *Canada (Attorney General)* v. *Ward*, [1993] 2 S.C.R. 689 at para. 103).

50 *Human Rights Act*, S.Y. 1987, c. 3.

51 *Human Rights Act*, R.S.N.S. 1989, c. 214.

52 *Criminal Code*, R.S.C. 1985, c. C-46, s. 181.

53 *Criminal Code*, R.S.C. 1985, c. C-46, s. 319.

54 *R.* v. *Lucas*, [1998] 1 S.C.R. 439 at para. 48.

55 *R.* v. *Keegstra*, [1990] 3 S.C.R. 697 at para. 269.

56 *Actio personalis moritur cum persona.* Neither the estate nor dependents of the deceased have an action after death. I. Saunders, 'Survival Actions' in K. Cooper-Stephenson, *Personal Injury Damages in Canada*, 2nd ed. (Toronto: Carswell, 1996) at 721–46. This inability to sue has been modified through statute, and these modifications will be discussed further below when legislative support for/limits on the value of life are reviewed.

57 Justice Sopinka for the majority in *Rodriguez*, supra, n1 at 584.

58 Ibid. at 605.

59 See also, e.g., the discussion of the right to life in *Sheena B.*, supra, n19.

60 Supra, n1 at 595.

61 All provinces have survival of actions legislation. See, e.g., *Survival of Actions Act*, R.S.N.S. 1989, c. 453 and *Trustee Act* and R.S.N.W.T. 1988, c. T-8.

62 I. Saunders, 'Fatal Accident Actions' in K. Cooper-Stephenson, supra, n56 at 651–720. All provinces and territories have fatal injuries legislation. See, e.g., *Fatal Injuries Act*, R.S.N.S. 1989, c. 163, and *Fatal Accidents Act*, R.S.N. 1990, c. F-6. Some federal legislation also contains elements that operate as fatal injuries legislation. See, e.g., *Canada Shipping Act*, R.S.C. 1985, c. S-9.

63 Supra, n1 at 608. Emphasis added.

6 Resolution of Conflicts among Values

1 Again, I take the legal system on its own terms. I am looking at the Canadian legal system as a whole to inform how values conflicts should be resolved for the withholding and withdrawal of potentially life-sustaining treatment.

2 I canvass only the limits on life and autonomy – and not dignity – for two reasons. First, the limits on dignity are less clear in the law than the limits on life and autonomy. Second, what is clear in the law with respect to life and autonomy is sufficient to answer the question of what the law should be with respect to voluntary withholding and withdrawal of potentially life-sustaining treatment. A consideration of the limits on dignity would simply add support to the claim that, in cases of internal conflict, autonomous decisions must almost always be respected even if the result is the death of the autonomous individual.

3 With the exception of the Northwest Territories which allows for claims for the non-pecuniary loss of 'loss of expectation of life.'

4 Unless there is a duty. See *Criminal Code* R.S.C. 1985 c. C-46, s. 219. Justice McLachlin (as she then was) makes a similar point in her dissenting opinion in *Rodriguez* v. *British Columbia (Attorney General)*, [1993] 3 S.C.R. 519 at para. 90 [hereinafter *Rodriguez*].

5 'Section 11(1). A person found guilty by a military court of a war crime may be sentenced to and shall be liable to suffer any one or more of the following punishments, namely: (a) Death (either by hanging or shooting).' *War Crimes Act*, S.C. 1946, c. 73. Until 1997, capital punishment was also available as a punishment for espionage and mutiny with violence under the *National Defence Act* (R.S.C. 1985, c. N-5, as am. by S.C. 1998, c. 35, s. 28).

6 Ipsos-Reid 2001 poll at <www.ipsos-reid.com/pdf/media/mr01251_3.pdf.> Support has been steadily declining – in 1987 it was 73%, in 1995 it was 69%, and in 2001 it was 52%.

7 *Kindler* v. *Canada [Minister of Justice]*, [1991] 2 S.C.R. 779 at 63.

8 *Rodriguez*, supra, n4 at 595–6.

9 Ibid. at 605.

10 *Agar* v. *Canning* (1965), 54 W.W.R. 302, aff'd 55 W.W.R. 384 (Man.C.A.); *Martin* v. *Daigle* (1969), 6 D.L.R. (3d) 634 (N.B.C.A.); *Pettis* v. *McNeil* (1979), 8 C.C.L.T. 299 (N.S.S.C.). A.M. Linden, *Canadian Tort Law*, 6th ed. (Toronto: Butterworths, 1997) at 66.

11 *Malette* v. *Shulman* (1990), 2 C.C.L.T. (2d) 1 at 10 (O.C.A.).

12 See the discussion of common-law illegality in G.H.L. Fridman, *The Law of Contract in Canada*, 3rd ed. (Toronto: Carswell, 1994), and S. Waddams, *The Law of Contracts*, 3rd ed. (Toronto: Canada Law Book, 1993). Justice McIntyre, for the Supreme Court of Canada, wrote in *Ontario (Human Rights Commission)* v. *Etobicoke (Borough)*, [1982] 1 S.C.R. 202: 'It is clear from the authorities, both in Canada and in England, that parties are not competent to contract themselves out of the provisions of such enactments [human rights codes] and that contracts having such effect are void, as contrary to

public policy. In Halsbury's Laws of England, 3rd ed., vol. 36, p. 444, para. 673, the following appears: "673. Waiver of statutory rights. Individuals for whose benefit statutory duties have been imposed may by contract waive their right to the performance of those duties, unless to do so would be contrary to public policy or to the provisions or general policy of the statute imposing the particular duty or the duties are imposed in the public interest."'

13 Saskatchewan is the exception. See *Mental Health Services Act*, S.S. 1984–85–86, c. M-13.1, as am. s. 24(2)(a)(ii).

14 *Mental Health and Consequential Amendments Act*, S.M. 1998, c. 36, as am., s. 19, *Mental Health Act*, R.S.B.C. 1996, c. 288, as am., ss. 8(a) and 31(1), *Mental Health Act*, S.A. 1988, M-13.1, as am., s. 29(1), *Mental Health Act*, R.S.N. 1990, c. M-9, as am., s. 6(3), and *Mental Health Act*, R.S.N.B. 1973 c. M-10, as am., s. 8.4(2).

15 Supra, n13.

16 Supra, n14.

17 *R. v. Big M. Drug Mart Ltd.*, [1985] 1 S.C.R. 295 at 337. While Chief Justice Dickson was discussing the *Charter*, these limits are also found in liberal individualism as a theory and in the Canadian legal system as a system grounded in that political philosophy.

18 See, e.g., *Mental Health Act*, R.S.O., c. M.7, as am. s. 20(5)(a)(ii), *An Act Respecting the Protection of Persons Whose Mental State Presents a Danger to Themselves or to Others*, S.Q. 1997, c. 75, as am., s. 7, *Hospitals Act*, S.N.S. 1989, c. 208, as am., s. 36, *Mental Health Act*, R.S.N.B. 1973, c. M-10, as am., s. 8, *Mental Health Act*, S.P.E.I. 1994, c. 39, as am., s. 13, *Mental Health Act*, R.S.N.W.T. 1988, c. M-10, as am., s. 13, *Mental Health Act*, S.Y.T. 1989–90, c. 28, as am., s. 13.

19 Again, I am exploring the legal system on its own terms. My responses to charges of positivism were given earlier and will not be repeated here.

20 *Winnipeg Child and Family Services v. G.(D.F.)*, [1997] 3 S.C.R. 925.

21 See, e.g., *Human Tissue Act*, S.M. 1987–88, c. 39; *Human Tissue Gift Act*, R.S.O. 1990, c. H-20; and *Human Tissue Donation Act*, R.S.P.E.I. 1992, c. 34.

22 'Subsection 487.05(1) A provincial court judge who on *ex parte* application is satisfied by information on oath that there are reasonable grounds to believe (a) that a designated offence has been committed, (b) that a bodily substance has been found (i) at the place where the offence was committed, (ii) on or within the body of the victim of the offence, (iii) on anything worn or carried by the victim at the time when the offence was committed, or (iv) on or within the body of any person or thing or at any place associated with the commission of the offence, (c) that a person was a party to the offence,

and (d) that forensic DNA analysis of a bodily substance from the person will provide evidence about whether the bodily substance referred to in paragraph (b) was from that person and who is satisfied that it is in the best interests of the administration of justice to do so may issue a warrant in writing authorizing a peace officer to obtain, or cause to be obtained under the direction of the peace officer, a bodily substance from that person, by means of an investigative procedure described in subsection 487.06(1) [includes the taking of blood by pricking the skin surface with a sterile lancet], for the purpose of forensic DNA analysis.

23 All provinces have public health acts which grant a wide range of powers to medical health officers to enable them to combat a variety of communicable diseases. See, e.g., *Health Act*, R.S.N.S. 1989, c. 195; *Health Act*, R.S.B.C. 1979, c. 161; *The Venereal Disease Prevention Act*, R.S.S. 1978, c. V-4. These powers can include the power to detain, examine, quarantine, and order treatment.

24 *Supra*, n18.

25 See the discussion of the 'balancing of competing interests' in *F.(S.)* v. *Canada (Attorney General)* (1997), 11 C.R. (5th) 232 (Ont.C.J. (Gen.Div.)) esp. at 252–7.

7 A Legal Regime for the Withholding and Withdrawal of Potentially Life-Sustaining Treatment from Competent Individuals

1 See, e.g., Bill S-13, *An Act to Amend the Criminal Code (Protection of Health Care Providers)* 2d Sess., 35th Parl., 1996, (1st reading 27 Nov. 1996) at s. 45.1(3)(a) and (b) (re: bleak prognosis); Canadian Nurses for Life Brief to the Special Senate Committee on Euthanasia and Assisted Suicide at 2–3, on file with the Library of Parliament and the author (re: type of treatment); and Bill S-13, ibid. at s. 45.1(1)(b) (re: physical pain requirement for provision of potentially life-shortening palliative treatment).

2 See, for e.g., *Procureur Général du Canada c. Hôpital Notre-Dame et Niemiec*, [1984] C.S. 426 (Que.Sup.Ct.); *British Columbia (Attorney General)* v. *Astaforoff*, [1983] 6 W.W.R. 322 (B.C.S.C.), aff'd [1984] 4 W.W.R. 385 (B.C.C.A.); *Malette* v. *Shulman* (1990), 2 C. C. L.T. (2d) 1 (O.C.A.); *Fleming* v. *Reid* (1991), 4 O.R. (3d) 74 (C.A.); *Nancy B.* v. *Hôtel-Dieu de Québec* (1992), 86 D.L.R. (4th) 385 (Que. Sup. Ct.); *Ciarlariello* v. *Schacter*, [1993] 2 S.C.R. 119.

3 The doctrine of informed consent can be traced through the following: *Masny Carter-Halls-Aldinger Co. Ltd.*, [1929] 3 W.W.R. 741 (Alta. Q.B.); *Mulloy* v. *Hop Sang*, [1935] 1 W.W.R. 714 (Alta. C.A.); *Parmley* v. *Parmley*, [1945] 4 D.L.R. 81 (S.C.C.); *Hopp* v. *Lepp* (1980), 112 D.L.R. (3d) 67 (S.C.C.); *Reibl* v. *Hughes* (1980), 114 D.L.R. (3d) 1 (S.C.C.); *Ciarlariello* v. *Schacter*,

supra, n2; *Norberg* v. *Wynrib*, [1992] 2 S.C.R. 226; and *Arndt* v. *Smith* (1997), 148 D.L.R. (4th) 48 (S.C.C.).

4 E.I. Picard and G.B. Robertson, *Legal Liability of Doctors and Hospitals in Canada*, 3rd ed. (Toronto: Carswell, 1996) at 55.

5 For example, s. 11(1) of the *Health Care Consent Act, 1996*, S.O. 1996, c. 2.

6 See, e.g., *Trainor* v. *Knickle*, [1996] P.E.I.J. No. 55 at para. 96, (S.C., T.D.), online: QL (PEIJ).

7 This standard was established in *Reibl* v. *Hughes*, supra, n3. It was most recently reviewed in *Arndt* v. *Smith*, supra, n3.

8 *Reibl* v. *Hughes*, supra, n3.

9 *Norberg* v. *Wynrib*, supra, n3.

10 *Fleming* v. *Reid*, supra, n2 and *Norberg* v. *Wynrib*, supra, n3.

11 *Re T.D.D.*, [1999] S.J. No. 143 (Q.B.), online: QL (SJ).

12 It should be noted that they are also the elements that are widely accepted as the elements of informed consent in the legal and philosophical literature. In their comprehensive review of the history of informed consent, Ruth Faden and Tom Beauchamp point to the following 'representative sources' to support this claim: R. Levine, 'The Nature and Definition of Informed Consent in Various Research Settings,' *Appendix: Vol. 1, The Belmont Report* (Washington, DC: DHEW Publication No. (OS) 78–0013, 1978), (3-1)–(3-91), esp. (3-3)–(3-9); T. Beauchamp and J. Childress, *Principles of Biomedical Ethics*, 2nd ed. (New York: Oxford University Press, 1983) at 70; M.A. Somerville, as prepared for the Law Reform Commission of Canada, *Consent to Medical Care* (Ottawa: Law Reform Commission, 1979) at 11ff, 24; President's Commission for the Study of Ethical Problems in Medicine and Biomedical and Behavioral Research, *Making Health Care Decisions*, Vol. 1, chapt. 1, esp. 38–9; A. Meisel and L. Roth, 'What We Do and Do Not Know about Informed Consent?' (1981) 246 J.A.M.A. 2473; C.V. Lidz and A. Meisel, 'Informed Consent and the Structure of Medical Care' in President's Commission, *Making Health Care Decisions*, Vol. 2, 317–410, esp. 318; M.P. Stansfield, 'Malpractice: Toward a Viable Disclosure Standard for Informed Consent' (1979) 32 Oklahoma L.Rev. 871; and the National Commission for the Protection of Human Subjects of Biomedical and Behavioral Research, *The Belmont Report* (Washington, DC: DHEW Publication No. (OS) 78–0012, 1978) at 10. R. Faden and T. Beauchamp with N. King, *A History and Theory of Informed Consent* (New York: Oxford University Press, 1986) at 294.

13 *Reibl* v. *Hughes*, supra, n3.

14 D. Checkland and M.Silberfeld, 'Decision-Making Capacity and Assisted Suicide' in C.G. Prado ed., *Assisted Suicide: Canadian Perspectives* (Ottawa: University of Ottawa Press, 2000), 95 at 102.

15 See D.C. Marson et al., 'Determining the Competency of Alzheimer Patients to Consent to Treatment and Research' (1994) 8(4) Alzheimer Dis. Assoc. Disord. 5 at 5.

16 *Nancy B.*, supra, n2.

17 *R.B.* v. *Children's Aid Society of Metropolitan Toronto*, [1995] 1 S.C.R. 315 [hereinafter *Sheena B.*].

18 *Sawatzky* v. *Riverview Health Centre Inc.*, [1998] M.J. No. 506 at para. 5 (Q.B.), online: QL (MJ). Similar sentiments re: ethical decisions belonging to the legislatures are expressed in *Tremblay* v. *Daigle*, [1989] 2 S.C.R. 530 and *Winnipeg Child and Family Services (Northwest Area)* v. *D.F.G.*, [1997] 3 S.C.R. 925.

19 See J.S. Janofsky, R.J. McCarthy, and M.F. Folstein, 'The Hopkins Competency Assessment Test: A Brief Method for Evaluating Patients' Capacity to Give Informed Consent' (1992) 43(2) Hosp. Community Psychiatry 132.

20 See, e.g., G. Bean et al., 'The Assessment of Competence to Make a Treatment Decision: An Empirical Approach' (1996) 41(2) Can. J. Psychiatry 85.

21 See, e.g., E. Etchells et al., 'Assessment of Patient Capacity to Consent to Treatment' (1999) 14(1) J. Gen. Intern. Med. 27.

22 See, e.g., B.W. Palmer et al. 'Treatment-Related Decision-Making Capacity in the Middle-Aged and Older Patients with Psychosis: A Preliminary Study Using the MacCAT and HCAT' (2002) 10(2) Am. J. Geriatr. Psychiatry 207.

23 By implication, see Justice Cory's reasons in *Rodriguez* v. *British Columbia (Attorney General)*, [1993] 3 S.C.R. 519 at 630. The Oregon legislation also includes a requirement that an individual who accesses assisted suicide be terminally ill (*Death with Dignity Act*, 127.805, s. 2.01).

24 Canadian Nurses for Life made the following argument at 2–3 in their written brief to the Special Senate Committee on Euthanasia and Assisted Suicide (on file with the Library of Parliament and the author): 'Providing basic nutrition and hydration has never been medical treatment because neither treat any illness or disease ... The following is the text of the resolution passed at the International Congress of the World Federation of Doctors who Respect Human Life which took place in Rome, 1–2 Dec. 1989. This federation has almost 300,000 members in 59 countries. "In every case of terminal illness, it is a cruel and anti-medical practice to withdraw nutrition and hydration and thus to cause the patient to die of hunger and thirst, which can only increase his suffering. Nutrition and hydration are a basic life-maintaining need even if administered intravenously or by gastric tube."'

25 Hemodialysis was developed in the 1940s and peritoneal dialysis was developed in the 1970s. *Canadian Medical Association Home Medical Encyclopaedia* (London: Dorling Kindersley, 1992) at 349.

26 For further debate about the ordinary/extraordinary distinction, see J. Rachels, 'More Impertinent Distinctions and a Defense of Active Euthanasia' in B. Steinbock and A. Norcross, eds., *Killing and Letting Die*, 2nd ed. (New York: Fordham University Press, 1994) 139 at 143–5, and T.D. Sullivan, 'Coming to Terms: A Response to Rachels' in B. Steinbock and A. Norcross, ibid. 155 at 158–61.

27 J.V. Zerwekh, 'The Dehydration Question' (1983) Nursing '83 47.

28 See, e.g., the testimony of Arn Schilder. Senate of Canada, *Proceedings of the Senate Special Committee on Euthanasia and Assisted Suicide [hereinafter Special Senate Cte.]*, (28 Sept. 1994) at 34 and 26.

29 Testimony of Dr Marcel Boisvert. *Senate Special Cte.*, (18 May 1994) at 34–5.

30 Ibid. at 44–5.

31 Ibid. at 35.

32 *Review Procedures for the Termination of Life on Request and Assisted Suicide: An Amendment of the Criminal Code and the Burial and Cremation Act (Termination of Life on Request and Assisted Suicide (Review Procedures) Act)*. Bill decreed 1 April 2002.

33 Robert F. Weir, ed. *Physician-Assisted Suicide* (Bloomington: Indiana University Press, 1997) 156–7 describing *State v. McAfee*, 385 S.E. 2d 651 (S.C. Ga. 1989).

34 See Justice Ryan in dissent in *Walker (Litigation Guardian of) v. Region 2 Hospital Corp.* (1994), 116 D.L.R. (4th) 477 (N.B.C.A.) and the majority in *Ney v. Canada (Attorney General)*, [1993] B.C.J. No. 993 (S.C.), online: QL (BCJ).

35 Justice Ryan in dissent in *Walker*, supra, n34 at 498, and the majority in *Ney*, supra, n34 at para. 58.

36 Supra, n34 at 488.

37 In *Eve v. Mrs (E.)* (1986), 31 D.L.R. (4th) 1 (S.C.C.) [hereinafter *Eve*], the Supreme Court of Canada reviewed the genesis and scope of the *parens patriae* jurisdiction in the context of a mentally incompetent adult. In *Beson v. Director of Child Welfare (Newfoundland)*, [1982] 2 S.C.R. 716, the Supreme Court of Canada explored the role of the *parens patriae* jurisdiction in the context of a province with a statutory child welfare regime and in a case involving an immature minor. In *Sheena B.*, supra, n17, the Court was presented with the issue by counsel but declined to address it as it was not raised by the facts of the case before the Court.

Unfortunately, this issue has not been resolved in the academic literature either. See F.X. Plaus and R.B. Brissenden, 'On Adolescence and Informed Consent' (1994) 14 Health L. Can. 69 (exploring the criteria for decisional capacity for adolescents but not the jurisdiction of the courts); S.I. Bushnell, 'The Welfare of Children and the Jurisdiction of the Court under *Parens*

Patriae' in K. Connell-Thouez and B.M. Knoppers, eds., *Contemporary Trends in Family Law: A National Perspective* (Toronto: Carswell, 1984) at 223–42 (exploring the meaning of '*parens patriae* powers' but simply assuming that the jurisdiction applies to all minors), and G. Sharpe, 'Consent and Minors' (1993) 13 Health L. Can. 197 (exploring only the common law and Ontario statutes).

38 *Butler* v. *Freeman*, Amb. 302.
39 *Earle of Shaftesbury* v. *Shaftesbury*, 2 P. Wms. 102; Gilb. Eq. Ca. 172.
40 *Eve*, supra, n37.
41 Ibid.
42 *Malette* v. *Shulman*, supra, n2, and *Fleming* v. *Reid*, supra, n2, both embraced by the majority in *Rodriguez*, supra, n23.
43 *Eve*, supra, n37.
44 Lord Hardwicke, in *Butler* v. *Freeman*, Amb. 302, quoted in John David Chambers, *A Practical Treatise on the Jurisdiction of the High Court of Chancery Over the Persons and Property of Infants* (London: Saunders and Benning, 1842) at 3.
45 *Earl of Shaftesbury* v. *Shaftesbury*, 2 P. Wms. 102; Gilb. Eq. Ca. 172, quoted in John David Chambers, *A Practical Treatise on the Jurisdiction of the High Court of Chancery Over the Persons and Property of Infants* (London: Saunders and Benning, 1842) at 3.
46 Lord Macclesfield, *Eyre* v. *Countess of Shaftesbury*, 2 P.W. 123, quoted at 613 in George Spence, *The Equitable Jurisdiction of the Court of Chancery*, vol.1 (Philadelphia: Lea and Blanchard, 1846).
47 'In the eye of the Court of Chancery, as of the common law, all persons are esteemed infants until they have attained the age of twenty-one years (a)…. Neither law nor equity know any difference between an infant of sixteen or seventeen and one turned of twenty, there being a precise time fixed for their coming of age, and the latter may be equally relieved with the former, for till he arrives at twenty-one he is, in consideration of the Court, an infant (c). All Courts must look upon a child of nineteen as a child of five years of age, and you are, by law, concluded from saying he is more capable at one period than another (d).' J.D. Chambers, supra, n44 at 13. 'The guardianship of chancery over infants extends to the age of twenty-one. An infant, in chancery, is not entitled, as of course, on arriving at the age of fourteen, to select a new guardian.' G.T. Bispham, *The Principles of Equity: A Treatise on the System of Justice Administered in Courts of Chancery* (Philadelphia: Kay and Brother, 1893) at 665.
48 *Eve*, supra, n37 at 14.
49 Ibid. at 29.

50 Ibid. at 28.
51 Ibid. at 15. See the discussion of *parens patriae* in *Malette* v. *Shulman*, supra, n2 and *Fleming* v. *Reid*, supra, n2. In these cases, the Ontario Court of Appeal explicitly limits the application of the jurisdiction to only a subset of the set of all mentally ill persons.
52 See, e.g., L. Mann, R. Harmoni, and C. Power, 'Adolescent Decision Making: The Development of Competence' (1989) 12 J. Adolescents 256, and F.X. Plaus and R.B. Brissenden, 'On Adolescence and Informed Consent' (1994) 14(3) Health L. Can. 68.
53 See, e.g., D.G. Scherer, 'The Capacities for Minors to Exercise Voluntariness in Medical Treatment Decisions' (1991)15(4) Law & Human Behavior 431, and D.G. Scherer and N.D. Repucci, 'Adolescents' Capacity to Provide Voluntary Consent' (1998)12(2) Law & Human Behavior 123.

Part III: Overview

 1 I will not discuss the following arguments: risk of misdiagnosis; loss of opportunity for cure; delay; harm to society; loss of hope; stunting of palliative care; stunting of research into cures for fatal diseases; violation of the social role of doctors as healers; erosion of trust in doctors; breach of the Hippocratic Oath; violation of physicians' values; and imposition of a bureaucratic burden on doctors. These arguments are not made as frequently in the literature as the arguments I do discuss. Furthermore, they are not as strong as the other arguments that I consider in this part and I wish to avoid the appearance of shooting fish in a barrel. Readers interested in discussions of these arguments are directed to A. Browne, 'Assisted Suicide and Active Voluntary Euthanasia,' (1989) 2 Can. J. L. & Juris. 35; and J. Downie, 'Voluntary Euthanasia in Canada,' (1993) 14 Health L. Can. 13.
 2 *Canadian Charter of Rights and Freedoms*, Part I of the *Constitution Act, 1982*, being Schedule – to the *Canada Act 1982* (U.K.), 1982, c. 11.

8 Unsustainable Distinctions

 1 An excellent collection of articles on the distinction between killing and letting die is B. Steinbock and A. Norcross, eds., *Killing and Letting Die*, 2nd ed. (New York: Fordham University Press, 1994). This collection includes many of the classic articles in the field as well as nine original contributions.
 2 The active/passive distinction has been the subject of much discussion in both the philosophical and legal literature. Leading proponents of the active/passive distinction include: Y. Kamisar, 'Against Assisted Suicide –

Even a Very Limited Form' (1995) U. Det. Mercy L. Rev. 735, and 'Euthana-
sia Legislation: Some Nonreligious Objections' in T. Beauchamp and S. Per-
lin, eds., *Ethical Issues in Death and Dying* (New York: Oxford University
Press, 1978) 220; and D. Callahan, 'Self-Extinction: The Morality of the
Helping Hand' in R. Weir, ed., *Physician-Assisted Suicide* (Bloomington:
Indiana University Press, 1997) 69.

3 Dan Brock characterizes the distinction in a similar manner: 'One kills
  when one performs an action that causes the death of a person (e.g., we are
  in a boat, you cannot swim, I push you overboard, and you drown), and
  one allows to die when one has the ability and opportunity to prevent
  the death of another, knows this, and omits doing so, with the result that
  the person dies (e.g., we are in a boat, you cannot swim, you fall overboard,
  I don't throw you an available life ring, and you drown).' D. Brock,
  'Physician-Assisted Suicide Is Sometimes Morally Justified' in Weir, ed.,
  supra, n2 86.

4 The most influential proponent of this position is James Rachels. See, e.g.,
  his 'Euthanasia, Killing, and Letting Die' in J. Ladd, ed., *Ethical Issues Relating to Life and Death* (New York: Oxford University Press, 1979) at 146,
  which is a longer version of the more frequently cited 'Active and Passive
  Euthanasia' (1975) 292 N.E.J.M. at 78–80; and J. Rachels, *The End of Life*
  (Oxford: Oxford University Press, 1986). One of the most active proponents
  of this position is D. Brock; see, e.g., 'Voluntary Active Euthanasia,' (1992)
  22 Hastings Center Report 10–22, and 'Physician-Assisted Suicide Is Some-
  times Morally Justified' in Weir, ed., supra, n2 86; 'Forgoing Food and
  Water: Is It Killing?' in J. Lynn. ed. *By No Extraordinary Means: The Choice to
  Forgo Life-Sustaining Food and Water* (Bloomington: Indiana University
  Press, 1986); 'Moral Rights and Permissible Killing' in J. Ladd, ed., *Ethical
  Issues Relating to Life and Death* (Oxford: Oxford University Press, 1979).
  Other leading proponents include: M. Tooley, 'An Irrelevant Consideration:
  Killing versus Letting Die' in Steinbock and Norcross, *Killing and Letting
  Die,* supra, n1 103–11; and J. Bennett, 'Acting and Refraining,' *Analysis* 28
  (1967) 30–1, and 'Shooting, Killing, Dying,' (1973) 2 Can. J. Philosophy
  315–23.

5 J. Rachels, 'Euthanasia, Killing, and Letting Die,' supra, n4 at 154.

6 See, e.g.: T.D. Sullivan, 'Active and Passive Euthanasia: An Impertinent
  Distinction?' in Steinbock and Norcross, supra, n1 at 131–8; P. Foot, 'Killing
  and Letting Die' in J.L. Garfield and P. Hennessey, eds., *Abortion and Legal
  Perspectives* (Amherst: University of Massachussetts Press, 1984), and 'Killing, Letting Die, and Euthanasia: A Reply to Holly Smith Goldman' (June
  1981) 41, 4 Analysis.

7 Rachels, 'Euthanasia, Killing, and Letting Die,' supra, n4 at 153.

8 *Airedale N.H.S. Trust* v. *Bland*, [1993] Appeal Cases 789 at 887 per Lord Mustill.

9 Again, Kamisar and Callahan are among the most influential proponents of this distinction, supra, n2. This distinction was also embraced by the President's Commission for the Study of Ethical Problems in Medicine and Biomedical and Behavioral Research, *Deciding to Forego Life-Sustaining Treatment: A Report of the Ethical, Medical, and Legal Issues in Treatment Decisions* (Washington, DC: Government Printing Office, 1983).

10 Kamisar, supra, n2.

11 The pacemaker example is taken from P. Hopkins, 'Why Does Removing Machines Count as 'Passive' Euthanasia?' (1997) 27 Hastings Center Report 29.

12 Examples of non-culpable causation of death are accidental killing and killing in self-defence.

13 P. Foot, 'The Problem of Abortion and the Doctrine of Double Effect' in Steinbock and Norcross, supra, n1 at 266. Foot continues at 267: 'The doctrine of double effect is based on a distinction between what a man foresees as a result of his voluntary action and what, in the strict sense, he intends. He intends in the strictest sense both those things that he aims at as ends and those that he aims at as means to his ends. The latter may be regretted in themselves but nevertheless desired for the sake of the end, as we may intend to keep dangerous lunatics confined for the sake of our safety. By contrast a man is said not strictly, or directly, to intend the foreseen consequences of his voluntary actions where these are neither the end at which he is aiming nor the means to this end. Whether the word "intention" should be applied in both cases is not of course what matters: Bentham spoke of "oblique intention," contrasting it with the "direct intention" of ends and means, and we may as well follow his terminology. Everyone must recognize that some such distinction can be made, though it may be made in a number of different ways, and it is the distinction that is crucial to the doctrine of double effect. The words "double effect" refer to the two effects that an action may produce: the one aimed at, and the one foreseen but in no way desired. By "the doctrine of double effect" I mean the thesis that it is sometimes permissible to bring about by oblique intention what one may not directly intend.'

9 Inconsistencies across Categories of Assisted Death

1 See, e.g.: E.D. Pellegrino, 'The False Promise of Beneficent Killing' in L.L.

Emanuel, ed., *Regulating How We Die: The Ethical, Medical, and Legal Issues Surrounding Physician-Assisted Suicide* (Cambridge: Harvard University Press, 1998) 71–91 at 80–2; S. Wolf, 'Gender, Feminism, and Death: Physician-Assisted Suicide and Euthanasia' in S.M. Wolf, ed., *Feminism and Bioethics: Beyond Reproduction* (New York: Oxford University Press, 1996) 282–317.

2 Testimony of Paddy Rodney. Senate of Canada, *Proceedings of the Senate Special Committee on Euthanasia and Assisted Suicide*, No. 15 (27 Sept. 1994) at 124.

3 See, e.g., the Law Reform Commission of Canada, *Euthanasia, Aiding Suicide, and Cessation of Treatment: Working Paper 28* (Ottawa: Supply and Services Canada, 1982) at 47.

4 The New York State Task Force on Life and the Law, *When Death Is Sought: Assisted Suicide and Euthanasia in the Medical Context* 102 (1994).

5 J.H. Pickering, 'The Continuing Debate over Active Euthanasia' (Summer 1994) Bioethics Bull. (ABA) 1 at 2.

6 For a discussion of the role of gender, race, class, and culture in the context of assisted death, see, e.g., 'Hazards of Death Control' in B. Logue, *Last Rights: Death Control and the Elderly in America* (New York: Lexington Books, 1993) 258–88.

10 Invalid Arguments

1 I. Kant, *Foundations of the Metaphysics of Morals* (L.W. Beck trans.) (Indianapolis: Bobbs-Merrill Educational Publishing, 1980).

2 J. Childress, 'Religious Viewpoints' in L.L. Emanuel, ed., *Regulating How We Die: The Ethical, Medical and Legal Issues Surrounding Physician-Assisted Suicide* (Cambridge: Harvard University Press, 1998) at 120–47 at 144–5. See also R.M. Hare, 'Euthanasia: A Christian View' 2 (1) (Summer 1975) Philosophic Exchange.

3 Indeed, s. 2(a) of the *Charter* guarantees that '2. Everyone has the following fundamental freedoms: (a) freedom of conscience and religion; (b) freedom of thought, belief, opinion and expression, including freedom of the press and other media of communication; (c) freedom of peaceful assembly; and (d) freedom of association.

4 The Seventh, Third, and Tenth Commandments, respectively.

5 For further discussion of the religious sanctity of life arguments, the reader is directed to R. Gillon, 'Suicide and Voluntary Euthanasia: Historical Perspective' in A.B. Downing, ed., *Euthanasia and the Right to Death* (Los Angeles: Nash, 1969), and G. Williams, *The Sanctity of Life and the Criminal Law* (New York: Knopf, 1957) Chapter 8.

6 See, e.g., L. Dionne, Director General, Maison Michel Sarrazin, Quebec testimony before the Senate Committee on Euthanasia and Assisted Suicide. Senate of Canada, *Proceedings of the Senate Special Committee on Euthanasia and Assisted Suicide* [*hereinafter Senate Special Cte.*], No. 13 (6 July 1994). See also E.H. Kluge, *The Ethics of Deliberate Death* (New York, 1981) 32–3. The theme of meaning through suffering is illustrated in V. Frankl, *Man's Search For Meaning: An Introduction to Logotherapy* (New York: Simon and Shuster, 1962).

7 For example, the Canadian Nurses Association testimony before the Senate Committee on Euthanasia and Assisted Suicide. *Senate Special Cte.*, No. 19 (5 Oct. 1994) at 5.

8 I use a tentative tone in this section because I do not have quantitative data to support my conclusions. Given the illegality of assisted suicide and euthanasia, there is a paucity of data on the experiences of family members and friends who assist death. It is difficult to, e.g., survey family members who have helped a loved one to die about the reconciliation and growth that occurred during the planning process. To do so would expose them to potential criminal liability.

   This possibility of criminal liability was almost realized in Russel Ogden's study of assisted suicide in the AIDS community in British Columbia. The BC coroner made vigorous attempts to pierce the veil of confidentiality Ogden had promised his research participants. Ogden successfully resisted these attempts.

9 Advocates of this argument include E.D. Pellegrino, 'The False Promise and Benefit of Killing' in Emanuel, supra, n2 at 73, and S. Wolf, 'Facing Assisted Suicide and Euthanasia in Children and Adolescents' in Emanuel, supra, n2 at 118.

10 Although palliative care includes pain control, palliative care is more than pain control and pain control can happen outside the palliative care context.

11 B.L. Mishara, 'Synthesis of Research and Evidence on Factors Affecting the Desire of Terminally Ill or Seriously Chronically Ill Persons to Hasten Death' (March 1998) Report to Health Canada, on file with Health Canada and with the author; J.V. Lavery, S.E.D. Shortt, 'The Desire to Die, or to Hasten Death in Terminal Illness: A Literature Synthesis' (March 1998) Report to Health Canada, on file with Health Canada and with the author; A.E. Chin, K. Hedberg, G.K. Higginson, and D.W. Fleming, 'Legalized Physician-Assisted Suicide in Oregon – The First Year's Experience' (1999) 340 N.E.J.M. 577; E.J. Emanuel, D.L. Fairclough, E.R. Daniels, and B.R. Clarridge, 'Euthanasia and Physician-Assisted Suicide: Attitudes and Experi-

ences of Oncology Patients, Oncologists, and the Public' (1996) 347 Lancet 1805; and R. Charlton, S. Dovey, Y. Mizushima, and E. Ford, 'Attitudes to Death and Dying in the U.K., New Zealand, and Japan' (1995) 11 J. Pallia-tive Care 42.

12 The most frequently cited estimate is that 5% of dying people in Canada receive palliative care. For a comprehensive description of the availability of palliative care in Canada, see the report commissioned by the Senate Committee on Euthanasia and Assisted Suicide and reproduced as Appen-dix M, 'Palliative Care in Canada,' in Special Senate Committee on Eutha-nasia and Assisted Suicide, *Of Life and Death: Report of the Special Senate Committee on Euthanasia and Assisted Suicide* [hereinafter *Of Life and Death*] (June 1995) A-85, and *Quality End-of-Life Care: The Right of Every Canadian* (Subcommittee to update *Of Life and Death* (Final Report: June 2000)). The 1995 report of the SUPPORT study revealed that 'for 50% of conscious patients who died in the hospital, family members reported moderate to severe pain at least half the time.' The SUPPORT Principal Investigators, 'A Controlled Trial to Improve Care for Seriously Ill Hospitalized Patients,' 274 (20), J.A.M.A. (1995): 1591–8 at 1591. See also N. MacDonald et al., 'A Quebec Survey of Issues in Cancer Pain Management' (2002) 23(1) J. Pain and Symptom Management 39.

13 See testimony before the Special Senate Committee on Euthanasia and Assisted Suicide of Brian Mishara, Elizabeth Latimer, and Balfour Mount. *Senate Special Cte.*, No. 2 (20 April 1994) at 26, No. 4 (4 May 1994) at 16, and No. 5 (11 May 1994) at 30, respectively. See also N. MacDonald et al., 'A Quebec Survey of Issues in Cancer Pain Management' supra, n12.

14 *Senate Special Cte.*, No. 6 (18 May 1994) at 35.

15 Total sedation is defined by the Senate Committee on Euthanasia and Assisted Death as 'the practice of rendering a person totally unconscious through the administration of drugs without potentially shortening that person's life.' *Of Life and Death*, supra, n12 at 33. It is also known as 'twilight sleep,' 'artificial sleep,' and 'snowing.'

16 See, e.g., Arn Shilder, British Columbia Persons with AIDS, testimony before the Special Senate Committee on Euthanasia and Assisted Suicide. *Senate Special Cte.*, No. 16 (28 Sept. 1994).

11 Slippery Slope Arguments

1 See G. Crelinston, 'Mercy Killing: Active Euthanasia Is Not Part of Medi-cine and It Should be Rejected' (21 Oct. 1991) *Montreal Gazette* at B3; Special Senate Committee on Euthanasia and Assisted Suicide, *Of Life and Death;*

Report on the Special Senate Committee on Euthanasia and Assisted Suicide [hereinafter *Of Life and Death*] (June 1995) at 56–7.

2 *Of Life and Death* (June 1995) at 56–7.

3 I am departing from the convention of describing the two types of slippery slopes as logical and psychological (although cited to a number of differing originating sources, I have traced the logical/psychological slippery slope distinction back to J. Rachels in S. Spicker and T. Engelhardt, eds., *Philosophical Medical Ethics: Its Nature and Significance* (Boston: Reidel, 1977) at 65). I have changed the name from 'psychological slippery slope' to 'empirical slippery slope' because there is not necessarily a psychological component to the empirical slippage and both psychological and non-psychological barriers can be placed on this slope.

4 Rachels, ibid. at 65.

5 Most notably, Y. Kamisar, 'Some Non-Religious Views against Proposed Mercy-Killing Legislation' (1958) 42 Minn. L. Rev. 969, 975–77. See also M.H. Kronberg, 'Hitler's Euthanasia Program – More Like Today's Than You Might Imagine' in N.B. Spannaus, M.H. Kronberg, and L. Everett, eds., *How to Stop the Resurgence of Nazi Euthanasia Today* (1988); Nat Hentoff, 'Contested Terrain: The Nazi Analogy in Bioethics' (1988) 18 Hastings Center Report; and R.J. Neuhaus, 'The Return of Eugenics' (1988) Commentary 15.

6 See, e.g., E.H. Loewy, 'Harming, Healing, and Euthanasia' in L.L. Emanuel, ed., *Regulating How We Die: The Ethical, Medical and Legal Issues Surrounding Physician-Assisted Suicide* (Cambridge: Harvard University Press, 1998) at 268.

7 D. Maguire, 'Deciding for Yourself' in R. Weir, ed., *Ethical Issues in Death and Dying*, 2nd ed. (New York: Columbia University Press, 1986) 284 at 286. Maguire uses the *retorqueo argumentum* technique in relation to absolute pacifism, sterilization, and the development and retention of nuclear weapons.

8 M.C. Bassiouni, T.G. Baffes, and J.T. Evrard, 'An Appraisal of Human Experimentation in International Law and Practice: The Need for International Regulation of Human Experimentation' (Winter 1981) 72 J. Crim. L. & Criminology 1597–1666.

9 For descriptions of this study, see S.B. Thomas and S.C. Quinn, 'The Tuskegee Syphilis Study, 1932 to 1972: Implications for HIV Education and AIDS Risk Education Programs in the Black Community' (Nov. 1991) 81 Am. J. Public Health 1498–1505 at 1501, and J. Jones, *Bad Blood: The Tuskegee Syphilis Experiment – A Tragedy of Race and Medicine* (New York: Free Press, 1981).

10 In these studies, funded by the CIA and the Canadian Government, sub-

jects were given LSD and other hallucinogens without their consent. They were also subjected to a variety of 'brainwashing' techniques. The studies are described in S. Bindman, 'Brainwash Victims to Get Compensation' (18 Nov. 1992) *Toronto Star* at A10; Law Reform Commission of Canada, *Biomedical Experimentation Involving Human Subjects: Working Paper 61* (Ottawa: Law Reform Commission of Canada, 1989) at 2; and A. Collins, *In the Sleep Room: The Story of the CIA Brainwashing Experiments in Canada* (Toronto: Key Porter Books, 1977).

11 Many appalling non-Nazi examples of abuse in research involving humans are described in H. Beecher, 'Medical Research and the Individual' in D. Labby, *Life or Death: Ethics and Options* (Seattle: University of Washington Press, 1968) 139.

12 See, e.g., H. Hendin, 'Seduced by Death: Doctors, Patients and the Dutch Cure' (1994) 10 Issues in Law & Medicine 123–68; H. Hendin, *Seduced by Death: Doctors, Patients and the Dutch Cure* (New York: W.W. Norton, 1996); H. Hendin, C. Rutenfrans, and Z. Zylicz, 'Physician-Assisted Suicide and Euthanasia in the Netherlands: Lessons from the Dutch' (1997) 277 J.A.M.A. 1720–22; R. Fenigsen, 'A Case against Dutch Euthanasia' (1989) 19 Hastings Center Report 22–30; C.F. Gomez, *Regulating Death: Euthanasia and the Case of the Netherlands* (New York: Free Press, 1991); and E. Pellegrino, 'The False Promise of Beneficent Killing' in Emanuel, supra, n6 87.

13 Hendin et al., supra, n12 at 1720.

14 Dr K. Gunning. Senate of Canada, *Proceedings of the Senate Special Committee on Euthanasia and Assisted Suicide* [hereinafter *Senate Special Cte.*], No. 17 (29 Sept. 1994) at 88.

15 For example, the Netherlands is more permissive with respect to the sale and possession of drugs such as marijuana. For an explanation of drug law and policy in the Netherlands <http://www.ministerievanjustitie.nl:8080/A_BELEID/FACT/CFACT7.HTM>. See also <http://www.ministerievanjustitie.nl:8080/A_BELEID/THEMA/DRUGS/qenqA.htm>.

16 The role of *overmacht* is explained infra in the discussion of the case law in the Netherlands. For a discussion of the defence of necessity in the context of euthanasia in Canada, see, e.g., Barney Sneiderman, '*Latimer* in the Supreme Court: Necessity, Compassionate Homicide, and Mandatory Sentencing' (2001) 64 Saskatchewan L.R. 511–44.

17 J. Griffiths, A. Bood, and H. Weyers, *Euthanasia and Law in the Netherlands* (Amsterdam: Amsterdam University Press, 1998) at 28.

18 R. Fenigsen, 'The Report of the Dutch Governmental Committee on Euthanasia' (1991) 339 Issues in Law & Med. 339 at 340.

19 Hendin et al., supra, n12 at 1722.
20 P.J. van der Maas, J.J.M. van Delden, and L. Pijnenborg, 'Euthanasia and Other Medical Decisions Concerning the End of Life' (1992) 22(2) Health Policy.
21 P.J. van der Maas, G. van der Wal, I. Haverkate, C.L.M. de Graaff, J.G.C. Kester, A. van der Heide, J.M. Bosma, D.L. Willems, and B.D. Onwuteaka-Philipsen, 'Euthanasia, Physician-Assisted Suicide, and other Medical Practices Involving the End of Life in the Netherlands, 1990–1995' (1996) 335 N.E.J.M. 1699–1705.
22 Ibid. at 1699.
23 Supra, n17 at 211.
24 This claim was made in witness statements sent to the Dutch witnesses in advance of a videoconference with the Special Senate Committee on Euthanasia and Assisted Suicide. See *Senate Special Cte.*, No. 21 (25 Oct. 1994) at 62.
25 Ibid. at 62.
26 See, e.g., Gunning, supra, n14 at 91, *Of Life and Death*, supra, n2 at A-120, and J. Keown, 'Euthanasia in the Netherlands' in *Euthanasia Examined: Ethical, Clinical and Legal Perspectives* (Cambridge: Cambridge University Press, 1995) at 280.
27 *Senate Special Cte.*, No. 21 (25 Oct. 1994) at 28–9.
28 Griffiths et al., supra, 17, refer to the following as an authoritative literature study of palliative care in the Netherlands: A.L. Francke, et al. *Palliative zorg in Nederland. Een inventarisatiestudie naar palliatieve zorg, deskundigheidsbevordering en zorg voor zorgenden* [Palliative Care in the Netherlands. A Survey of Studies of Palliative Care, Promotion of Expertise, and Support for those Giving Care] (Utrecht: *Nederlands Instituut voor Onderzoek van de Gezondheidszorg*), 1997.
     Further information dispelling misperceptions of palliative care in the Netherlands can also be found on the web site for the Dutch Ministry of Justice <http://www.minnjust.nl>. For example, the site reveals that the Dutch government has set aside NLG 7 million a year for a period of five years for further efforts to improve palliative care in the Netherlands.
29 Fenigsen, supra, n12 at 25.
30 L. Pijnenborg, P.J. van der Maas, J.J.M. van Delden, C.N.C. Looman, 'Life-Terminating Acts without Explicit Request of Patient' (1993) 341 Lancet 1196 at 1197.
31 Ibid.
32 Fenigsen, supra, n12 at 25.
33 Keown, supra, n26 at 285.

34 Ibid. at 286.
35 Supra, n17 at 210.
36 During the day-long videoconference with the Special Senate Committee on Euthanasia and Assisted Suicide, several of the Dutch experts reported concern about the 1990 LAWER figures. *Senate Special Cte.*, No. 21 (25 Oct. 1994) at 26–7. See also supra, n30.
37 Hendin et al., supra, n12 at 1720. See also James Bernat, 'Ethical and Legal Issues in Palliative care' (2001) 19(4) Neurologic Clinics.
38 Supra, n12 at 341.
39 Supra, n17 at 23.
40 R. Dworkin, 'Assisted Suicide: What the Court Really Said' (25 Sept. 1997) N.Y. Rev. 40 at 43–4.
41 Supra, n17 at 25.
42 Supra, n40 at 44.
43 Supra, n21.
44 2.4% explicit request in accordance with legal guidelines and 0.36% no explicit request in accordance with legal guidelines but discussed or wish stated (2.4%+.36% = 2.76%).
45 Voluntary/non-voluntary is calculated as follows: explicit request 2.4%; no explicit request 0.7% (wishes known 52%, wishes not known 48%); voluntary = 2.4%+52% of 0.7% and non-voluntary = 48% of 0.7%.
46 45% of 20%.
47 51% of 20%.
48 5% of 20%.
49 43% of 19%.
50 42% of 19%.
51 15% of 19%.
52 H. Jochemsen and J. Keown, 'Voluntary Euthanasia under Control? Further Empirical Evidence from the Netherlands' (1999) 25 J. Med. Ethics 16.
53 G. van der Wal, P.J. van der Maas, J.M. Bosma, B.D. Onwuteaka-Philipsen, D.L. Willems, I. Haverkate, P.J. Kostense, 'Evaluation of the Notification Procedure for Physician-Assisted Death in the Netherlands' (1996) 335 N.E.J.M. 1706 at 1707.
54 *Termination of Life on Request and Assisted Suicide (Review Procedures) Act*. Bill approved 28 Nov. 2000 by the Lower House of Dutch Parliament and by the Upper House of Dutch Parliament (Senate) 4 April 2001 (Upper House of the States General, Parliamentary year 2000–2001 no. 137; 26 691). Decreed 1 April 2002 [hereinafter *Review Procedures Act*].
55 'Statistics from 1996 and 2000' Ministerie van Buitenlandse Zaken <http://www.minbuza.nl>.

56 Article 293: 'A person who takes the life of another person at that other person's express and earnest request is liable to a term of imprisonment of not more than twelve years or a fine of the fifth category.' Supra, n17 at 308.

57 Article 294: 'A person who intentionally incites another to commit suicide, assists in the suicide of another, or procures for that other person the means to commit suicide, assists in the suicide, is liable to a term of imprisonment of not more than three years or a fine of the fourth category, where the suicide ensues.' Ibid.

58 Ibid. at 307.

59 I will not review *all* of the cases involving euthanasia in the Netherlands. Rather, a select group will be reviewed with the goals of illustrating the evolution of the courts' responses to euthanasia and clarifying the current legal status of euthanasia in the Netherlands as delineated by the courts.

60 *Nederlandse Jurisprudentie* 1952, no. 275.

61 The court said 'because, as far as the Court is aware, this is the first time that a case of euthanasia has been subject to the ruling of a Dutch judge.' Supra, n17 at 44.

62 Ibid. at 44.

63 *Nederlandse Jurisprudentie* 1973, no. 183.

64 Gomez, supra, n12 at 30.

65 Ibid. at 31.

66 *Nederlandse Jurisprudentie* 1982, no. 63.

67 'A conditional sentence of six months subject to one year probation. As a special restriction, the court ordered that she be put under house arrest for the first two weeks of her probation.' Supra, n17 at 59.

68 Ibid. at 59.

69 Ibid.

70 Ibid. at 60.

71 *Nederlandse Jurisprudentie* 1985, no. 106.

72 Supra, n17 at 323–4.

73 *Nederlandse Jurisprudentie* 1985, no. 709.

74 '(1) The request for euthanasia must be voluntary; (2) the request must be well-considered; (3) the patient's desire to die must be a lasting one; (4) the patient must experience his suffering as unacceptable for him (the Board emphasized that there are only limited possibilities for verifying whether suffering is unbearable and without prospect of improvement. The Board considered it in any case the doctor's task to investigate whether there are medical or social alternatives that can make the patient's suffering bearable.); (5) The doctor concerned must consult a colleague. Supra, n17 at 66.

75 Ibid. at 67.
76 *Nederlandse Jurisprudentie* 1994, no. 656.
77 Supra, n17 at 332.
78 Ibid. at 331.
79 Ibid. at 332.
80 *Prins: Nederlandse Jurisprudentie* 1995, no. 602 and, on appeal, *Nederlandse Jurisprudentie* 1996, no. 113. *Kadijk: Tijdschrift voor Gezondheidsrecht* 1996, no. 35.
81 Supra, n17 at 83.
82 Ibid. at 350–1.
83 *Review Procedures Act*, supra, n54, c. II, art. 2(1).
84 Ibid., art. 2(2).
85 Ibid., art. 2(3).
86 Ibid, c. III.
87 J.J.M. van Delden, L. Pijnenborg, P.J. van der Maas, 'Dances with Data' (1993) 7 Bioethics 323 at 327.
88 Supra, n17 at 301.
89 H. Kuhse, P. Singer, P. Baume, M. Clark and M.Rickard, 'End-of-Life Decisions in Australian Medical Practice' (1997) 166 Med. J. Australia 191 at 191.
90 Ibid.
91 Griffiths et al., supra, n17 at 127.
92 E. Westermarck, *The Origin and Development of Moral Ideas*, vol. 1 (London: Macmillan, 1924) at 394–413.
93 Ibid. at 387 and 392.
94 G. Bosshard et al., 'Open Regulation and Practice in Assisted Dying: How Switzerland compares with the Netherlands and Oregon' (2002) 132 Swiss Med. Weekly 527.
95 'Oregon's Death with Dignity Act: Three Years of Legalized Physician-Assisted Suicide' Portland, OR: Oregon Health Division, 22 Feb. 2001. It is obviously early in this social experiment but the preliminary results run counter to the slippery slope argument.
96 *Of Life and Death*, supra, n1 at 54.
97 N. Searles, 'Silence Doesn't Obliterate the Truth: A Manitoba Survey on Physician Assisted Suicide and Euthanasia' (1996) 4 Health L. Rev. 9.
98 'Home Mercy Killings Common: Ontario Coroner' (21 July 1997) *Montreal Gazette* A6.
99 D.E. Meier, C.-A. Emmons, S. Wallenstein, T. Quill, R.S. Morrison, and C. Cassel, 'A National Survey of Physician-Assisted Suicide and Euthanasia in the United States' (1998) 338 N.E.J.M. 1193–201. This article also includes

references to and some discussion of prior surveys conducted on this issue in the United States.

100 *Senate Special Cte.*, No. 16 (28 Sept. 1994) at 24.

12 The *Canadian Charter of Rights and Freedoms*

1 Section 7 of the *Canadian Charter of Rights and Freedoms*, Part I of the *Constitution Act 1982*, being Schedule B to the *Canada Act 1982* (U.K.), 1982, c. 11 provides that '[e]veryone has the right to life, liberty and security of the person and the right not to be deprived thereof except in accordance with the principles of fundamental justice.' Section 15.(1) provides that '[e]very individual is equal before and under the law and has the right to the equal protection and equal benefit of the law without discrimination and, in particular, without discrimination based on race, national or ethnic origin, colour, religion, sex, age or mental or physical disability.' Section 1 allows limits to be placed on some *Charter* rights: 'The *Canadian Charter of Rights and Freedoms* guarantees the rights and freedoms set out in it subject only to such reasonable limits prescribed by law as can be demonstrably justified in a free and democratic society.'

2 *Rodriguez* v. *British Columbia (Attorney General)*, [1993] 3 S.C.R. 519 [hereinafter *Rodriguez*].

3 The *Rodriguez* decision prompted a considerable number of articles and case comments. The most interesting of these include: B. Sneiderman, 'The Rodriguez Case: Where Do We Go from Here – A Multi-dimensional (6-Layered) Approach' (1994) 2 Health L.J. 1; K. Kilback, 'To Be Human: Selective Reflections on the Sanctity of Life in *Rodriguez*' (1994) 2 Health L.J. 39; R. Mykitiuk and J. Paltiel, 'Terminal Care: Terminal Justice – The Supreme Court of Canada and Sue Rodriguez' (1994) 5 Constitutional Forum 38(6); I. Dundas, 'Rodriguez and Assisted Suicide in Canada (Case Comment) (1994) 32 Alberta L.Rev. 811; M.A. Somerville, '"Death talk" in Canada: The Rodriguez Case (Case Comment) (1994) 39 McGill L.J. 602; L.E. Weinrib, 'The Body and the Body Politic: Assisted Suicide under the Canadian Charter of Rights and Freedoms' (Case Comment) (1994) 39 McGill L.J. 519; B. Freedman, 'The Rodriguez Case: Sticky Questions and Slippery Answers' (Case Comment) (1994) 39 McGill L.J. 644; E. Keyserlingk, 'Assisted Suicide, Causality and the Supreme Court of Canada' (1994) 39 McGill L.J. 708; A. Jackman, '"Solutions in Sciences Outside of the Law?" *Rodriguez* v. *British Columbia (A.G.)*' (1994) 17 Dalhousie L.J. 206.

4 Supra, n2 at 583.

5 Ibid. at 595.
6 Justice McLachlin's analysis is found ibid., at 621–3. See also L Weinrib, supra, n3. In this paper, Lorraine Weinrib offers a critique of Justice Sopinka's importation of traditional s. 1 considerations into the s. 7 analysis.
7 Supra, n2 at 595.
8 Ibid. at 595–6.
9 Ibid. at 597–8.
10 Ibid. at 620.
11 Ibid. at 559.
12 Ibid. at 598.
13 Ibid. at 606.
14 Ibid.
15 See Chapter 8.
16 See Chapter 8.
17 Supra, n2 at 607–8.
18 Ibid. at 630–1.
19 Ibid. at 607.
20 Ibid.
21 Ibid. at 608.
22 Ibid. at 608.
23 See, e.g., N. Searles, 'Silence Doesn't Obliterate the Truth: A Manitoba Survey on Physician Assisted Suicide and Euthanasia' (1996) 4 Health L. Rev. 9; T.D. Kinsella and M. Verhoef, 'Alberta Euthanasia Survey: 1. Physicians' Opinions about the Morality of Active Euthanasia' (1993) 148 C.M.A.J. 1921; and T.D. Kinsella and M. Verhoef, 'Alberta Euthanasia Survey: 2. Physicians' Opinions About the Accepetance of Active Euthanasia as a Medical Act and the Reporting of Such Practice' (1993) 148 C.M.A.J. 1929.
24 Gallup polls consistently place support for voluntary euthanasia at greater than 75% for the past ten years. M. Otlowski, *Voluntary Euthanasia and the Common Law* (Oxford: Clarendon Press, 1997) at 262.
25 Supra, n2 at 608.
26 *Dagenais v. Canadian Broadcasting Corp.*, [1994] 3 S.C.R. 835 *per* Lamer C.J.
27 Supra, n2 at 595.
28 Ibid. at 613.
29 Ibid. at 614.
30 Lamer C.J.C., ibid. at 569, and McLachlin J., ibid. at 626.
31 Freedman, supra, n3 at 656. Lorraine Weinrib more thoroughly articulates this argument in Weinrib, supra, n3 at 636–41.

Index

motive, 93; no defence in cases of
murder, 38; mercy, 37; relevant to
sentencing, 38, 165n4; self-interest
as, 34–5. *See also* intent
multiculturalism, 60, 170n41
murder, 5, 16, 17, 29, 32, 37, 38, 64
Myers, Cheryl, 41

Nancy B., 4, 74
Nancy B. v. *Hôtel-Dieu de Québec*, 17–
18, 20, 137, 156n19
Nazi Germany: human experimentation in, 108–10; involuntary euthanasia in, 107–8; not relevant to
Canada, 108
necessaries of life, legal duty to provide, 15–17, 18
negligence. *See* criminal negligence
Netherlands: abuses related to
euthanasia in, 117–18; availability
of euthanasia in, 112–13; Committee of Procurators-General, 122;
Dutch Association of Voluntary
Euthanasia, 124; Dutch Voluntary
Euthanasia Society, 109; guidelines, 120–2; incidence of assisted
death in, 118–19; incidence of
euthanasia in, 111–12; involuntary
euthanasia in, 117; LAWER study,
115–16, 128; legal status of euthanasia and assisted suicide in, 119;
non-voluntary euthanasia in, 115,
116, 124–5; nursing homes in, 114;
palliative care in, 113–15; physician's obligation to consult in, 121–
2, 123, 124; Regional Review Committees, 127; Remmelink Report,
116–17; reporting rates in, 119;
Requirements for Due Care (2002),
126–7; Requirements of Careful

Practice, 125, 126; Supreme Court
of the Netherlands, 122–6. *See also*
Dutch case law
New Brunswick, 54; Court of
Appeal, 24, 81; *Medical Consent of
Minors Act*, 21–2
Ney v. *Canada (Attorney General)*, 25,
81
Nova Scotia: College of Physicians
and Surgeons, 42; *Hospitals Act*, 20;
Human Rights Act, 59; prosecutorial discretion in, 42–3
nurse, 141, 176n24
nursing homes, 114
nutrition, artificial, 3, 69, 77, 93, 94,
176n24

Odgen, Russell, 129–30
Ontario, 23, 30–1, 35; euthanasia in,
130; *Health Care Consent Act*, 19, 21,
55, 168n27, 169nn28–30; High
Court, 23; prosecutorial discretion
in, 39–40, 41–2; Provincial Court
(Family Division), 24
opiates, 8
opioids, 8

pain: control of, 4, 7, 87, 102–5, 114,
139, 183n10; and competency, 97;
and discomfort, 78–9; psychological, 78; unrelievable physical, 69,
77–9, 104, 124. *See also* morphine;
palliative care; suffering
palliative care, 3, 7, 29, 32, 39, 78, 87,
95, 103–5, 113–15, 120–1, 139,
184n12; *Criminal Code* provisions
regarding, 29, 32, 95; potentially
life-shortening, 3, 6, 7, 29–32, 95,
139–40
parens patriae jurisdiction of the